Lessons of Kosovo

Lessons of Kosovo

The Dangers of Humanitarian Intervention

Edited by Aleksandar Jokic
Introduction by Burleigh Wilkins

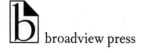 broadview press

NATIONAL LIBRARY OF CANADA CATALOGUING IN PUBLICATION

Lessons of Kosovo : the dangers of humanitarian intervention / edited by Aleksandar Jokic ; introduction by Burleigh Wilkins.

Includes bibliographical references.
ISBN 1-55111-545-X

1. Humanitarian intervention—Yugoslavia—Kosovo (Serbia)
2. North Atlantic Treaty Organization—Yugoslavia—Kosovo (Serbia)
3. Humanitarian intervention—Moral and ethical aspects. I. Jokić, Aleksandar

KZ6377.5.K66L48 2003   341.5'84'094971   C2002-905697-7

Broadview Press, Ltd. is an independent, international publishing house, incorporated in 1985. Broadview believes in shared ownership, both with its employees and with the general public; since the year 2000 Broadview shares have traded publicly on the Toronto Venture Exchange under the symbol BDP.

We welcome any comments and suggestions regarding any aspect of our publications — please feel free to contact us at the addresses below, or at broadview@broadviewpress.com

North America
Post Office Box 1243,
Peterborough, Ontario,
Canada K9J 7H5
Tel: (705) 743-8990
Fax: (705) 743-8353

3576 California Road,
Orchard Park, New York
USA 14127

customerservice@broadviewpress.com
www.broadviewpress.com

United Kingdom
Thomas Lister, Ltd.
Unit 3 & 4A
Old Boundary Way,
Burscough Rd.
Ormskirk, Lancashire
L39 2YW
Tel: (01695) 575112
Fax: (01695) 570120
books@tlyster.co.uk

Australia
UNIREPS
University of
New South Wales
Sydney, NSW, 2052
Tel: + 61 2 96640999
Fax: + 61 2 96645420
info.press@unsw.edu.au

Broadview Press Ltd. gratefully acknowledges the financial support of the Government of Canada through the Book Publishing Industry Development Program for our publishing activities.

Cover design and typeset by Zack Taylor, www.zacktaylor.com.

This book is printed on acid-free paper containing 30% post-consumer fibre.

Eco-Logo Certified.
30% Post.   Printed in Canada

Contents

For Milica Djordjevic (1908-1999),
the perfect grandparent

Preface

Aleksandar Jokic

This book is one of two volumes that are the result of an ongoing project under the general name "International Law and Ethics Conference Series" (ILECS), which is concerned with exploring issues regarding the changing global order. Envisaged originally as a way of facilitating dialog between leading moral, legal, and political philosophers from the United States and Western Europe and their Eastern European counterparts, ILECS had adopted a two-part model consisting of a conference each June (since 1997) at Belgrade University and a follow-up conference in the US. Although undoubtedly operating against a background of the Anglo-American style of analytical philosophy, ILECS has sought always to reflect actively on the inter-disciplinary nature of its enterprise and to recruit experts who are not primarily philosophers.

The two volumes — one focusing on theoretical and philosophical issues, the other on the particular case of Kosovo — offer essays from 15 scholars with backgrounds in various disciplines — philosophy, international law, anthropology, political science, international studies, and Slavic studies — from different countries — United States, Yugoslavia, Germany, and Australia. The chapters are based on presentations delivered at the pair of ILECS conferences held under the title "Ethics of Humanitarian Intervention: Grounds for Internationalizing Internal Conflicts," held on June 23-25, 2000 at Belgrade University and October 13-14, 2000 at Portland State University.

The completion of the two volumes would not have been possible without financial contributions from a number of sources. The Belgrade meetings were supported by generous grants from the Open Society Foundation for Yugoslavia and Goethe Institute in Belgrade. The follow-up conference was funded by the Machette Foundation and the Conflict Resolution Graduate Program at Portland State University. The work on editing this volume was supported, in part, by the John D. and Catherine T. MacArthur Foundation.

In terms of intellectual input, it is not possible to list all those whom I wish to thank for providing valuable comments at the conferences and through other forms of communication that influenced the final shape of this volume. Special thanks are due to Dr. Robert Gould, Director of the Conflict Resolution Program at PSU, who has worked to provide a welcome venue for ILECS. Jovan Babic, my ILECS Co-Director, was involved with this project at every critical juncture. Burleigh Wilkins took on the task of writing a critical Introduction to each volume, a pleasure to read in its own right, intended to be useful to students as well as professionals by singling out a set of issues from each article for further examination. Finally, my colleagues Joseph White and Jim Chesher at the Center for Philosophical Education (CPE) at Santa Barbara City College, the official home of ILECS as the place where it originated, deserve my deep appreciation for their enduring encouragement and support.

I have certainly profited immensely from putting together this volume and engaging with its themes. I hope that it will prove to be a rich source of intellectual stimulation to advance conceptual understanding of intervention and related ideas in philosophy as well as in the other disciplines represented here.

Introduction

Burleigh Wilkins

If the "plain letter of the law" has any applicability to international law, it is this: states shall not intervene militarily or otherwise in the affairs of other states. This is stated explicitly in the Charter of the United Nations (UN). Since the UN was founded in the aftermath of World War II, the desire of member states to prevent any further interventions is understandable. An exception was provided: when a conflict within a state poses a threat to international peace, security military intervention by the UN is warranted. Indeed, the UN Charter provides for an international police force, though nothing ever came of this provision. The Charter and other UN documents also assert that human rights are to be protected, but the responsibility for the protection of human rights seems to rest on the governments of the states where the violation of these rights occurs. The prohibition of aggressive wars — i.e., wars not fought in self-defense — seems firmly established as a principle of international law, but the question of what protection if any the UN should provide to individuals when their human rights are violated by the government, or with the complicity of the government, of the country in which they live remains a contentious issue. There is the temptation to treat any human rights violations involving armed conflicts within a state as threats to international peace and security, and at times the UN Security Council has yielded to this temptation. Perhaps a more promising tack would be to regard international law as a legal system similar in many respects to municipal legal systems. Since all legal systems contain principles which under some circumstances may oppose one another, it is arguable that respect for state sovereignty and respect for human rights are two such principles. Historically the respect for state sovereignty has been allowed to trump respect for human rights, but now it has become arguable that when states fail to respect the human rights of their citizens (or others who reside within their boundaries), they may be held accountable by the UN. Intervention in a variety of forms–including, ultimately, military force — has

9

come to be regarded by some as justifiable. The question which this collection of essays addresses is this: is military humanitarian intervention justifiable and, if so, under what circumstances?

This is one of two paired volumes. The first, *Humanitarian Intervention as a Moral and Philosophical Issue*, consists primarily of reflections by philosophers on the more abstract aspects of humanitarian intervention. The second, *Lessons of Kosovo: The Dangers of Humanitarian Intervention*, contains essays dealing more concretely with issues concerning the legal and moral dimensions of intervention by NATO or by the UN—all of them arguing from various points of view that the NATO intervention in Kosovo lacked clear justification, and that this raises important doubts as to the wisdom of "humanitarian" intervention in other situations.

Lessons of Kosovo:
The Dangers of Humanitarian Intervention

In this volume the contributors grapple with the question of whether the North Atlantic Treaty Organization (NATO) intervention was legally or morally acceptable. The contributors, despite significant differences among them, all have doubts on this score, and several argue vehemently that the intervention was both legally and morally unjustified. But if NATO was legally or morally deficient in its actions, could the UN have fared better? Despite the failures of the UN in Bosnia and Rwanda, people who speak seriously of "the international community" think that the UN should "do something" to prevent human rights abuses and that the UN, and not NATO, should have intervened in Kosovo.

Georg Meggle's "Is This War Good? An Ethical Commentary" is a painstaking piece of careful philosophical analysis. Meggle lays out a set of necessary conditions for the justification of humanitarian intervention. These conditions can be seen mainly as a spelling out of a proportionality requirement, and accordingly much of his emphasis falls upon what he calls "damage minimization." Since he recognizes that some "moral weighing" of his damage minimization requirements may be necessary, he should, I think, have developed more fully some of his intuitions—e.g., that there may be obligation to offer assistance in case of an emergency even at the cost of harm to the intervening party. How much harm should the intervening party be expected to bear? How do we compare the possible harm to "the intervention subject" that emergency assistance might bring with the probable harm the subject would suffer over a fairly long period of time if there is no intervention to protects its rights? Like Ellis (in the companion volume to this one), Meggle downplays the significance of the motive in performing a humanitarian intervention: "What really counts in an emergency is to receive genuine assistance — not the motives behind the act bringing about this help (or not)." But suppose for every act of intervention someone like Marjorie Cohn, whose paper on Kosovo appears later in this volume (Chapter 6), is able to trot out plausible explanations in terms of motives aimed at promoting the economic or geopolitical interests of the intervening parties. Would this not make a difference? What "really counts" for those in need of assistance may not always be the same as what really counts, all things considered.

Richard Falk takes the idea of the international community seriously, and in "Humanitarian Intervention After Kosovo" he explores the moral and tactical deficiencies of NATO intervention there and attempts to formulate lessons for future interventions. The Kosovo intervention itself he describes as "*necessary*" (to prevent further "genocidal cleansing") and "*impossible*" (because of deep divisions among the European states). After a judicious exploration of what went wrong in Kosovo, he concludes that there can be no overarching response to circumstances as diverse as Kosovo and East Timor. Despite his sensitivity to the variety of circumstances, Falk does, however, venture some "conclusions" for future cases in which humanitarian intervention may be an option. If the UN framework of legal restraint on the use of forces is to be rejected, there is a strong burden of proof on those who would depart from this framework (as NATO did); humanitarian intervention can be justified only if there is a credible threat of genocide or some distinct humanitarian catastrophe and only if there has been a sincere effort to prevent their occurrence by diplomatic means; a case for humanitarian intervention is weakened by tactics of warfare which result in civilian harm and by punitive measures imposed on an adversary after hostilities have ceased. NATO and the US are to be faulted, if Falk is correct, on all these scores, but Falk, holds out hope for future success. I think of Falk as an honest idealist or internationalist who fails perhaps to take induction seriously enough. In his various writings he admits to numerous past failures on the part of the international community where both trials for war crimes and humanitarian interventions are concerned, but, he is not willing to give up. The protection of human rights is so important that the search for adequate procedures must continue.

Aleksandar Pavkovic, in his "Humanitarian Intervention in Nationalist Conflicts: A Few Problems," takes NATO's intervention in Kosovo to be an exemplary case of an attempt to save lives of innocent people in a conflict in which each party to the conflict regards the civilian, non-armed population of the other side as a serious threat. In the view of each side, there are no innocents among the civilian population of the opposing side. Outside military interventions in such conflicts usually support a militarily weaker side against the stronger one and thus enable the supported side to expel and kill the civilians of the unsupported side; this is, Pavkovic claims, what happened in Kosovo. In such a case, the military intervention saves lives primarily of one group but not of the other. Are military interventions in such conflicts humanitarian? While Pavkovic is right to raise this question, his negative answer seems too quick. A military intervention in such conflicts may indeed fail to save lives of some innocent people of the non-supported group, but this failure does not, necessarily, detract from its value as a humanitarian intervention, provided that it has succeeded in saving a large number of innocent lives from both groups.

In his "Interdependence and Intervention," Ernst Otto Czempiel attempts an overview of what he calls "Euro-Atlantic" (the area covered by the Cold War). The interdependence of states is a fact of life, according to Czempiel, meaning that no state can achieve its objectives without cooperation of other states. Non-violent intervention is morally justified when human rights are threatened, and democratization is a necessary means to implement the protection of human rights. Czempiel does not discuss the "liberal democracies" which have emerged in Eastern Europe after the collapse of the Soviet system, but I think he would regard these democracies as part of a transition to liberal democracies that will respect human rights. He points to policies by the European Union (EU) with evident approval. Membership in the EU is highly sought after for economic reasons, and it can impose conditions of democracy and a respect for human rights upon states wishing to become members. So long as interventions are non-violent, people can accept them or reject them; apparently, Czempiel believes that this warrants intervention in the affairs of other states. But the price of resisting may be very high, a fact which he ignores. Diplomatic sanctions and economic hardships may occur, but non-violent coercion, he says, is nevertheless acceptable. But consider the reaction of the EU to the emergence of the neo-fascist Haider as a political force in Austria; some commentators saw this as aimed more at Germany than Austria, as a warning that extreme right-wing forces would not be permitted to gain ascendancy in Germany. Then the EU abruptly halted its intervention in Austria, as though fearful that it had gone too far. Perhaps Czempiel would regard all of this as an example of the difficulty of fine-tuning an intervention, while others might see it as an unwarranted intervention in the affairs of a sovereign state, one that happens to be committed to both democracy and the protection of human rights. Czempiel does not mention the European Court of Human Rights, which is unfortunate, I think, because its success shows that his optimism concerning human rights in Europe is well-founded.

"Biased 'Justice': Humanrightsism and the International Criminal Tribunal for the Former Yugoslavia" is a detailed and forceful criticism by Robert M. Hayden of what he calls "Human Rightsism." His paper focuses on what he believes to be military misconduct by NATO in Kosovo and judicial misconduct by the International Criminal Tribunal for the Former Yugoslavia. NATO deliberately bombed civilian targets, but its personnel risk no prosecution by the ICTY, and the ICTY selects individuals, mainly Serbians, for prosecution in accordance with the wishes of the West, especially the US. Hayden raises hard questions about why Human Rights Watch and other human rights organizations have largely ignored the war crimes committed by NATO when similar acts by, for example, Russia or China would not be overlooked. Hayden believes there has been a "usurpation" of the "human rights culture" by dominant powers such as the US—i.e., it has been transformed into a culture of "humanrightsism" justifying the use of power by the world's most powerful states against weaker ones. Where Hayden sees usurpation others might see perhaps only a convergence of opinions and interests. However, Hayden's highly professional criticism of the ICTY for being unduly deferential to prosecutors in a number of trials, including the highly publicized case of the Bosnian Serb Tadic, is extremely disturbing. The politicalization of intervention is perhaps unavoidable, but the politicalization of a judicial tribunal is intolerable.

In her carefully argued "The Myth of Humanitarian Intervention in Kosovo," Marjorie Cohn maintains that the motivation behind the intervention was to preserve US hegemony in the region and to assure our access to the oil of the Caspian Sea region. Russia wants Caspian Sea oil to run through its territory to Western Europe while the US wants the oil pipelines to run through Turkey and then shipped across the Black Sea and piped to the Adriatic via Bulgaria, Macedonia, Kosovo, and Albania. The American bombings of the bridges at Novi Sad and other points on the Danube River blocked the passage of tankers carrying oil directly to Europe from the Caspian oil fields. Not so incidentally, according to Cohn, former US secretaries of state Alexander Haig and James Baker earned large consulting fees from oil companies working in the Caspian Sea region; moreover, the Trepca mines in Kosovo contain rich deposits of minerals such as zinc and lead. Of all the countries in the region only Serbia, as evidenced by its initial resistence to the fragmentation of Yugoslavia, had the will and resources to block US foreign policy objectives, and, according to Cohn, Kosovo provided an excuse or pretext for US action to reduce the importance of Serbia, as the Gulf War had reduced the importance of Iraq.

The literature on humanitarian intervention is of course deadly serious, and rightly so. But there is one paper, Milan Brdar's "Humanitarian Intervention and The (De)Nazification Thesis As a Functional Simulacrum," which manages to be both serious and delightful. The idea that there is such a thing as an autonomous referential object in the real world (by means of which we could evaluate, for example, the truth or falsity of Cohn's explanatory theory) has become, according to Brdar, a fairy tale of undergraduate philosophy seminars. In its place there is a postmodern emphasis upon "the sign"—in this case the "Serbs" which serves as a "negative totem operator" and "as a transfer of evil symbolics." According to Brdar, the symbol "Serbs" works as an "actual transfer of an invariant scheme of evil." In order for the "modern and civilized" image of the West to flourish in the narcissistic collective consciousness there is a need for a "Monster"—national tribalism—to stand in its path: "This Monster is necessary for Narcissus to enjoy his own perfection." The "semantic killing" of the negative totemic operator prepares for the real killing of those who represent the "wild tribe" which stands in the way of the prevalence of Western values and interests. "Serbs" has taken on a function like "Bourgeoisie" in Communist propaganda and "Jews" in Nazi propaganda. According to Brdar, "anti-Serbian discourse is a discourse of suppressed and pathological desire operating by projection of the unconscious drive against the Other."

Brdar knows his way around the philosophy of language and can speak with expertise about symbols and "regimens of discourse," but what I find especially disturbing is his account of how the media came to accept a picture of Serbs as modern-day Nazis and how public relations firms helped persuade Western intellectuals to forget the anti-Nazi role of Serbians and the pro-Nazi role of Croatians and Muslims in World War II. Once an image of Serbian atrocities gained prominence in the media it became a relatively simply matter to exclude or downplay the atrocities of their opponents.

In "The Aftermath of the Kosovo Intervention: A Proposed Solution," Aleksandar Jokic does two things. First, he raises fundamental questions of fairness concerning condemnations by the media and some politicians of so-called "Serbian nationalism" as if somehow Serbia alone among states should not be permitted to harbor nationalist sentiments. Second, he proposes a partition of Kosovo, with Albanians being granted the independence they desire, and then a division of Bosnia, with the Republika Srpska being granted permission to join Serbia. I fear, however, and this is acknowledged by Jokic, that this would be unacceptable to the Muslim government of the Bosnian/Croat Federation entity in Bosnia and Herzegovina and its NATO supporters. Furthermore, if Republika Srpska were allowed to leave Bosnia, surely the Croatians in Bosnia would demand to be united with Croatia. Dissolving Bosnia in this fashion would complete the deconstruction of Yugoslavia along the same lines it was originally constructed in December 1918, the exception being that an entirely new Muslim political entity would emerge on the territory of former Yugoslavia. Having accepted the dissolution of Yugoslavia, the international community would, paradoxically, balk at one more dissolution, even if this would, arguably, put a genuine end to ethnic conflict in the former Yugoslavia (as contrasted to the artificial end to conflict in Bosnia and Herzegovina which results entirely from the presence of NATO troops).

I

Is This War Good?
An Ethical Commentary[1]

Georg Meggle[2]

The almost unanimous approval in Germany of NATO's war against Yugoslavia is attributable to what is called its "humanitarian aim." The goal of our humanitarian intervention is to stop genocide—or, as it is sometimes described, to prevent "a second Auschwitz." Those who are against Auschwitz must approve of this war. This is the heaviest piece of moral artillery to be wheeled out on our side during our moral war. It is certainly the most effective form of artillery, universally appealing right across the political spectrum, including former pacifists. But is this argument valid? Is this war good? Is this war really *morally* good?

I believe this question, at least the fundamental problem itself, can be answered relatively simply. It is certainly simpler than many other moral questions. Nevertheless, many of us find it very difficult to come up with a genuinely well-founded opinion on the ethical legitimacy of NATO's war against Yugoslavia—assuming we actually try to reach an opinion in the first place. I do not want to deny anyone the right to make up their own mind, but perhaps my comments will make it easier for some people to decide. I therefore invite you to consider with me step-by-step the fundamental moral decisions and the factual assumptions on which our moral assessment of NATO's intervention depends. Even if you still waver in your final opinion, as long as now you at least know why you do, I will have achieved my aim.

Self-Defense and Emergency Assistance

Let us start by taking the customary tack of self-defense and assistance in an emergency. If someone makes an attempt on my life and I cannot ward off his attack in any other way, I may defend myself by killing him before he kills me. Note the use of "may"—I am under no compulsion to do so. I might not value my life so much that I am prepared even to kill in order to save it. Self-defense is a right, not an obligation.

By contrast, whenever emergency assistance is concerned, it is not my life which is at stake but that of at least one other person. Say a murderer wants to kill a defenseless child. If there is no other way of saving the child's life, may I try and kill the murderer? Of course I may. Indeed, it is probably my duty to do so. Although I may choose to relinquish my own life, I may not be able to refrain from saving the child's. In other words, we have a right both to self-defense and to grant assistance in an emergency—but the latter might also be an obligation. (Whether and the extent to which we are duty-bound to assist depends not only on the scale of the threat but also on what sort of risk can reasonably be expected of me in view of my own right to life. Moreover, the risk I am prepared to take doubtless also depends on just how important the victim's life is to me.)

This approach based on reference to cases of self-defense and emergency assistance is almost always chosen when weighing up the moral justification of a license or even a duty to kill. It is also used in other cases—including those in which war is involved. It is used to justify not only recruitment, but also waging war itself. After all, the general assumption goes, states are individuals too. And any individual, be it a single person or a collective of people organized in the form of a state, may defend its existence, even if this might mean the end of the attacking individual. Wars of defense are nothing more than cases of a state's self-defense, and wars of assistance (regardless of whether they are fought within the framework of a defense pact) are nothing more than cases of international emergency aid. Hence, according to the main argument, they are morally justified. And consequently, as far as the right to join wars (the *jus ad bellum*) is concerned, these wars are described as "just wars." So far, so good—perhaps.

But at this point a problem occurs. States themselves consist of individuals and thus of groups of individuals. Although the chief aim of a state is supposed to be to protect its citizens, not every state actually serves this purpose. What about cases in which the state apparatus turns against its own citizens, or against individual groups of its citizens? Do they too have a corresponding right to self-defense if things vital to them (existence and human living conditions) are threatened? Of course they do. This is the famous right of resistance—a moral right that the threatened group has *vis-à-vis* its own state, even if such a right is not enshrined in the state's laws or is actually ruled out in them. Consequently, external parties have the right to provide assistance in an emergency in such cases if the group under threat is unable to help itself.

However, groups—for example, political parties, ethnic or religious groups, etc.—may be threatened not only by states but also by other groups.

The respective state is responsible for countering such threats in line with its main aim, its role of protector. However, this role still leaves much to be desired in some cases; moreover, the repression, expulsion, or destruction of one group by at least one other group sometimes suits those in power, and as well as concealing it they might even encourage or initiate it. In this case, too, if the state ignores its responsibility, outsiders may come to the aid of those not sufficiently able to defend themselves.

Let me ask you a question: did you find it as easy to swallow the justification of self-defense and emergency assistance in the last two cases as the previous ones? If so, you have already crossed a critical boundary — the frontier of the state concerned. Those who concur with the principle that we may come to the aid of a group or population under threat in the last two cases evidently believe that the provision of assistance itself is more important than the source of this help, be it domestic or foreign.

And rightly so. If Hitler had not embarked upon foreign conquest and had only maintained concentration camps in Germany, should the rest of the world have stood idly by because his policy of extermination was kept local? Well, the world might have done so, but under no circumstances would this have been acceptable behavior. This is where pacifism becomes a crime, and the view that "No more Auschwitz!" outweighs "No more war" is correct.

One of the moral premises most frequently used at present is also correct: if a second Auschwitz can be prevented, it must be prevented, regardless of its location. This can be easily generalized: violations of human rights are not domestic affairs. Compared to the violation of human rights, the violation of national borders is the lesser evil and, in fact, is no evil at all in the event of violations on the scale of Auschwitz. State sovereignty is not the highest good.

If we reply that people as such have a right to organize themselves in the form of states — in other words, if we say that the question of states is itself a human rights issue — we have to bear in mind that there are serious and less serious human rights. The right to live on this or that side of the Bavarian border is certainly less serious than the right to life itself.

Humanitarian Intervention: The Concept

Let us get down to business. Interventions by outside states can be justified in precisely this manner. We are not talking just about sending aid parcels and supplying weapons but also about military operations in the narrow sense, that is, those in which the various armed services deploy the various means at their disposal. The so-called "humanitarian interventions" can at least be justified in this way, as long as this term is used to mean interventions which closely fit the above justification strategy. The following definition fits best of all:

(HI) An intervention on the part of a state or a group of states X in another state Y to benefit Z (certain individuals or groups) is a *humanitarian intervention* iff X undertakes this intervention with the intention of preventing, ending, or at least reducing current serious violations of human rights *vis-à-vis* Z (certain individuals or groups) which are caused, supported, or at least not prevented by Y on the territory of Y.

Whether the conditions ought to include the stipulation that the members of the threatened group Z are citizens of Y (or at least were previously citizens of Y) is a moot point. Should a rescue operation in which the state X tries by means of military action to rescue *its own* citizens from a crisis area in Y be termed humanitarian intervention? Let us not go into this at the moment. In the following I am going to deal only with the current case in which those on whose behalf the intervention was started are citizens of *another* state. Using the symbol Y is thus rather fitting.

According to (HI), humanitarian interventions are actions directed towards a particular purpose. They have an aim: the action subject X intends by his intervention in Y to protect the group Z from the serious violations of human rights with which it is threatened. It is this *humanitarian intention* which makes the intervention humanitarian, or rather, which is supposed to make it humanitarian. Although according to (HI) the intervening X (the "intervention subject") believes and hopes that the intervention will also actually achieve the proclaimed aim, whether this hope is indeed fulfilled depends on more than just the strength of his belief and perhaps on completely different matters. Even if the intervention subject is naturally banking on the success of his intervention, everyone knows that not every purposeful action is successful, and interventions are no exception.

We would therefore do well to draw a distinction between interventions in the sense of *attempts* and *successful interventions*. An intervention is successful iff it actually achieves its aim in the way intended, i.e., by means of the intervention. Unless otherwise stated, "interventions" shall in the following be taken to mean only attempted interventions. Of course, it is not the intervention itself which is being attempted; instead, an attempt is made to achieve the proclaimed aim. Humanitarian interventions are special salvation attempts, attempts which, if they succeed, mean salvation for the group threatened.

Furthermore, we have to distinguish between a subjective and an objective interpretation of the definition above. According to the *subjective interpre-*

tation, a humanitarian intervention only applies if the intervention subject X *believes that Z is threatened* and that this threat must be countered by means of intervention.

Humanitarian interventions in this sense need not be reactions to actual threats; it would be enough if they were reactions to merely supposed attacks. Thus, under certain circumstances such interventions could be regarded as humanitarian without a hair of anybody's head being harmed prior to the intervention. According to this interpretation, an intervention is humanitarian iff the intervention subject itself regards it as such.

On the other hand, many will already have understood the above definition—and this corresponds to the *objective interpretation*—to mean that a humanitarian intervention only applies if *Z is actually threatened*, and X believes he is able to counter this threat by means of intervention. X thus does not merely *believe* that Z is threatened, but actually *knows* this to be the case. In this interpretation, therefore, humanitarian intervention is supplemented by the objective components of the actual threat. X then performs the intervention not merely with the intention of countering an emergency (perhaps merely assumed by X) suffered by the victim; the emergency actually exists—and X pursues with his intervention the aim of providing the victim with emergency assistance.

Those performing humanitarian intervention naturally believe that the threat they have assumed actually does exist. From the viewpoint of the intervention subject, humanitarian intervention is always objective. Whether this view is correct is, of course, quite a different matter.

Humanitarian interventions must (in order to be such) be associated with appropriate humanitarian intentions (of emergency assistance); according to the subjective interpretation, humanitarian interventions are such merely by virtue of their intentions. This is not the case regarding acts of self-defense and emergency assistance, at least as far as criminal law is concerned. According to criminal law, these actions are exclusively defined by reference to objective characteristics of a situation of self-defense substantiated by a present illegal attack. According to Section 32, paragraph 2, of the German Criminal Code, "self-defense" constitutes the defense required to protect oneself or another person from such an attack. Moreover, pursuant to paragraph 1 of Section 32, those who perform such an act are not acting illegally. No mention is made of intentions. They only become involved in supposed acts of self-defense, that is, when somebody wrongly assumes a need for self-defense to exist.

This difference between acts of self-defense or emergency assistance on the one hand and humanitarian interventions as a special (perhaps merely supposed) case thereof cannot be emphasized too strongly. What makes an action an act of self-defense is exclusively defined by objective characteristics of the situation; the action subject's viewpoint and the intention he has is irrelevant to whether what he is doing constitutes self-defense or not. In short, self-defense is something objective. By contrast, humanitarian interventions are (at least also) subjective. An intervention is humanitarian (assuming the group Z is suffering an emergency situation) if it is connected with the right humanitarian intention.

Having sorted out the concept of humanitarian intervention, let us now turn to the question of moral justification.

Justifying Humanitarian Interventions

In order to be morally justified by analogy with emergency assistance, humanitarian interventions must also correspond to their self-perception as cases of emergency assistance. Hence, among the group to be protected by the intervention there must prevail a situation of emergency, that is, a situation that corresponds to the scale of assistance. The threatened group must be suffering or directly threatened by serious violations of human rights. This condition is not fulfilled trivially in the case of humanitarian interventions.

Furthermore, the intervention must also be the final means available that can avert the danger or at least reduce the threat to Z. An intervention is thus only morally permissible if this danger cannot be prevented without intervention. Let us sum up these two points of view as follows:

> An HI is morally permissible only if
> (1) serious violations of human rights cannot be prevented in any other way.

Any violation of human rights does not necessarily provide permissible grounds for intervention, otherwise a war of humanitarian intervention could be waged against countries like the US. After all, the US's use of the death penalty constitutes a clear violation of human rights in Amnesty International's view. This raises the extremely difficult question of how serious violations of human rights need to be in order to justify an intervention. I suggest that *pro argumento* we do something for the time being which we otherwise should not: let us settle the argument about where violations of human rights cross the boundary at which intervention is deemed necessary by definition. Let us say, for instance, that massive crimes must have been carried out against humanity on the scale we have been made to believe caused NATO to intervene in the Kosovo crisis, that is, involving all the massacres, systematic rape, mass expulsion, etc., which have been cited by the US and other states as reasons for intervention. In the following, we shall refer to the scale of crimes contained in these reports as the *Kosovo Dimension (KD)*. Then, our first stipulation reads as follows:

An HI is morally permissible only if
(1) massive crimes against humanity (KD) cannot be prevented in any other way.

In addition to sparing me the trouble of exact quantification, this rough stipulation also saves me the certainly much more painstaking task of verification. (As soon as we start drawing up opinions about the specific case, it will of course be impossible to avoid these painstaking tasks.) Although the Kosovo Dimension is fortunately somewhat lower down the scale of everything represented by Auschwitz, it — and this is exactly what my stipulation is driving at — ought to be sufficiently terrible in order to allow it to be considered a reason for humanitarian intervention. In other words, the Kosovo Dimension should be a genuine *reason* for humanitarian intervention.

The fact that a means is required to achieve an aim does not yet mean that the usage of this means also makes sense. Not every necessary means is also a *useful means*. To take a very trivial example, if you want to catch fish in a pond, you must cast a line or set fish traps, etc. But none of these necessary, alternative means is any good if there are no fish in the pond in the first place. Or, to use an example closer to home, to make yourself comfortable in your freezing house you have to light the fire. However, this is not going to do a lot for the comfort factor if you have a house full of gelignite which will blow up as soon as the first sparks waft around. The fact that a means is necessary is not sufficient; it must be an expedient means which will help the aim to be achieved. This demand should also hold for humanitarian interventions and their moral permissibility.

An HI is morally permissible only if
(2) the type of intervention (a) is expedient to the aim of intervention.

This stipulation takes us into an examination of the conditions dealt with in theories of just warfare under the category of justice *in* war (of *ius in bello*). The first condition dealt with what it takes to make the launch of an intervention morally right; now we are concerned with the moral limitations surrounding the intervention as a means to an end.

These limitations do not come out of the blue. They result from the corresponding moral limitations for general actions of self-defense and emergency assistance. Even in a situation of self-defense, the victim and those coming to his aid may not resort to any action whatsoever merely because such a situation has arisen. We state that the action must be "required," meaning that apart from the expedience mentioned above, the *counteraction* taken must be *the mildest possible in the circumstances*. To return to our example with the defenseless child threatened by a murderer, of course I may (if I have to) neutralize the killer, but not for instance by cutting his throat *if* I am sufficiently skilled in karate to knock him out with a couple of blows until the police arrive — and if by not resorting to my knife I do not put my own life at much greater risk than by using it.

As (in the case of military interventions), referring to "the mildest possible counteraction" could sound cynical, I shall formulate the new condition (b) as follows:

An HI is morally permissible only if
(2) the type of intervention (b) enables the aim of intervention to be achieved with the least possible harm to the intervention precipitator.

This translation is strictly geared towards the previous consideration, which only mentions that the party against whom the emergency assistance is directed must not be harmed more than necessary. Accordingly, the new condition (b) is also aimed only at the harm done to the party who provided the reason for intervention — in short, at the enemy against whom (or to be more accurate: against whose massive crimes against humanity) the intervention is directed, the "intervention precipitator."

The harm befalling the intervention precipitator is not the only — and not the most important — damage that must be considered in the moral assessment of interventions. Those threatening those providing emergency assistance were just mentioned. Let us leave them aside for the time being. Those who in the course of normal self-defense or emergency assistance may not be harmed are clearly identified by the criminal regulations reserved for such cases: self-defense or emergency assistance may only be directed against the *aggressor*, not against *outsiders' legal interests*. The well-aimed sniper's bullet against the terrorist holding hostages, if this really is the last chance of saving the hostages, may be justified under criminal law, yet ceases to be so as soon as another innocent person is jeopardized by this bullet.

This ban is thoroughly acceptable within the framework of criminal law. Within moral consideration (our activity here), however, it will be impossible to maintain it under all circumstances. At this point we ought to embark upon a process of weighing-up similar to that acted out for or against utilitarianism in any introductory seminar course. To borrow one of the most common exercises, let us assume that a terrorist has taken 20 hostages, and let us assume we are all absolutely certain that, as his demands have not been met, he will blow himself up together with all the hostages in the next few seconds. Should the SAS marksman who already has his sights trained on the terrorist be allowed to fire, even if he cannot completely rule out the chance of hitting an innocent passer-by who suddenly appears and strays into his line of fire? If you hesitate to answer yes, would you do the same if the terrorist had taken 50 hostages? Or what about 200? Or 1,000? These reflection games are terrible, but ethics is not supposed to be a barrel of laughs.

The Kosovo Dimension easily outweighs all bank-robber scenarios. Those who in view of this scale of difference accept humanitarian intervention as I have defined it as a *prima facie* option have already made up their minds. For moral reasons they are willing to overstep the bounds of what (in related contexts) is permissible under criminal law. We are thus entering a field where what is forbidden by criminal law is morally allowed. Military interventions that do not put external parties at risk simply do not exist. Even military interventions with the highest of humanitarian intentions are no exception. It is impossible to approve of humanitarian interventions and at the same time rule out others being put at risk.

This certainly does not mean that this hazard can be neglected in future. On the contrary: whenever during an operation a threat to external parties cannot be ruled out, everything must be done to ensure that this threat is minimized. This means in particular:

An HI is morally permissible only if
(2) the type of intervention (c) minimizes the threat to external parties.

Whosoever these external parties just mentioned might be, they certainly include neither those who precipitated the intervention and against whom the intervention is ultimately directed (in order to put a stop to their crimes), nor the intervention subject himself. Stipulation (b) dealt with the intervention precipitators; the intervention subject has so far been neglected by the previous stipulations. This omission is filled by condition (d):

An HI is morally permissible only if
(2) the type of intervention (d) minimizes the harm or threat to the intervening party himself.

Just to cite the extreme case, for example, this stipulation prevents an intervening state from simply using its own citizens as cannon-fodder to make intervention successful. The concept of harm or danger naturally encompasses a little more than the loss of human life. Not to be killed is not the only human value.

Stipulations (a) to (d) listed under (2) cover the core of what is often also described as the demand to *keep things in proportion*. I cannot go into the tricky question here of whether our above stipulations cover every aspect of proportion—and if they do not, how we could do justice to these outstanding points of view. This is not a great loss, as the necessary conditions outlined so far are perfectly adequate to judge NATO's intervention.

To be on the safe side, however, and to make sure that nobody regards the sum of these conditions as sufficient merely for the purpose of experimentation, I would like to include a safeguarding clause (even though many might believe it to be a matter of course):

An HI is morally permissible as long as
(3) it does not itself involve massive crimes against humanity.

This means that a humanitarian intervention is morally justified only if it does not involve the same things it is supposed to be combating and from which the entire *raison d'être* of humanitarian interventions stems. Humanitarian interventions that, in comparison to the crimes they are supposed to prevent, themselves constitute massive crimes against humanity, cannot be morally permissible. Humanitarian interventions may not for their part provide grounds for morally justified humanitarian counter-interventions.

Humanitarian Interventions and International Law

One stipulation for the moral permissibility of humanitarian interventions is still lacking from our necessary conditions—namely, one whose necessity has been the subject of the greatest controversy in the whole debate so far about the war in Kosovo:

An HI is morally permissible only if
(?—4—?) the intervention is sanctioned by (a) international law
and (b) in particular by a resolution passed by the UN Security
Council.

Why is this demand lacking? Quite simply because the world is not yet ready for this stipulation to make sense *now*. International law is not sufficiently developed, and the Security Council's resolution procedure still has a long way to go.

The situation in Kosovo was (as we should have known before the start of the war) an extremely precarious situation. It concerned the relationship between law and morality. Moral questions are very closely linked to legal questions—and this is precisely why we must draw a sharp distinction between the two so that this close connection cannot lead to any confusion. If something is legally necessary, it is generally morally necessary too. Note the "generally": it is not always so (otherwise, there would be no need whatsoever to discuss the moral justification of legal regulations). Isolated cases are conceivable in which it is not merely morally permissible but even morally necessary to violate existing laws, in which case what is legally necessary could even be morally forbidden. Of course, solid reasons are always going to be needed for such exceptions in view of the moral value (which cannot be assessed too highly) of binding legal norms, and these reasons probably exist only in very rare cases.

This potential difference between law and morality occurs in all areas of law, including current international law. Cases *are* conceivable in which violation of the international laws presently in force is not only morally allowed but may in fact be morally imperative. Such a case would be my fictitious Auschwitz scenario above: Auschwitz and all the other concentration camps exist in Germany alone, at a time of no German wars of aggression. Moreover, if it is also assumed that this Nazi Germany is a member of the Security Council with the power of veto, show me those who, in response to this situation, would be prepared to demand what at present many seem willing to blindly sign petitions for: respect for international law *whatever the consequences*. If the world complied with current international law, the consequence would be that the world would be forced to stand by and watch. Yet morality demands precisely the opposite. The Auschwitz Dimension cries out for humanitarian intervention even in contravention of valid international law and, obviously, even without the Security Council's approval (which anyway would not be forthcoming in the above situation owing to Nazi Germany's veto). In order to make this questionable stipulation concerning international law a necessary condition, international law must be changed so that, in the case of this fictitious Auschwitz scenario, the morally necessary humanitarian intervention would no longer be blocked despite the veto of a member of the Security Council.

In order to make myself clear, I would now like to add a few points.

1. The Kosovo Dimension is, as mentioned above, not identical with the Auschwitz Dimension.

2. Yugoslavia is not Nazi Germany. Neither is Serbia.

3. Yugoslavia is not a member of the Security Council. In view of the Kosovo Dimension, merely invoking Auschwitz is not enough to reach the same conclusion for the actual Kosovo crisis as for the above fictitious Auschwitz crisis.

Another aspect has so far been neglected in the debate surrounding the validation of the war in Kosovo under international law. This debate assumes that if in addition to NATO the UN was also in favor of this war, everything would be fine. This is at present legally correct, but in moral terms potentially wrong. It takes more than UN support for an intervention (even a humanitarian intervention) to be morally acceptable. As we have seen above, a few other conditions have to be met as well. And these could then be violated, even with the approval of the Security Council.

This discussion so far constitutes a brilliant victory for the renowned German tradition of hermeneutics. Its domains are the diverse relations between wording and deeper sense. If the *letter* of international law really is opposed to the war, how can its *spirit* be determined so that the *essence* of international law can be reconciled with our humanitarian consciousness and traditions? This is the question which humanitarian writers, intervention ministers, and other experts on international law argued while NATO flew over 20,000 missions over the former Yugoslavia. Let us postpone the apologetic exegesis of international law until tomorrow. Today's question is: is this war morally good?

Is This War Good? The Relevant Questions

Is this war good? Is NATO's intervention in Yugoslavia morally justified? Now that the central concepts have been explained and the most relevant moral demands are known, "all" we now need to answer this question is the facts. As usual, these can be divided into three categories: the clear facts, the less clear ones, and those we do not yet know. We should try to support our case on the first category, the clear facts, but unfortunately it is this group which is the smallest — which is probably always the case as far as relevant facts during times of war are concerned. Therefore, at such times one has to make do with the less clear facts, making the resulting moral judgment less solid.

Is our intervention in Yugoslavia morally permissible? This question can now be formulated more precisely. Have all the requirements which need to be met for such an intervention to be morally legitimate actually been met? We know what these requirements are, so let us subject the current NATO intervention — from now on I will often just say *the intervention* for short — to the test of these demands.

The intervention covers a great deal. It can stand for the decision to intervene militarily, the launch of the intervention, the manner of the intervention (e.g., air raids instead of ground troops), the same thing but in more detail (e.g., only bombs dropped from a great height, thus magnifying the risk of collateral damage), the manner of the intervention today, etc. These are very different things. And similarly, moral judgment of these different things can also differ. However, it should always be clear what these and other things mean when we are talking about *the intervention*.

We must ask ourselves the following questions:

1. Was or is the intervention really necessary to eliminate the reason for the intervention?

2. Is the manner of the intervention actually beneficial for its aim?

3. Is the intervention being carried out such that for the intervening agents themselves the damage and the threat caused is kept to a minimum?

4. Is the intervention taking place such that it is accompanied by the least damage required to achieve the aim of intervention being inflicted on the intervention precipitator?

5. Is the intervention being carried out such that the risk to outside parties is minimized?

6. Is the intervention on our part connected with massive crimes against humanity?

An assessment of the intervention requires answering this list of questions as a whole. What "least possible damage" is supposed to mean in the three areas of damage to be taken into account (intervention subject, intervention precipitator, outside parties) can only be more closely identified by considering the minimization of the overall damage. In doing so, we will not be able to dodge morally weighting the various damage minimization requirements. Do moral reasons not make us devote priority to minimizing damage to third parties over minimizing damage to the intervention precipitator—and over minimizing damage suffered by the intervention subject? It certainly cannot be said that the less harm suffered by the intervening party (at the cost of third parties), the more moral the intervention.

We are dealing with the moral evaluation of a concrete intervention—with the assessment of an *action*, not of an *actor*. Thus what counts for this intervention assessment is primarily its *consequences*, not the (supposed or actual) *intentions* linked to it. Do we really have to remember that these are two different things? And that history contains enough examples of how the best intentions can lead to the most appalling consequences? And vice versa, that even the worst intentions can sometimes result in good? We primarily take intentions into account when we are assessing the actor (the person, the acting institution); we study the consequences when we want to judge the act itself.

This distinction has a clear application: The mere fact that an intervention is humanitarian (i.e., it is associated with a humanitarian intention) does not by itself make an intervention good—not by a long chalk. The reason for this was stated above: the conditions for the moral justification of a humanitarian intervention are not merely fulfilled by virtue of the existence of a humanitarian intention.

This separation between assessing an intention and assessing the consequences takes much of the alleged moral point out of the speculation about the true intentions of the intervening party. What really counts when somebody is in an emergency is for them to receive genuine assistance—not the motives behind the act bringing about this help (or not). These intentions and motives at most become relevant if we analyze reasons for equivalent behavior in future cases.

During moral evaluations, one often falls into the *fictitious da capo trap*. You married the wrong woman, you are in a right mess, and you wonder what the best thing is for everyone, including the kids. The last thing that is going to help is, "I told you so"—as if you could simply slip out of the current situation and leap back to before you got together and then take the right decision this time. The relevant question is: what should be done now?

All well-meaning advice concerning what the various sides should or should not have done beforehand so that the question "Intervention—yes or no?" would not have had to be asked in the first place are equally irrelevant for a moral assessment of the intervention. Being wise after the event should be put to good use in managing similar situations better *in future*; it is no good for a moral assessment of the *current* situation, which we evidently did not manage better. Reference to the genesis of the current situation helps us to understand it; it does not solve the moral problems which only emerge once we are in the middle of it.

Notes

1. This is the English version of a talk I gave at several universities in Germany when NATO attacked Yugoslavia in spring 1999. For the original German version see: *Ist dieser Krieg gut? Ein ethischer Kommentar, Der Kosovo-Krieg und das Völkerrecht*, ed. Reinhard Merkel (Frankfurt/M.: Edition Suhrkamp, 2000).

2. For Georg Henrik von Wright and Sarah Rebecca Meggle. My title stems from talks I gave in early May 1999 in Leipzig, Münster, and Frankfurt am Main. Apart from Georg Henrik von Wright and my daughter, I would also like to express my grateful thanks for the help received from Jovan Babic, Kurt Bayertz, Lutz Eckensberger, Günther Grewendorf, Franz von Kutschera, Wolfgang Lenzen, Weyma Lübbe, Matthias Lutz-Bachmann, Thomas Metzinger, Richard Raatzsch, Veronika Reiss, Sabine Rieckhoff, Peter Rohs, Mark Siebel, and my right hand throughout this time, Christian Plunze.

2

Humanitarian Intervention After Kosovo

Richard Falk

In the aftermath of the cold war, conflicts internal to states have captured center stage in global politics. Numerous humanitarian catastrophes have occurred in this period since 1989, partly as a result of weak structures of governance, producing the phenomenon of "failed states," especially in sub-Saharan Africa. Also, the emergence of human rights as items ranked rather highly, although selectively, on the global policy agenda has generated support for "humanitarian intervention."[1] This support also reflects the growing influence of TV in building public pressure to act in the face of severe humanitarian abuse.

Such a background has challenged the capacities of the United Nations to provide politically acceptable and logistically effective responses.[2] Although not paralyzed by ideological stalemates, disagreements persist among the permanent members of the Security Council as to the proper balance in particular situations between sovereign rights and humanitarian intervention. Furthermore, geopolitical realities restrict an interventionary option to circumstances where the country involved is relatively weak or is induced to give consent. The whole pattern of response has also been affected in this period by the quality of global leadership provided by the United States, and the extent to which the nature of this leadership has been buffeted to and fro by domestic political tensions, particularly as exhibited by the US Congress, as in the struggle over the US relationship to the UN.

Such a set of circumstances poses a series of difficult challenges directed at the relevant international institutions and international law norms. It is partly a matter of reconciling doctrine with practice, partly a matter of evaluating the world order significance of these various moves toward a new humanitarian diplomacy that is being shaped by contradictory pressures — the post-colonial revival of interventionary diplomacy and the emergence of support for the international implementation of minimum human rights in the face of severe governmental abuses and criminality.

Many of these concerns are brought into focus by a consideration of the legal and world order controversy surrounding the NATO War over Kosovo waged against Yugoslavia in 1999. This consideration is also guided by the inspirational influence of Georges Abi-Saab's career as scholar and humanist, embodying such a delicate balance between fidelity to the craft of law and lawyering and a preoccupation with humane values.[3]

A Point of Departure

Perhaps more fundamentally than any recent international occurrence, the NATO initiative on behalf of the Kosovars has provoked extreme divergent interpretations of what is truly at stake, about the prudence of what was undertaken, and about the bearing of law and morality on this course of events. This divergence of perspective can be suggestively framed by reference to the positions adopted by two highly respected and morally engaged international figures: Vaclev Havel, acclaimed president of the Czech Republic, and Robert Fisk, renowned correspondent and feature writer for the British newspaper, *The Independent*.

Acknowledging that the tactics adopted by NATO have given rise to controversy, Havel in an address to the Canadian Senate and House of Commons on April 29,1999, goes on to affirm what was for him beyond controversy about the Kosovo undertaking:

> But there is one thing no reasonable person can deny: this is probably the first war that has not been waged in the name of "national interests," but rather in the name of principles and values. If one can say of any war that it is ethical, or that it is being waged for ethical reasons, then it is true of this war. Kosovo has no oil fields to be coveted; no member nation in the alliance has any territorial demands on Kosovo; Milosevic does not threaten the territorial integrity of any member of the alliance. And yet the alliance is at war. It is fighting out of a concern for the fate of others. It is fighting because no decent person can stand by and watch the systematic, state-directed murder of other people. It cannot tolerate such a thing. It cannot fail to provide assistance if it is within its power to do so.[4]

Robert Fisk writes with equal fervor in criticism of what NATO has done:

How much longer do we have to endure the folly of NATO's war in the Balkans? In its first fifty days, the Atlantic alliance failed in everything it set out to do. It failed to protect the Kosovo Albanians from Serbian war crimes. It failed to cow Slobodan Milosevic. It failed to force the withdrawal of Serb troops from Kosovo. It broke international law in attacking a sovereign state without seeking a UN mandate. It killed hundreds of innocent Serb civilians — in our name, of course, while being too cowardly to risk a single NATO life in defense of the poor and weak for whom it meretriciously claimed to be fighting. NATO's war cannot even be regarded as a mistake; it is a criminal act.[5]

Although written in the midst of the war, the essential lines of Fisk's critical analysis remain untouched by subsequent events, except that Milosevic did eventually submit to NATO bombing, although only after wresting several important political concessions from the Russian negotiators. This "diplomatic solution" has produced the withdrawal of Serbian military and police forces, the safeguarding of Kosovo through the presence of a strong NATO-led international peacekeeping force, and a central post-conflict administering and reconstruction role for the UN.

A difficulty of assessment arises because in crucial respects *both* of these seemingly contradictory positions are persuasive. The Western mind, especially in its legal dimensions, tends toward an either/or resolution of adversarial lines of interpretation, as modeled through judicial litigation. However arbitrary in a particular case, there is always a winner and a loser in a judicial setting. It is jurisprudentially problematic to regard *both* ethnic cleansing as intolerable by the international community and to condemn the form and substance of the NATO interventionary response designed to prevent it. And yet just such a doctrinal tension seems to follow from the perspectives of international law and world order. My attempt here is to defend such a double condemnation as posing the essential normative challenge for the future: *genocidal behavior cannot be shielded by claims of sovereignty, but neither can these claims be overridden by unauthorized uses of force delivered in an excessive and inappropriate manner.*

The main line of argument can be anticipated. So long as a purely textual analysis of the relevant norms is relied upon, there exists no satisfactory way to reconcile the divergencies between humanitarian imperatives and the prohibition upon interventionary force unauthorized by the UN. The only mode of assessment that can achieve a limited reconciliation depends on a contextual analysis along the lines of "configurative jurisprudence," or closely related, "incidents jurisprudence." Of course, contextual complexity creates ample opportunity for sharply divergent lines of factual and legal interpretation, as is illustrated by the sharp controversies about the legality of the American intervention in the Vietnam War among those who regarded themselves as adherents of a configurative approach.[6] Nevertheless, what the configurative approach enables, indeed entails, is a comprehensive assessment that includes an embrace of complementary norms, as well as an appraisal of what has been done in the name of law and an evaluation of whether preferable policy alternatives to the course taken were available to those with the authority to make decisions. For these reasons, the configurative orientation enhances the quality of legal debate even if it is generally unable to resolve the underlying legal controversy. Enhancing debate is particularly important for a democratic society whose essence arguably lies in the core societal commitment to resolve controversy by nonviolent communicative discourse.

In the setting of Kosovo, such a style of contextual assessment alone allows the double condemnation, yet helps disclose a course of action that might have avoided both ethnic cleansing and recourse to warfare and its conduct in a morally and legally dubious fashion. In this respect, the Kosovo precedent is critically examined to enable a more constructive line of response in the event of a comparable future challenge, or at minimum to encourage a more promising line of discussion and reflection. Admittedly, a retrospective contention that an alternative course of action might have produced a preferable outcome is an instance of counter-factual reasoning and, as such, is necessarily highly speculative. Such uncertainty is unavoidable if the position taken, as here, is one that is critical of what was done under NATO auspices, but does not endorse the view that, in this event, nothing effective should or could have been done about meeting the challenge of ethnic cleansing. Attempting to find a preferable path of action for future responses to genocidal behavior and crimes against humanity inevitably involves an acceptance of such hypothetical reasoning. Such reasoning may itself be more or less convincing depending on the integrity and skill of its presentation of facts and legal considerations.

Depicting the Fearful Policy Dilemma

There is no reasonable doubt that the Albanian majority population of Kosovo was being placed in severe jeopardy by actions taken under the authority of the Milosevic government in Belgrade during the 1990s. These policies involved fundamental denials of human rights, including the right of self-determination to "a people." The essence of these denials encouraged Serbian atrocities designed to intimidate Albanian Kosovars or to coerce their mass exit, clearing the way for less-obstructed Serb dominance, the underlying goal of this ethnic cleansing. Such factual one-sidedness is itself not entirely accurate as the formation of the KLA (Kosovo Liberation Army) dedicated to waging an armed struggle to achieve an independent Kosovo involved a variety of violent provocations that provided an ongoing pretext and rationale for harsh Serb security measures.[7] Considering the demographic balance in Kosovo—9: 1 in favor of the Albanians—the Serbian pressure to intimidate was undoubtedly intense, but the result was one of unmistakable repression of the majority population with a deliberate ethnic thrust that was genocidal in its overall effects.

It was also reasonable in light of earlier Serb tactics in Bosnia—as epitomized by concentration camps, numerous massacres and crimes against humanity, and the brutal annihilation in 1995 of some 7,300 Bosnian Muslims sheltered by the UN safe haven of Srebenica—that international action of significant magnitude was urgently needed if full-scale ethnic cleansing in Kosovo was to be avoided. The Serb massacre of 40 persons in the Kosovo town of Racak, 18 miles southwest of Pristina, in January 1999, was widely portrayed by Europe and Washington as the final warning bell and was so presented by the media.[8] Sources sympathetic with Serb viewpoints continue to insist that the "civilians" were actually KLA "fighters" killed in an encounter with Serb security forces, and then made to appear as massacre "victims" by local Albanians. The dominant Euro-American perception was that something had to be done, and quickly, or else the Bosnian ordeal would be reproduced catastrophically in Kosovo with damaging consequences for the future of Europe and for the credibility of the trans-Atlantic alliance with the US.

Beyond this, it was evident to many influential leaders and advisors, particularly in the US, that the UN was ill-suited for this mission. It was seen as having failed in Bosnia, in part due to the absence of political will by those who were committed to its peacekeeping mission there and partly due to friction within the Security Council as to the proper course of action to be adopted, whether that of neutrality and impartiality, or on behalf of the ethnic group being victimized.[9] In the context of Kosovo these problems seem even more formidable than had been the case in Bosnia. In the months before the war, China and Russia appeared ready to veto any call for UN intervention, as well as any mandate that conferred upon NATO or any other entity such a right. In this respect, the only prospect for an effective humanitarian intervention *appeared* to depend on acting outside of the UN and in violation of the basic letter and spirit of its Charter. Such an "appearance" was reinforced, but also undermined, by strong independent pressures to endow NATO with renewed credibility and meaningful security roles in the emergent post-cold war setting of a Europe unthreatened by an *external* adversary. Also of apparent significance was the post-cold war opportunity to reassert the hegemonic role of the US with respect to European security policy. Without archival access, which will not be available for years, the impact of these pressures on shaping the response to ethnic cleansing and human rights abuse in Kosovo is impossible to evaluate, especially as their relevance is officially denied.

It was also maintained by the pro-intervention side that diplomatic remedies had been exhausted. Richard Holbrooke visited Belgrade repeatedly in 1998 and early 1999 to induce Milosevic to accept a diplomatic solution, which consisted of the deployment of a NATO peacekeeping force in Kosovo, substantial interim autonomy for the province, and a commitment to hold a referendum on its future in three years. This diplomatic package was presented as a non-negotiable set of demands to Yugoslavia at Rambouillet, and its rejection by Belgrade and only reluctant acceptance by the KLA provided a political mandate for NATO military action. In essence, recourse to military intervention arguably occurred after all reasonable opportunities for peaceful settlement had been sufficiently explored. Under these circumstances, it was alleged that waiting any further would have exposed the endangered Kosovar population to grave risks and irreversible harm and would have made impossible a successful humanitarian intervention.

The anti-intervention argument is comparably coherent.[10] It takes the fundamental view that NATO's recourse to war was legally unacceptable without explicit authorization by the UN Security Council and that NATO could not validly act on its own in this setting.[11] It rejects as legalistic the textual claims that the NATO use of force was not directed at "the territorial integrity or political independence" of Yugoslavia and, therefore, was not prohibited by Article 2(4) of the Charter. It also rejects the parallel contention that NATO was not bound by Article 53 of the Charter, since as an alliance it was not formally a Chapter VIII "regional organization" and its undertaking was not strictly "an enforcement action." In this reading of the Charter, all uses of non-defensive force are strictly controlled by the UN Security Council; to bypass its authority on the basis of a self-serving evasion of prospective vetoes is unacceptably to take law into one's own hands. Indeed, one justification for the veto is precisely to prevent uses of force that are not responses to an armed attack in the absence of a political consensus among the permanent members. And here, with the initiative being one of collective action by the Western powers within NATO, the bypassing of UN authority is seen as a devastating constitutional blow at that authority's most basic prohibition inscribed in international law governing recourse to force by states outside the domain of self-defense. It is likely to be viewed with particular alarm by China and Russia, which understandably view their veto power as a protection against threats of "a tyranny of the majority," and as providing a measure of insulation from US "hegemonic" claims. It also provides these governments with "a precedent" for their own contested claims to use force against dissident minority peoples and territorial units in Chechnya and Tibet.

Beyond this, the anti-interventionists do not accept the argument that diplomatic means were properly used or exhausted. They point to the exclusion of Russian diplomatic participation prior to NATO's recourse to war, the rigidity of the Holbrooke/Rambouillet formula, and the absence of any evident diplomatic effort to induce China and Russia to accommodate the Security Council majority by shifting their veto to an abstention.[12] Critics of the NATO intervention compare this pattern of pre-war negotiation with the success of the war-ending diplomacy based on a major Russian role and face-saving gestures offered Belgrade that included a willingness to "conceal" the dominant role of the NATO-led peacekeeping force beneath a UN cover story. It is notable in this regard that the war-ending diplomatic text, Security Council Resolution 1244, barely mentions NATO and, if "innocently" read, would suggest that Kosovo is fundamentally subject to UN peacekeeping authority.[13] The contention is that flexible diplomacy might have achieved an acceptable result along the lines of Resolution 1244 and that, had it been tried without success, a subsequent recourse to force under NATO auspices would then have seemed far more reasonable. Still, such reasonableness with respect to recourse to war would still not have met the objections relating to the modalities of force relied upon by NATO, nor altogether overcome the Article 2(4) prohibition on non-defensive force.

These objections fueled a parallel debate relating to the means chosen to conduct the war.[14] Those who defend NATO point to the outcome, which is viewed as submission by Belgrade and in effect an acceptance of the essential features of the Rambouillet framework. They also point to the political constraints that precluded other interventionary options, such as reliance on ground troops or upon a more focused bombing strategy that would have subjected NATO aircraft to more risks from Yugoslav anti-aircraft defenses. Public support in the NATO countries for intervention was supposedly conditioned on the prospect of minuscule casualties, making recourse to higher risk options politically unavailable to the leaders of NATO countries, who felt themselves accountable to their respective electorates.[15]

Also, as President Clinton acknowledged shortly after the suspension of the Kosovo bombing, his expectation had been that Milosevic would either give in to threat diplomacy or, at worst, submit after a few days of bombing, which in this initial phase was in fact generally confined to military targets, reinforced by primary reliance upon "smart" weaponry.[16] In light of expert military advice, it was arguable that such an expectation on the part of the NATO political leadership was reasonable and that, when proved wrong, it was then necessary to carry on with the military effort, intensifying the attack until it reached its goals. To have abandoned the effort midway, it is maintained, would have wrecked NATO's credibility in relation to the future of European security, and sent the wrong signals to future tyrants and oppressors. It would also have given a green light to the accelerated ethnic cleansing undertaken in Kosovo as soon as the war commenced, a response given guidance and direction by Belgrade. This latter assessment of complicity at the highest level of the Yugoslav government is reinforced by the indictment of Milosevic and his closest aides on various criminal charges by the UN International Criminal Tribunal for Yugoslavia.

Critics of the manner in which the NATO intervention was carried out see the situation very differently. They perceive alternative lines of action as having been available and far preferable on humanitarian grounds to a high altitude bombing campaign. In this regard they favor helping the KLA in securing an independent Kosovo or insisting on a NATO strategy that combined ground assault with lower altitude air attacks. They also reject the extension of NATO bombing after its initial failure to induce submission by Milosevic, especially the decision to target key components of the civilian infrastructure of Serbia. The expansion of the bombing campaign resulted in heavy damage to the water and electricity supply systems; caused severe pollution through the destruction of chemical factories and oil refineries; and introduced such unacceptable weaponry and tactics as B-52 attacks, cluster bombs, and depleted uranium ordinance.[17]

Such critics also highlight the effects of the bombing as doing severe damage to Kosovo and its inhabitants, inducing a heavy flow of refugees that approached one million, as well as destroying many cities and towns, and causing the death of hundreds, if not thousands, of civilians in Kosovo. These critics are also inclined to regard the massive Serb resort to ethnic cleansing by the most brutal means as largely *an effect* of the bombing rather than as merely accelerating a plan that would otherwise have been carried out in a more gradual manner. A related criticism is that the severity of NATO's strategy combined with the Serb responses to it have produced a set of circumstances that is resulting in a second cycle of ethnic cleansing in Kosovo, which is being carried forth successfully by Kosovar Albanians against Serbs and gypsies, while under the supposedly protective gaze of the UN/NATO peacekeeping operation.

Putting these two major lines of interpretation together leaves one with the disturbing impression that humanitarian intervention on behalf of Albanian Kosovars was *necessary* but, under the circumstances, *impossible*. It was necessary to prevent a humanitarian catastrophe in the form of ethnic cleansing. It was impossible due to the *political* unavailability of an appropriate means. The selection of such a means was blocked by deep divisions among leading European states and by the resolve to insist on a NATO solution. It also reflected the refusal by the citizenry of the NATO countries, especially Germany and the US, to be prepared to bear the considerable and uncertain human costs that might have followed from the adoption of a legally and morally more acceptable form of intervention. As this phrasing suggests, the most helpful form of legal appraisal is one of *degree*, conceiving of legality and illegality by reference to a spectrum. The more "reasonable" a response, the closer to the legality end of the spectrum. In relation to Kosovo, the contention here is that there were plausible options available to give the action taken a higher degree of legality (without compromising the humanitarian mission), and thereby improving its status as a precedent for the future.

Rejecting Legalism

Although, admittedly, no jurisprudential approach to legal analysis leaves an entirely satisfied impression under the circumstances that existed in Kosovo, reliance on legalistic analysis is particularly unfortunate for the future of international law. It puts international lawyers in the uncomfortable role that Immanuel Kant accused them of in *Perpetual Peace*, namely, that of being "miserable consolers." There is no ultra-literalistic reading of the Charter provisions that does not strain credulity as to the intentions of the founders of the UN. The basic undertaking of the Charter was to assign exclusive control over non-defensive uses of force to the Security Council and to accept the limits on response that this entailed as a result of vesting the five permanent members with a right of veto. In the setting of the Gulf War this Charter framework supporting collective security was reaffirmed by the entire Security Council; although China had misgivings about the recourse of force under the UN flag, it abstained, thereby creating an impression of unanimity, which indirectly reinforced the decision by the World Court in the Nicaragua case that placed strict limits on claims to exercise force in self-defense.[18]

Furthermore, the idea that NATO can use force freely without the expected accountability of regional actors to the Charter system by refraining from denoting its undertaking as "an enforcement action" is to strain political and moral credulity to the breaking point. It would appear that a military alliance would be subject to greater constitutional constraints than a regional organization as understood by Chapter VIII. Indeed, if its actions do not qualify as "collective self-defense" under the Charter, then the full weight of Article 2(4) would appear applicable. Such an analysis bears directly on NATO, which was set up in 1949 as a means to institutionalize the defense of Europe against the threat of a Soviet attack, with no indication of any claim to respond to intrastate strife even within the alliance area, much less beyond it.

Similarly, the legalistic contentions of those that point to the domestic jurisdiction and veto powers as precluding humanitarian intervention occupy untenable ground. It is correct that normal textual readings are on their side and that the Charter system cannot be legally bypassed in the manner that NATO attempted to do. Yet, it is equally true that to regard the textual barriers to humanitarian intervention as decisive in the face of genocidal behavior is politically and morally unacceptable, especially in view of the increasing qualifications imposed on unconditional claims of sovereignty by the growth of an international human rights tradition.[19] It is true that the UN was not constituted in a setting that addressed the challenges of intrastate conflict, and indeed the understanding among the founders was that such an agenda would be treated as falling within the "domestic jurisdiction" limitation on UN competence to act. But a series of normative developments over the years have eroded the clarity of this distinction: the Genocide Convention, the blurring of inside/outside distinctions (in relation to the territorial state) under the various pressures of "globalization," and the spread of democracy and of the media capacity to report human tragedy in real time has generated a new global ethos of responsibility in relation to humanitarian emergencies.[20] Admittedly, this ethos is unevenly implemented on the level of political action, as the earlier experiences in Bosnia and Rwanda illustrate, but, in the setting of Europe and given the perceived failures of the recent response in relation to Bosnia, the pressure to act was legitimized in a manner that superseded legalistic restraints.

In essence, the textual level of analysis, upon which legalists rely, cannot give a satisfactory basis for NATO intervention, nor can it provide a suitable rationale for rejecting the humanitarian imperative to rescue the potential victims of genocidal policies in Kosovo. Nor does textualism help focus attention on whether the means chosen were legally acceptable in light of the goals being pursued. A more nuanced attention to context is required to reformulate the debate in a manner that corresponds with the broad injunction to seek a global security system that contributes to the achievement of "humane governance" on a global scale. Otherwise, the self-marginalization of international law and international lawyers is assured in contemporary situations involving claims to use force, consigning their vocational fate to the demeaning roles of "apologist" or "utopian." No less demeaning is to conflate law and policy by mechanically deferring to "practice" and "effective power" as vindicating extensions of the notions of legality with respect to the use of force.

The Geopolitical Prerogative

Another framework for assessment involves rationalizing special exemptions from the constraining impact of international law by reference to the special role of the US as a self-anointed guardian of international order, exempt from any inhibiting constraints of international law. The fact that the US chose to act within the collective framework of NATO is of mild relevance, suggesting some diminution of an essentially unilateral geopolitical prerogative. Yet, not too much should be made of recourse to NATO, due to its control by Washington. Revealingly, in the text of his book on the Bosnian negotiations that produced the Dayton Agreement at the end of 1995, Richard Holbrooke reprints the text of a letter he later wrote to President Clinton, in which he unwittingly confirmed the prevailing view of NATO as a US pawn: "Of the many organizations in Yugoslavia in the last five years, only NATO — that is, the US — has been respected."[21]

Variations of this view have graced the pages of recent issues of *Foreign Affairs*, masquerading as a debate between two prominent American international law specialists, Michael Glennon and Thomas Franck (with some additional commentary from the former and widely respected Executive Director of the United Nations Association of the United States, Edward C. Luck). Glennon grounds his argument on the premise that the Charter was drafted to cope with interstate violence, while the contemporary world is beset with a series of intrastate challenges that can only be met by coercive forms of peacekeeping (that is, without the consent of the relevant government), or what he refers to as "the new interventionism."[22]

In rationalizing the Kosovo initiative, Glennon perceives the basic issue as one in which "justice (as it is now understood) and the UN Charter seemed to collide." He goes on immediately to contextualize the claim of justice by reference to what "enlightened states now believe ... to be just," and then implicitly identifies this mandate with a validation of the NATO response to Kosovo.[23] It seems unavoidable to wonder whether Glennon's use of "enlightened" is not a late twentieth-century updating of the now unfashionable "civilized." The normative pretension seems indistinguishable! Glennon does condition this affirmation with cautionary language about the risks of validation, given its ad hoc character and the vagueness of the guidelines, but concludes with the view that "the cost of abandoning the old anti-interventionist structure" is not high as "[t]he failings of the old system were disastrous."[24] The essence of Glennon's careful argument is that the currently most powerful Western governments have an implicit authority to pursue lines of coercive diplomacy that accord with their sense of justice.[25] However, the viability over time of such diplomacy will depend on the capacity of such geopolitical actors to place "the new interventionism" within an appropriate principled framework of decision that comes to be widely accepted by the rest of the international community[26] and thereby legitimated. In effect, Kosovo was an acceptable first step toward reformulating the relationship of power to justice, positing an alternative to the anachronistic Charter conception, but this approach will only be enduringly vindicated by overcoming its appearance of being an ad hoc move.[27]

The response of Franck, also an evident supporter of the NATO initiative, is to contend that the Charter framework is far more adaptive than Glennon lets on, that it can be used to address intrastate challenges whenever a Security Council consensus exists, and that in this sense it is in essence no different than the case presented by interstate violence where the Council can be paralyzed by a veto.[28] Franck points to a series of well-known instances of coercive peacekeeping that has achieved Security Council backing, such as Bosnia, Somalia, Rhodesia, South Africa, Haiti, and Iraq.[29] He accepts the veto in this instance as but a trivial obstacle to NATO action, nothing more than a cautionary indication of serious opposition to a geopolitically preferred course of action. The veto does not operate for Franck as an unconditional bar to such action: "NATO's action in Kosovo is not the first time illegal steps have been taken to prevent something palpably worse."[30] The hegemonic power enjoys the privileged position of neglecting the restraints of international law for the sake of pursuing objectives that it deems to be of sufficient importance, as was the case in relation to Kosovo. For Franck, the basic Charter framework continues to be a useful foundation for world order, although subject to a legitimated dynamic of geopolitical nullification.

From my perspective, the debate between Glennon and Franck, while interesting, misses the essential feature of the Kosovo challenge, which is what I have earlier referred to as "the fearful dilemma." By endorsing the Kosovo response as carried out by NATO, their focus is upon finding an acceptable political rationale; thus, their focus is on what the US should do in circumstances where its preferred line of policy is blocked by a veto in the Security Council. Does one really want to encourage such a geopolitical prerogative even if softened, as in Glennon's position, by an advisory that in the long term legitimacy is important and can only be achieved through community acceptance of some new framework of principled action? Such a world order precedent seems dangerous and irresponsible and must be tested by reference to the acceptability of comparable conceivable claims made in the future by a geopolitical adversary, such as Russia and China. As earlier suggested, the invocation of Kosovo by the highest Russian officials to validate their brutality in Chechnya is a reminder that geopolitical arguments for abandoning legal constraints can be turned in many directions.[31]

But even more centrally, both Glennon and Franck finesse the questionable modalities of the NATO response to Kosovo as casting considerable doubt on the central claim of an enactment of justice. They focus the argument on whether there was a fit occasion for an effective response to a credible challenge of ethnic cleansing, but without questioning the legally, morally, and politically dubious nature of the response itself.[32]

The main problem with presupposing the validity of NATO's response is that it focuses exclusively on the injustice of Milosevic's policies in Kosovo and does not consider the injustice of the NATO response, including the decision to withhold reconstruction aid from Belgrade and to maintain sanctions despite the likelihood of widespread suffering by the Serbian population, especially during the winter months in 1999-2000. My contention is that, unless this double injustice is placed in focus, no jurisprudential appraisal will be generally convincing, nor should it be. At most, it will help those firmly within the NATO circle of support to find the most satisfying world order spin for their preferred course of action, and it will widen the gap between NATO critics and supporters to such a degree as to render constructive dialogue impossible. I would also view in the same manner those who one-sidedly condemn NATO for bypassing the UN, defying international law applicable to the use of force, and ignoring legal restraints relevant to the initiation and conduct of war. They, too, unacceptably simplify the search for a conclusion, seemingly resigned to a response of helplessness, regressive insensitivity to the humanitarian challenge posed by ethnic cleansing and sustained, severe human rights abuse evident in Kosovo over a period of years, and intensifying during 1998.

Against this background, my argument centers on the need to ground a legal appraisal and an appeal to justice on the contextual reality of Kosovo, which includes the inability and unwillingness of NATO to fashion a response commensurate to the challenge or to craft a humanitarian policy that included Serbia. Because of this fundamental circumstance, no clear line of legal inference can be persuasively drawn in relation to what was done: in effect, it was justifiable to act, but not in the manner undertaken. As such, the Kosovo precedent is flawed as a foundation for future action.[33]

The Configurative Option

The argument being made is that an assessment of the NATO response to the humanitarian crisis in Kosovo cannot be usefully resolved by a reliance on positivist styles of legal appraisal, underpinned by a mixture of geopolitical and humanitarian preoccupations. I regard the Glennon/Franck debate as an instance of positivist style. Both scholars view the legal controversy from the perspective of its rule-oriented character, Glennon arguing that the Charter legal regime be cast aside as obsolete, Franck responding that the Charter is still useful, but that in this instance it is acceptable to disregard its constraint; the other more manifestly positivist style involves interpreting the Charter rules as either allowing or precluding the NATO initiative. Such lines of appraisal in this setting cannot illuminate the complexity of the decision arising from the apparent dilemma of either intervening without appropriate legal authorization or watching on the sidelines while ethnic cleansing of an embattled minority takes place. The best that it can do is either to set international law aside or to mount legalistic arguments on one side or the other by strained reasoning insensitive to the main doctrinal contradiction embedded in *this* factual context. To some extent every set of circumstances that gives rise to factual controversy exhibits these features to varying degrees. In some settings the hierarchy among legal considerations is sufficiently clear as to give decisive weight to textual factors and positivist lines of reasoning, as when Indonesia attacked East Timor in 1975 or Iraq attacked Kuwait in 1990.[34]

Jurisprudential options, then, are to be considered as tools of illumination rather than as expressive of an ontological truth and are to be evaluated primarily by whether they engender constructive debate about policy choices and past decisions. In this regard, the role of international law and lawyers is to clarify decisional contexts, to recommend preferred options, and to engender useful societal debate in the setting of controversial issues of great public significance.

In relation to Kosovo, the analysis set forth here is based on respect for the Charter framework relating to force, the acceptance of a humanitarian imperative, and criticism of the manner in which the response was fashioned. It is now necessary to explain the main lines of criticism.

THE FAILURE TO PURSUE DIPLOMATIC REMEDIES

An authoritative assessment of whether a negotiated diplomatic solution for Kosovo was ever sought in good faith is not possible without unimpeded access to the minds and secret communications of the principal players on both sides. Nevertheless, there are preliminary conclusions that can be reached on the basis of available information and circumstantial evidence. Without entering into the factual detail needed to support such assertions, the diplomatic stance of the American Secretary of State, Madeleine Albright engenders a strong sense that the US government was opposed to any sort of flexibility in dealing with Belgrade in the lead-up to the war and, further, was similarly opposed to entrusting the United Nations with any role relating to an agreed process of offering the people of Kosovo protection.[35] Such inflexibility was exhibited in a number of ways, including an insistence on the exclusive reliance on an American negotiator in discussions with Milosevic, the exclusion of Russia and China from the effort to find a diplomatic solution based on a political compromise, and the drafting of conditions for the NATO peacekeeping role in Kosovo in such an uncompromising fashion as to assure that Belgrade could not possibly accept the final round of diplomatic proposals made in February 1999 to representatives of the Federal Republic of Yugoslavia and of Kosovar Albanians at Rambouillet Castle, a former French royal hunting ground near Paris.

This impression of inflexibility contrasts revealingly with the approach accepted after the war strategy had failed to achieve either a pre-war surrender or the expected quick collapse of resistance in Belgrade. At this point a prominent Russian negotiator, Vladimir Chernomyrdin, was given a central role, along with the Finnish President, Martti Ahtisaari. The outcome of this diplomacy was a return to a set of arrangements at least nominally under the auspices of the UN and in which the Russians (despite being non-members of NATO) were given an active role in the Kosovo peacekeeping process. Even the Kosovars have not yet *formally* benefited from the submission of Belgrade. At Rambouillet, Kosovo was promised immediate autonomy with a referendum in three years to allow the population to decide upon their future status, including the option of secession and independence. Such a promise to apply the right of self-determination for Kosovo disappeared in the agreed Security Council Resolution 1244, although, arguably, the substantial attainment of de facto independence for Kosovo was a result of the war and could not have been achieved even if the Rambouillet terms had been accepted. Also helpful to the Albanian Kosovar side was the removal of all Serb military and paramilitary forces and the reconstruction of the police.

There are several conjoined points here. First of all, flexible diplomacy was not pursued. Second, there are reasonable grounds for supposing that a more flexible approach might have averted ethnic cleansing without recourse to war. Third, and most importantly, whether or not flexible diplomacy would have succeeded, which we cannot know at this point, the failure to attempt it raises serious doubts about the alleged necessity of the NATO initiative. This last point requires some clarification. It needs to be recalled that the basic undertaking of the UN Charter as famously enunciated in its Preamble is "to save succeeding generations from the scourge of war." Arguably, the overriding ambition of international law in this century has been to take such a pledge seriously, although not absolutely, as the acceptance of a limited right of self-defense and of an interventionary duty to prevent genocide concedes. The recourse to war by NATO in these circumstances seems to have cast aside the legal, moral, and political commitment to make recourse to war *a last resort* after all reasonable attempts to achieve a peaceful settlement have failed. This

45

is a serious allegation from the perspective of both international law and world order, as well as respect for the UN system. Its seriousness is magnified by the fact that three permanent members of the Security Council, including the main architect of the UN, established this precedent under the full glare of the global media.

Note that it is often argued that the failure of the UN to itself evolve a collective security system does justify greater latitude in interpreting the occasions on which it is *reasonable* for a state to use force.[36] This latitude allows for uses of force to uphold its vital security interests or to serve the cause of humane governance that the Charter appears on its face to foreclose. In this regard, Articles 2(4) and 51, although important guidelines, are no longer dispositive in relation to inquiries as to legality. However, a recourse to force should be clearly presented as the consequence of an energetic and credible good faith attempt via flexible diplomacy to find a peaceful solution, and the failure to do this severely compromises the normative status of the NATO initiative. This is so regardless of the legal rationale selected to justify its action. NATO's way of proceeding also weakens the argument for bypassing the UN and the restrictive constraints of international law. The UN was justifiably criticized along comparable lines for its apparent unwillingness to uphold war prevention goals by reliance on flexible diplomacy in the setting of the Gulf Crisis.[37]

The situation is somewhat less clear with respect to the modalities of force. The widespread reliance on strategic bombing by the Allies in World War II appeared to flaunt the prohibition on indiscriminate military tactics, but also to establish a pattern of practice that was repeated to a substantial degree in the Korean and Vietnam Wars and again in the Gulf War, as well as in a range of other war settings. At the same time, the NATO initiative was not a war in the conventional sense, but was based on a claim of "humanitarian intervention." As such, it would seem subject to stricter standards of constraint relative to the use of force, especially with regard to civilian harm, and particularly in reference to the population that is being protected. NATO's style of high altitude bombing after the first few days inflicted deliberate heavy damage on civilian targets of a wide variety, as it relied on mastery of the air, smart weaponry, and a proclaimed intention to continue the bombing on an intensifying scale until Belgrade "submitted" to diplomatic demands without conditions. The magnitude and effects of such a bombing campaign are difficult to reconcile with the humanitarian claims made by NATO spokespersons. Such difficulty is compounded by NATO's reliance on tactics of warfare that minimized the risk of harm to the intervening forces, while shifting such risks to civilians in Yugoslavia, including Kosovo. In that sense, the absence of casualties among the military forces of NATO during the bombing campaign while

2,000 or more civilians in Serbia and Kosovo were killed seriously damages the humanitarian rationale for the action. It also makes skeptical observers wonder whether the primary motives for intervention were other than those publicly relied upon, such as keeping NATO alive and testing new weaponry and war-fighting doctrine. An additional sub-text seeming influential among American policymakers was to demonstrate that contrary to the teaching of "the Vietnam syndrome," internal wars can be fought and won at acceptable costs.[38]

A Concluding Note

Several relatively clear conclusions emerge from a configurative assessment of the NATO initiative:

1. there is a strong burden of persuasion associated with the rejection of the UN framework of legal restraint on the use of force as generally understood;[39]

2. this burden can be initially met if there is a credible prospect of genocide or of some distinct humanitarian catastrophe otherwise occurring;

3. such a burden cannot be discharged fully if diplomatic alternatives to war have not been fully explored in a sincere and convincing manner;

4. the humanitarian rationale is also sustained or undermined by the extent to which the tactics of warfare exhibit sensitivity to civilian harm and the degree to which intervenors avoid unduly shifting the risks of war to the supposed beneficiaries of intervention to avoid harm to themselves;

5. the humanitarian rationale is also weakened if there were less destructive alternative means to protect the threatened population than those relied upon; and

6. the humanitarian rationale is further weakened if punitive measures are imposed on the adversary after a termination of hostilities has been negotiated, especially if indiscriminate sanctions are maintained.

The post-war Kosovo experience will also inform our sense of the precedent. It is already evident that the K-FOR/UNMIK peacekeeping process has failed to prevent a new phase of ethnic cleansing, that is, a lethal coercive process by which the Serbs and Romas are induced to leave Kosovo or endure the deadly consequences of remaining behind.[40] It is also evident that NATO has not been fulfilling its responsibility for economic and social reconstruction, including the reintegration of returning refugees, as well as its offers of stability to the South Balkans as a region.[41] It will also be important that K-FOR remains a strong enough presence over a period of years to ensure that

Belgrade does not reimpose an oppressive structure of rule over Kosovo. It is finally important that NATO countries take responsibility for restoring the civilian infrastructure of Serbia and the neighboring Balkan countries, as proposed by the UN Secretary General Kofi Annan in a speech on June 20, 1999, to a meeting of the Organization of Security and Co-operation in Europe (OSCE). Washington managed to exert enough pressure on Belgrade by way of its economic leverage to persuade the new Serbian leadership to hand Milosevic over to the tribunal in The Hague for criminal prosecution; this trial has been going on for months, so far without resolution. Such an approach has cast a dark backwards shadow on the Gulf War, which exacted a severe toll on the Iraqi civilian population as a result of sustaining sanctions over a period of more than eight years.[42]

In sum, unfortunately, the NATO initiative on behalf of Kosovo, offers us a badly flawed precedent for evaluating future claims to undertake humanitarian intervention without proper UN authorization. But precisely because these flaws are evident, it is possible that "the lessons of Kosovo" will exert pressure to view war in the future as more of a last resort and will insist on the *humanitarian* character of a *humanitarian* intervention. It may also build support for providing the UN with independent enforcement capabilities, enabling a more timely and effective response to some humanitarian catastrophes with a minimum intrusion of geopolitical considerations. At this point, such an approach may seem far-fetched, given the hostility to the UN that persists in Washington, but over time the efficiency and legitimacy of global governance would seem to depend on establishing just such a capability.

Of course, even with such an enhanced UN capability, the capacities to engage in humanitarian intervention would be exceedingly limited, and should not be exaggerated. A political consensus of permanent members of the Security Council would still be normally needed to provide the mandate. Such a consensus could be blocked for geopolitical reasons, as when the events are situated within a state aligned to a powerful country. Also relevant is the scale of the interventionary operation required. To rescue the peoples of Chechnya, Tibet, or Kashmir would require an operation of such magnitude as to be impracticable, as well as to pose too serious a threat of major, unmanageable warfare.

The events in East Timor, following so soon after Kosovo, also provide grounds for both concern and hope. The concern arises because of the UN failure to provide the population greater security at the time of a referendum on the future of the country that had an expected outcome quite likely to unleash an Indonesian backlash. The harshness of the Indonesian response to the overwhelming vote for independence by the East Timorese, while greater than reasonably expected, should not have come as a surprise, given the

Indonesian record of abuse over a period of almost 25 years. But East Timor also offers grounds for hope. A political mandate was agreed upon in the Security Council, effective pressure to back down was exerted on Jakarta, an appropriate UN peacekeeping and post-conflict operation was put into operation quickly, with strong regional participation. It is too soon to pronounce the UN effort in East Timor as a success, but it seems to have, at the very least, rescued the population from an extreme condition of abuse and danger and significantly moved along the process of respecting the declared will of the people to have an independent sovereign state of East Timor.

Each instance of humanitarian catastrophe presents the organized international community with a particular challenge based on an array of contextual features. There is no overarching response that fits this variety of instances. The focus needs to be kept on the opportunities to mitigate human suffering and injustice, while taking due account of constraints on effective action.[43]

Notes

1. For an excellent overview see Sean D. Murphy, *Humanitarian Intervention* (Philadelphia, PA: University of Pennsylvania Press, 1996).

2. Such a process was problematic from its turbulent inception. See the very balanced and illuminating analysis of Congo Operation by Georges Abi-Saab, *The United Nations Operation in the Congo 1960-1964* (Oxford: Oxford University Press, 1978).

3. See particularly Georges Abi-Saab, *Cours Général de Droit International Public* (The Hague, Netherlands: Martinus Nijhoff, updated 1987 lecture series at Hague Academy); for wider views on the relations between international law and world order see Abi-Saab, "The Changing World Order and the International Legal Order: The Structural Evolution of International Law beyond the State-Centric Model," *Global Transformations: Challenges to the State System*, ed. Yoshikazu Sakamoto (Tokyo, Japan: United Nations University Press, 1994) 439-61.

4. Vaclav Havel, "Kosovo and the End of the Nation-State," *New York Review of Books* (10 June 1999): 4-6.

5. Robert Fisk, "Who Needs NATO?," *The Progressive* (22 July 1999): 22-23.

6. For the full range of these controversies see Richard Falk, ed., *The Vietnam War and International Law*, 4 vols (Princeton, NJ: Princeton University Press, 1968-76).

7. For a critical account of KLA and its role see Chris Hedges, "Kosovo's Next Masters?" *Foreign Affairs* 78, 1 (1999): 24-42.

8. For the position of the US Government in the buildup to the NATO air campaign, see the essay of James B. Steinberg, Deputy Assistant to the President for National Security Affairs, "A Perfect Polemic: Blind to Reality in Kosovo," *Foreign Affairs* 78, 6 (1999): 128-33.

9. For a harsh assessment of UN role, see David Rieff, *Slaughterhouse: Bosnia and the Failure of the West* (New York: Simon and Schuster, 1995); recently restated in Rieff, "The U.N. Remains a Bright, Shining Lie," *Wall Street Journal* (18 November 1999). For a more balanced account see Susan L. Woodward, *Balkan Tragedy: Chaos and Dissolution after the Cold War* (Washington, DC: Brookings, 1995).

10. For a helpful legal assessment see Bruno Simma, "NATO, the UN and the Use of Force: Legal Aspects," *European Journal of International Law* 10, 1 (1999). Professor Simma deftly clarifies the "illegality" of the NATO campaign, while taking *legal* account of the humanitarian justifications for international action. For overall legal assessment see Case Concerning Military and Paramilitary Activities in and against Nicaragua (*Nicaragua v. United States of America*), Meritz Judgment, ICJ Reports 1986, 14.

11. The only independent basis for NATO action would be under the authority of Article 51 as an exercise of collective self-defense, which clearly did not fit the facts of Kosovo however construed.

12. Such a prospect is not far-fetched, it would seem, as Russia and China endorsed earlier UN Security Council resolutions that declared the humanitarian crisis in Kosovo as falling within the domain of Chapter VII, endangering international peace and security, and thereby not shielded by the domestic jurisdiction principle of Article 2(7). See Security Council Res. 1199, 23 September 1998, S/RES/1199 (1998), and Res. 1203, 24 October 1998, S/RES/1203 (1998). These resolutions were balanced in the sense of calling also on the KLA to comply with obligations to refrain from violence, imposing an arms embargo on both sides.

13. For text see S/RES/1244 (1999), containing the extraordinary dispositive language as follows: "*Decides*, on the deployment in Kosovo, under United Nations auspices, of international civil and security presences...." Such terminology hardly accords with the insistence by Washington and Brussels that the UN merely ratified the NATO victory. This formulation should also be compared with the dictatorial language and tone of the Rambouillet agreement with its explicit empowerment of NATO, especially in its famous Annex B, which gave NATO extensive powers throughout *the whole* of Yugoslavia. I share the view that it was "unreasonable" not to attempt to reach a "1244" solution *prior* to recourse to war.

14. Overall critique well-formulated by Michael Mandelbaum, "A Perfect Failure," *Foreign Affairs* 78, 5 (1999): 2-8.

15. Such a pragmatic argument for adopting legally dubious tactics is self-serving, undermining the central objectives of the law of war to set limits on the pursuit of belligerent objectives. A variant of this argument was relied upon by the US government to justify the use of atomic bombs against Hiroshima at the end of World War II, contending that such weapons saved numerous American lives. Such an assertion has been contested, disguising the real motive of use, which was to gain the upper hand geopolitically in the Pacific with respect to the Soviet Union.

16. See John M. Broder, "Clinton Underestimated Serbs, He Acknowledges," *New York Times* (26 June 1999): A6.

17. For a summary overview of the environmental damage, including radioactive contamination resulting from widespread use of uranium-tipped anti-tank shells, see Joe Cook and Frances Williams, "Nato Uranium 'Polluting Yugoslavia,'" *Financial Times* (22 July 1999): 3. The news story presents the preliminary conclusions of a 14-member UN team of scientists and other experts, known as the Balkans Task Force of the United Nations Environmental Program.

18. Although a textual reading of Article 27(3) of the UN Charter includes the requirement that a Security Council decision be supported "by an affirmative vote of nine members including the concurring votes of the permanent members," UN practice, going back to the Soviet boycott of the Security Council during the early stages of the Korean War, has treated absence or abstention as not preventing the Security Council from reaching valid decisions.

19. For a rationale in support of this trend toward limiting sovereignty see Kofi Annan, "Two Concepts of Sovereignty," *The Economist* (18 September 1999): 49-50.

20. For an excellent theoretical exploration see R.B.J. Walker, *Inside/outside: International Relations as Political Theory* (Cambridge, UK: Cambridge University Press, 1993); for overall assessment of globalization, see David Held et al., *Global Transformations: Politics, Economics, and Culture* (Cambridge, UK: Polity, 1999).

21. Richard Holbrooke, *To End a War* (New York: Random House, 1998) 339.

22. See Michael J. Glennon, "The New Interventionism: The Search for a Just International Law," *Foreign Affairs* 78, 3 (1999): 2-7.

23. Glennon 2.

24. Glennon 3.

25. Note needs to be taken of the opposition by China and Russia to forcible modes of intervention by NATO. Thus, two powerful but "unenlightened" states were opposed to this non-UN consensus.

26. For such an attempt, see Tom J. Farer, "A Paradigm of Legitimate Intervention," *Enforcing Restraint: Collective Intervention in Internal Conflicts*, ed. Lori Fisler Damrosch (New York: Council on Foreign Relations, 1993) 316-47.

27. Glennon develops this position at the end of his essay, esp. at 7.

28. Thomas M. Franck, "Break It, Don't Fake It," *Foreign Affairs* 78, 4 (1999): 116-18; see also Franck, "Lessons of Kosovo," *American Journal of International Law* 93 (1999): 864-67.

29. Franck 116.

30. Franck 118.

31. See Note 12.

32. It should be acknowledged that favorable to the response has been the attitude of the majority of Kosovo inhabitants, the return of the refugees, and the rescue of the Albanian Kosovars from the ordeal of Serb domination.

33. Such an analysis resembles in some respect the argument of Simma, note 10, that NATO's campaign was illegal, yet the humanitarian considerations meant that it was only "a thin red line" that separated legality from the rescue operation. Cf. here Antonio Cassese, "*Ex iniuria ius oritur*: Are We Moving towards International Legitimation of Forcible Countermeasures in the World Community?," *European Journal of International Law* 10, 1 (1999): 23.

34. In such circumstances, there are countervailing "legal" arguments, but of such an insubstantial character as to be generally ignored. For instance, Indonesia argued in 1975 that their invasion was in response to an invitation from the pro-integrationist faction in East Timor; Baghdad contended in 1990 that Kuwait was an artificial creation of British colonialism that deprived Iraq of a valuable portion of its sovereign territory.

35. On the first point, it is possible that Albright shared the view that flexibility was unnecessary because the bluff of air strikes would induce surrender without the actuality of war.

36. See W. Michael Reisman, "Kosovo's Antinomies," *American Journal of International Law* 93 (1999): 867-69; for fuller exposition, see Reisman, "Allocating Competencies to Use Coercion in the Post-Cold War World: Practices, Conditions, and Prospects," *Law and Force in the New International Order*, ed. Lori Fisler Damrosch and David J. Scheffer (Boulder, CO: Westview Press, 1991) 26-48; for earlier rationale along a similar line see Julius Stone, *Aggression and World Order: A Critique of United Nations Theories of Aggression* (Berkeley, CA: University of California Press, 1958).

37. Richard Falk, "Reflections on the Gulf War Experience: Force and War in the UN System," *The Gulf War and the New World Order: International Relations of the Middle East*, ed. Tareq Y. Ismael and Jacqueline S. Ismael (Gainesville, FL: University of Florida Press, 1994) 536-48.

38. The Gulf War allegedly established the same proposition for international wars.

39. That is, without various forms of strained interpretation. E.g., see Steinberg, note 8. Also, for presentation range of pro-NATO legal arguments, see Paul Williams and Michael P. Scharf, "NATO Intervention on Trial: The Legal Case That Was Never Made," *Human Rights Review* (2000).

40. See Steven Erlanger, "Chaos and Intolerance Prevailing in Kosovo Despite U.N.'s Efforts," *New York Times* (22 November 1999): A1, A12.

41. See Ben Steil and Susan Woodward, "A European 'New Deal' for the Balkans," *Foreign Affairs* 78, 6 (1999): 95-105.

42. Cf. John Mueller and Karl Mueller, "Sanctions of Mass Destruction," *Foreign Affairs* 78, 5 (1999): 43-53.

43. Portions of this chapter have been drawn from Richard Falk "Kosovo, World Order, and the Future of International Law," *American Journal of International Law* 93 (1999): 854-64.

3

Humanitarian Intervention in Nationalist Conflicts: A Few Problems

Aleksandar Pavkovic

Saving Lives by Killing People[1]

Could the saving of innocent lives justify killing other people who are not threatening anyone, that is, who are equally innocent? And if so, how could saving innocent lives justify acts of war, which involve killing people who are not threatening anyone?

In our attempt to answer these two related questions let us start with an imaginary but realistic example in which the act of killing innocent people is justified by the saving of lives.

Due to an accident, a passenger ship starts taking water on one side and is in danger of rolling over. In order to prevent this and save the lives of hundreds of passengers, the captain has no other option but to flood the compartments on the other side, knowing that this act is likely to (or will) kill dozens of trapped crew and passengers.

In order for this killing to be justified by the saving of lives, it is, I believe, necessary:

1. That the action leading to the killing of the innocent be the only available action which could have saved the endangered lives. It is not *only* a less risky or a less costly option than other available actions but the only action that could have been undertaken to save these lives. In our example, the captain decided to flood the compartments *not* because any other attempts to right the ship and save the passengers were less likely to succeed. He decided to do this *not* because he regarded the death of a dozen crew and third-class passengers as less costly than the death of the equal, or greater, number of the first-class

passengers whose lives were in danger. He decided to do this because, to the best of his knowledge at the time, there was no other way of saving the threatened passengers. We can call this condition the *No Other Option condition*.

2. That causing the death (or killing) of the innocent people be an action of the kind that can be justified by reference to its consequences in the saving of lives. Some types of killing cannot, I believe, be justified in this way. In our example, the captain ordered that the compartments be flooded *not* because he wanted to kill the members of the crew in those compartments because they had witnessed his complicity in some criminal acts (e.g., of extortion or blackmail): his action was not a murder of potential witnesses against him. If it were, that action could not be justified by reference to the lives saved by its performance. Probably there is no generally accepted list of actions that cannot be justified in this way—but the murder of witnesses of one's own criminal acts is surely one of those. This condition will be called *the Justifiability condition*.

3. That the action leading to the death of the innocents may reasonably be expected to save more lives than it terminates. The captain ordered the flooding of the compartments knowing that they held a much smaller number of crew and passengers than the total number of passengers and crew threatened by the rollover of the ship. Had that not been the case, and the number of those killed had been greater than the number of those saved, he (and we) would have considered his action irrational and senseless (if not devious). As in (2) above, there is no generally accepted formula of proportionality, stating that one killed person could, in such emergencies, justify the saving of X number of lives. This condition we shall name the *Death Minimization condition*.

The No Other Option condition in (1) could be justified by the humanist principle of the equal and paramount value of each human life. This principle asserts that no human life is less or more valuable than any other and that an individual's life is not comparable in value to anything else but another human life.

The Death Minimization condition in (3) follows from the same principle, and the description of the action as that of saving innocent lives. If the saving of lives is expected to lead to more deaths than those saved, either this was not intended to be an action of saving lives or else the principle of the equality of human lives was intentionally breached in the belief that the lives of those killed were less valuable than those saved.

The Justifiability condition in (2) is, however, more controversial. Some—those usually inclined towards deontological ethical views—would argue that no non-accidental or intentional killing (or perhaps no action whatsoever) can be justified by its beneficial consequences, while others—usually the consequentialists of various kinds—would argue that every type of action, however wrong it may appear to be, could be justified, at least to some extent, by its beneficial consequences. The position I take here is a pluralist one, according to which actions, in general, can be justified both by their intrinsic moral characteristics and by their beneficial consequences. In some cases, however, I hold that the intrinsic moral characteristics of an action cancel any justification by its beneficial consequences; in such cases the beneficial consequences following from such an action are considered irrelevant to its justifiability. Some cases of killing for specific self-interested reasons, I believe, fall into this category. Thus, any beneficial consequences of a killing committed to prevent the disclosure of other immoral or criminal acts of the killer or his associates are irrelevant for the moral judgment on, or justification of, that act. In other words, any other description of that act which would make it morally neutral or morally permissible (such as "killing for the sake of saving other lives") is incompatible with the initial and true description of that act as a case of killing for specific self-interested reasons. In contrast, killing for altruistic reasons—for example, killing a terminally ill relative or friend who is in great pain—may also be truly described as a mercy-killing; under that description the act is morally permissible and justifiable by its consequences.

There are at least two arguments in support of my view that some acts of killing are not justifiable by their beneficial consequences. First, one can point to harmful or unacceptable consequences of a policy that would allow individuals to commit irreversibly harmful acts, such as killing, provided that these also have beneficial consequences. The policy of permitting killing provided it saved some lives would encourage people to kill for self-interested reasons in such circumstances where this would save someone's life. For example, killing a witness of one's criminal acts could be justified by the fact that the victim's donated organs would save the lives of many ill people. The general policy advice would be: if you kill anyone, be sure that, as a consequence of his death, at least some lives are saved. This is not the kind of policy advice consequentialists would endorse or give. Quite independently of this, a policy prescription that would allow killing for self-interested reasons, provided specific beneficial consequences were to follow, would threaten the rule of law, at least as it is understood in modern liberal democracies: the monopoly on the use of deadly force would be taken from the state and, so to speak, privatized. Second, this policy would breach the principle of equal value of each human life: some lives would, in accordance with this policy, be less valuable and thus become expendable. Some innocent people could be justifiably killed for the personal gain of others, provided that their deaths saved lives. While these two arguments are not, necessarily, conclusive they provide at least some reasons for accepting the Justifiability condition.[2]

Having thus outlined three necessary (but not sufficient) conditions for justifying killing by the saving of lives it causes, I can now address the question: how could the saving of lives justify the waging of war against another state? A core activity of war consists in killing people; thus, one could argue, the killing of people is one of the main instruments of war. This makes war a rather poor candidate as a means of saving lives. In spite of this, each side in World War I and World War II argued that its waging of war was justified by its intent to save peoples' lives. Some of those justifications were often so transparently deceptive that, after the wars ended, they could not be taken seriously. In the next section we shall not consider the justifications offered for any war in the past but rather consider a very narrow category of wars, those waged in order to stop the killing of non-threatening and unarmed civilians, people who are in this essay called "innocents."

Saving Lives by Waging War

A state or group of states may wage war against another state with the intention of stopping the systematic killing of innocents taking place in that state. In such a case, from the fact that the systematic killing is taking place, it is obvious that the state in question is pursuing a policy of killing innocent civilians or a policy of condoning such killing by non-governmental agencies. In view of this systematic killing and the underlying governmental policy, a victorious war waged to replace this government or to stop this pursuit of its murderous policies would, in all likelihood, save innocent lives. Yet, like any other war, this would result in killing of innocents as well. It is for this reason that such a war would need to satisfy three conditions based on the three necessary conditions outlined in the preceding section.

First, waging war against the allegedly murderous government or state must be the only way to stop the killing of innocents. In some cases, the killing will be organized by the state and carried out by state agents for ideological reasons. The best known example in recent history is the Khmer Rouge killing of Cambodian civilians. Between 1975 and 1979 the revolutionary Khmer Rouge government in Cambodia forced most urban dwellers out of the cities and towns into the countryside where they were put to work under extremely brutal conditions. As a result, several hundred thousand civilians died or were intentionally killed.[3] If all diplomatic efforts (including threats and sanctions) to induce the government to stop or prevent such killing have failed, and the government's ideological commitment to that kind of killing indicates that no further efforts of this kind would succeed, then the No Other Option condition appears to be satisfied.

Second, waging war in such circumstances must be justifiable by reference not only to broadly defined beneficial consequences but, specifically, to the saving of lives. For example, various oppressed groups wage liberation wars against their conquerors or oppressors and justify the killing and destruction caused by the intended beneficial consequences of such wars—the liberation of their group from an unjust or oppressive rule. This broadly defined beneficial consequence is not equivalent to the saving of innocent lives. Unjust and oppressive (foreign or domestic) governments do not, necessarily and as a matter of policy, kill their non-threatening and unarmed subjects. The removal of such a government by war cannot, therefore, always be justified by the saving of lives of innocents. The converse, however, does hold: a government which organizes or condones killing of its non-threatening unarmed subjects is certainly an oppressive and unjust government. Thus, those wars that stop the killing of innocents may also lead to the removal of oppressive and unjust governments. Even so, the justification by reference to the first beneficial consequence differs from the one that refers to the second.

There are also wars that are waged with the intention of gaining control over a people and the territory on which they live against the wishes of that people. Any such war is a war of conquest (where "conquest" is broadly interpreted as any imposition of control over a territory) and is the very opposite of a war of liberation. These wars also result in the end of violence and killing. Are they then justified by the saving of lives? Among philosophers, Michael Walzer appears to think some such wars are: the Vietnamese invasion of Cambodia in December 1978, which removed the Khmer Rouge government from power and replaced it with a Vietnamese-controlled regime, also ended the systematic killing of innocent civilians by the Khmer Rouge. This result justifies the war the Vietnamese waged against the Khmer Rouge government—although it does not justify their imposing a government of their choosing on Cambodia.

This example is not meant to demonstrate that waging wars of conquest is, in general, justifiable by the saving of lives, only that in some cases such wars can be so justified. Is there also a kind of war—like killing for self-interested reasons—which cannot be so justified? At times, governments wage wars to cover up evidence of their own incompetence or malfeasance or to distract the attention of their constituencies from unacceptable or dubious aspects of their rule. If a war of this kind leads to the killing of innocents, then it resembles killing carried out in order to remove evidence of criminal acts in at least one way: in both cases people are killed in order that the evidence of wrongdoing be covered up. Further, governments sometimes wage wars of conquest (broadly defined) in order to enable their individual members or their associates to exploit the resources of the conquered territory for personal gain. This kind of war resembles killing for the purpose of robbery; such a murder (and any similar war) is not, in my opinion, justifiable by the saving of lives. This indicates that there are some kinds of war which are not justifiable by the fact that they save lives; these examples, however, do not provide the necessary or sufficient conditions for such unjustifiable wars.

Third, if a war turns out to have caused a larger number of deaths than it saved, it cannot be justified by reference to the lives saved; therefore, in order to be justifiable by the saving of lives, war needs to be waged with the reasonable expectation of saving more lives than causing deaths. Various aspects of modern warfare make it quite difficult to satisfy this requirement. For example, if a life-saving government uses any modern weapons of mass destruction, it may cause, unintentionally but predictably, a larger number of deaths than lives saved. Likewise, a life-saving government cannot control the way its enemy will fight back — the enemy may choose to expose its own side to the greatest possible number of casualties. If a government intent on going to war is to justify the waging of its war by reference to the lives saved, it would need to wage this war in the way which avoids predictable but unintended casualties among the non-threatening civilians.

Such a problem arises in any war in which saving lives is dependent on a military victory over a resisting enemy. Military victory can be achieved only by the use of appropriate or proportionate force against the enemy forces. But the use of appropriate force (in particular, weapons of mass destruction) to this end, in the face of a strongly resisting enemy, may indeed lead to more deaths than saved lives. Thus, the means required to achieve victory may be incompatible with a death minimization strategy which aims to minimize the deaths of all warring parties. In such a case, the fulfillment of the Death Minimization condition is conceptually incompatible with the requirement of military victory: in order to satisfy the condition, the life-saving government would have to give up victory in a war that would be too costly in human lives.

From time immemorial military commanders and political leaders have, however, adopted a *partial* death minimization strategy: in their pursuit of military victory, they often strive to minimize, both for prudential and for ethical reasons, only the number of deaths of their own co-nationals and their allies. In some circumstances a partial death minimization strategy of this kind is incompatible with the above Death Minimization condition, requiring, as a reasonable expectation, that the war will cause less deaths than lives saved. For example, one's own military personnel can be protected by using weapons of mass destruction against a technologically inferior enemy. High altitude aerial bombing or long-range artillery or missile bombardment of a technologically inferior enemy effectively minimizes death among the military personnel of its technologically superior adversary. But the use of unguided weapons of this kind poses a greater risk of death to innocent civilians than the use of ground forces and their close-support aircraft targeting military facilities (the latter, however, increases the death toll among the life-saving military personnel). It is also difficult to estimate and to control the death toll among the civilians exposed to weapons of the kind, and, unless the estimate of lives to be saved is very large, it is difficult to reasonably expect that the use of the weapons of mass destruction will lead to a smaller number of deaths than lives saved.

Unlike the life-threatening disasters caused by accidents or by natural phenomena (floods, earthquakes, and the like) war is an intentional activity whose main instrument is the use and the threat of use of deadly force. If its use is to be justified by the saving of lives, as we have seen above, one needs to restrict its scope and aim. This may not only reduce its effectiveness as an instrument of war but may also change the nature of the war waged for that purpose. If so, the wars waged with the intention of saving the lives of enemy subjects are specially restricted wars, in so far as the use of deadly force in them is restricted to minimize deaths. In their aim, these specially restricted wars resemble humanitarian interventions such as the operations launched to assist the victims of large-scale natural disasters such as famines, earthquakes, and the like. The aim of any humanitarian intervention, apart from providing assistance to the victims, is to remove either the potential causes of death and injury or the individuals from the area in which they are exposed to the risk of being killed. Specially restricted wars of this kind also aim to remove the potential causes of death and to protect the endangered individuals from violence and death. This gives some ground for the argument, readily espoused by politicians and media in the interventionist countries, that specially restricted wars for the sake of saving lives of innocents are a species of humanitarian intervention.

Against this argument one can point out significant differences between violent and war-like interventions as opposed to non-violent or ordinary humanitarian interventions. In non-violent humanitarian interventions, the principal aim — the saving of lives — is achieved by the use of means other than deadly military force or the threat of such force. As a result, in non-violent humanitarian interventions, interventionist personnel are not exposed to the risk of being intentionally killed by those who resist their intervention — and, of course, those whose lives are to be saved (the victims) are not exposed to the same risk of being killed, unintentionally, by those who are supposed to save their lives. In non-violent interventions, the interventionist personnel can thus safely seek to minimize both the deaths in their own group and of the victims without bringing into question their humanitarian aim — the saving of lives. In violent humanitarian interventions, a partial death minimization strategy, aiming to minimize the deaths *only* among the interventionist personnel and allowing as many deaths among innocent people of the opposing side as required for a military victory, may bring into the question the intervention's over-all aim of saving the lives of innocents. Humanitarian interventions in which the risk of death is minimized only for the interventionist personnel may turn out not to be that humanitarian, after all. This becomes quite apparent in cases of military interventions in nationalist conflicts.

But in spite of all these difficulties facing humanitarian military interventions, one may still argue that the war by Vietnam against the Khmer Rouge government in 1978-79 fulfilled the above three conditions necessary for such an intervention. One could argue that the war caused fewer deaths than it saved, partly because the Khmer Rouge military resistance to the Vietnamese military was weak, the Vietnamese did not resort to indiscriminate bombing of any targets close to civilian centers, and the Cambodian civilian population mostly welcomed the Vietnamese forces. Apart from the war, there was no other way of stopping the Khmer Rouge government from pursuing its policy of killing civilians, and, during the 10 years of occupation, the Vietnamese officials did not, systematically or otherwise, exploit Cambodia's resources for their own personal gain.[4] Nationalist conflicts, as we shall see, create conditions which are quite unlike those under which the Vietnamese intervention was carried out.

Saving Lives in Nationalist Conflicts

A nationalist conflict is a war between two or more national groups over political control of a single territory. Each national group is mobilized to support the use of violence against the other national group(s). The very presence of members of a national group on the contested territory is considered by its opponent(s) as an obstacle to their political control of the territory. In consequence, each member of the opposing national group on the contested territory is considered to be a threat of some kind. Hence, members of the war-mobilized national groups do not, in general, consider the non-threatening and unarmed civilians of the opposing national group as "innocents." This view explains, at least in part, the intentional mass killing of unarmed civilians, including women and children, by any party in such a conflict.

A stronger warring party in a nationalist conflict would resist any outside military intervention aiming to save the lives of innocents because it would regard the saving lives of the enemy population as aiding their enemies' war effort. By protecting the war-mobilized civilian population of the weaker party, such an intervention could enable that party to hold or to conquer the territory which the stronger party considers its own. For the same reason the weaker party or parties would welcome such an intervention.

Irrespective of this contest over territory, a military intervention against one warring party, with the intention of saving the lives of its enemies, may enable members of the "enemy" group(s) to kill innocent members of the group against which the military intervention is directed. Since the former do not consider the latter as innocents, they would not consider this impermissible, and there would be no effective constraint to prevent them from doing so.

In the context of a nationalist conflict, an interventionist war for the sake of saving lives may, therefore, lead to the deaths of innocents in at least three ways:

1. first, as in any war, military action aiming to defeat or subdue the military forces may, unintentionally — and unnecessarily — lead to the death of innocents among all warring groups;

2. second, interventionist military action may lead to the death of conscripts belonging to the resisting group, who are resisting the interventionist force simply because the latter is attacking their group and its territory; these conscripts are not engaged in killing or threatening to kill innocents of the enemy group and are, therefore, innocent themselves;

3. third, military actions against one group may enable the members of the other, adversary, group to kill innocents from the group against which the action is directed.

In a nationalist conflict with the already established inter-group hostility and violence, one can expect that a military action against one group will enable the other, adversary, group to proceed to kill members of the group exposed to this action. Therefore, in such a case the interventionists would have at least to share responsibility for the deaths of these innocents: without their military intervention, it is unlikely that these murders of members of one party to the conflict would have been committed.

In a war waged to save one group of innocents from a murderous and unpopular government, such as Vietnam's war against the Khmer Rouge regime, the interventionist force, targeting a relatively small and isolated group of people and its military force, may find it easier to avoid inflicting civilian casualties, and the conscripts may find it safer to surrender to the interventionist forces than to fight for a government they do not support. During their invasion of Cambodia, the Vietnamese forces found it relatively easy to avoid civilian casualties as the towns had been evacuated before their arrival, the civilians welcomed their invasion, and many members of the Khmer Rouge conscript force surrendered or fled. In cases of nationalist conflicts, evacuating one's own civilians from any territory is considered a defeat and is avoided at all costs—thus exposing civilians to military action. For soldiers, conscripted or volunteer, to surrender to the enemy or its allies is considered highly risky—and this is only one reason why they are not likely to surrender. And, for the reasons mentioned above, the civilian population of the opposing side is seen as a threat and is therefore exposed to selective or mass killing. An outside military intervention in such a conflict faces a wider range of ways of causing deaths to innocents than a military intervention against a murderous and unpopular government. This makes it less likely that the Death Minimization condition would be satisfied in a nationalist conflict.

But an outside military intervention in such a conflict may face additional difficulties of satisfying the No Other Option as well as the Justifiability condition. Let us start with the No Other Option condition. Nationalist conflicts are a result of a series of decisions made by political and community leaders of the national groups inhabiting one and the same territory. The leaders of one national group at some point decide to use force or to condone the use of force against members of the other national groups. In the present scenario of an impending life-saving military intervention by outside powers, these leaders have also decided to at least condone the mass murder of innocents from the enemy national group.

At each stage, these leaders had options other than the use of force and condoning mass murder. This is a major difference between natural disasters resulting in mass deaths and human-engineered mass killing. Since the warring parties have other options than to participate in mass killing, the interventionist party also has other options than to intervene by force to stop the mass killing. In most natural disasters, there are no options of any kind for preventing or avoiding mass deaths. If the interventionist party has the military power to intervene in the conflict, it is likely that it also has (or is capable of gaining) influence over the warring parties in the conflict. If the interventionist party has an option to influence the warring parties to desist from the use of force and from killing, then that military intervention is not the only option it has to stop the killing.

In order for the No Other Option condition to be fulfilled, the interventionist party must have exercised all other options at its disposal to stop or prevent killing, including that of using all the influence it has on any warring parties in the conflict. While it is often difficult for outside observers to establish whether all the options of this kind have been exercised, if it is shown that the interventionist party, before its military intervention, failed to exercise an option it had to prevent or stop the killing, that would make clear that in this case the No Other Option condition has not been fulfilled.

Military powers capable of effective intervention in nationalist conflicts often (but not always) support, politically and militarily, one of the warring parties in the conflict. In cases in which no warring party is supported by a major military power, such as that of Rwanda in 1994, the latter fails to intervene, in spite of huge losses of innocent lives. But if a potential (life-saving) interventionist power is already supporting the territorial claims of one warring party and provides it with military support in its armed struggle, it has already opted for the use of force as a way of resolving this conflict. In doing so, the potential interventionist party may have already forgone the option of using its influence on one of the warring parties to desist from the use of force. The former may have good reasons for doing so; for example, it may have good reasons for believing that the other warring party (or parties) in this conflict would kill innocents, regardless of whether the party it supports desists from its use of force or not. But, in such a case, regardless of its reasons for forgoing this option, a military intervention is not the only option the interventionist party had in its attempt to avoid or stop mass killing.

This kind of support for one of the warring parties in the conflict may make it difficult for the eventual military intervention to satisfy the Justifiability condition as well. In many cases, military support to warring parties—in weapons, training, and logistic support—is hidden from the public because it is not legally authorized; in order to keep it hidden, the potential interventionist government publicly (and falsely) denies giving any such support. Suppose now that in such a case its allied warring party faces military defeat by its adversary. Such a defeat may lead to the disclosure of the support and of the accompanying lies. Now suppose further that in order to prevent such an exposure, the implicated government intervenes in the conflict, thus winning the war for its almost defeated ally, and justifies its intervention by reference to the innocent lives it saved.

This scenario has obvious and intentional similarities with a case in which the captain orders compartments of his listing ship flooded with the intention of killing a few crew members in them who witnessed his extortion or blackmail (and also of righting his ship as described in the original scenario). By flooding the compartments he succeeds in saving many more lives, but the saving of lives was not his primary or only intention. Similarly, in the above scenario, while the military intervention saved innocent lives, the interventionist government would not have ordered it had it not been threatened by the disclosure of its lies and its illegal military support. Under these conditions, one could argue, its military intervention, which led to the (unintentional) killing of innocents, cannot be justified by the saving of innocent lives: under these conditions, killing innocents cannot be justified by the saving of (other) innocent lives.

No doubt, an interventionist power can surmount difficulties such as these and thus satisfy both the No Other Option and Justifiability conditions. For example, if a potential interventionist power remains neutral in a nationalist conflict and if all or some warring parties reject all non-military attempts by the interventionist and other parties to make them desist from using force, military intervention may indeed be the only option for stopping mass killing. However, in such a situation the life-saving interventionist force may face resistance from all or most warring parties and from their war-mobilized populations; this resistance in turn may increase the death toll on all sides, including the interventionist military personnel. Satisfying these two conditions in this way may make it more difficult to satisfy the Death Minimization condition.

A good illustration of how these difficulties may arise is provided by NATO's military intervention in 1999 in the nationalist conflict in the province of Kosovo (or Kosova) in Yugoslavia.

Saving Lives in Kosovo?

The war NATO waged against the Federal Republic of Yugoslavia, from March to May 1999, has been justified by reference to the saving of lives of Yugoslav citizens of Albanian nationality in the province of Kosovo who were, it was alleged, exposed to mass killing by the special forces and paramilitaries of the Yugoslav government. NATO politicians and journalists often referred to this military action as a humanitarian intervention. Let us now see whether this military action satisfies the three conditions for justification of killing by reference to saving lives.

THE DEATH MINIMIZATION CONDITION

In keeping with their proclaimed aim, the NATO military followed a death minimization strategy: NATO aircraft did not target the areas inhabited by civilians and flew at high altitude to avoid the exposure of its aircraft crews to anti-aircraft fire. These two policies failed to achieve the desired minimization of deaths: in pursuing the second, the aircraft had to fly so high as to make it very difficult to distinguish military from civilian targets; this led to the bombing of civilian residential quarters, hospitals, civilian traffic, and even Albanian refugee groups. Further, the NATO command did not seek to minimize deaths of Yugoslav army conscripts who were not engaged in killing or threatening to kill innocents. For example, they systematically bombed the defensive positions of the Yugoslav army, which was attempting to prevent the Albanian military forces from crossing into the territory of Yugoslavia from Albania.[5]

Upon the mutually agreed deployment of its ground forces in Kosovo in June 1999, NATO command pursued a policy of restricted protection of the non-Albanian population of Kosovo— Serbs, Montenegrins, the Roma, and the Turks—from the Kosovo Albanian forces. In pursuit of this policy, NATO forces prevented Albanian access to several enclaves populated by non-Albanians including Serbs but studiously avoided any confrontation with the Kosovo Albanian armed forces or individuals who were expelling, kidnapping, killing, or threatening to kill the non-Albanian inhabitants or the alleged Albanian collaborators outside these protected areas. During the first few months of its occupation of the province, the NATO forces failed to prevent the murder and kidnapping (involving suspected murder) of several thousands of non-Albanian civilians (as well as the expulsion from Kosovo of over 100,000 non-Albanians). They also failed to find and bring to justice the great majority of the perpetrators of those murders and kidnappings.[6]

This indicates that NATO's strategy was at its core a traditional partial minimization of deaths, primarily restricted to its own personnel and that of its ally, the Albanian Kosova Liberation Army (the KLA). The saving of lives of the non-Albanian population or the Albanian inhabitants accused of past collaboration with the Serb government was throughout the war and in its immediate aftermath a secondary concern, which was not allowed to interfere with the primary purpose of minimizing the deaths among its own forces and its allies.

Whatever the strategy, did NATO military intervention satisfy the Death Minimization condition—did it save more lives than it caused deaths? There are two distinct questions here. Was the NATO military intervention intended and carried out so as to save more lives than it caused deaths? Did that military intervention in fact save more lives than it caused deaths?

The major difficulty for any attempt to answer the second question is the absence of any reliable evidence as to how many lives the intervention in fact saved. To find that out, one would have to discover the plans of the Serbian and Yugoslav government under Slobodan Milosevic, as well as the plans of paramilitary organizations operating in Kosovo to carry out the mass killing of Albanian innocents prior to the NATO attack in March 1999. There is no evidence advanced so far[7] that, prior to that attack, Milosevic's government carried out any mass killing of innocents outside of immediate areas of fighting between its forces and the KLA. Neither the Yugoslav forces nor the KLA pursued a policy of saving the lives of innocents in the area of their military operations.[8]

In view of these policies of the two warring parties, had they continued to fight and had the area of their clashes continued to widen, many more innocents would have been killed in the course of their fighting; this would have happened, even if the Yugoslav government (or the KLA) had no plans for the mass killing of innocents. But given the steady advance of the Yugoslav military and its obvious military superiority over the KLA, it was likely that the

former would confine the area of the KLA's activity to a few sparsely populated mountainous areas. Had that happened, the death toll among innocent
civilians from the military operations would have, in fact, decreased. In order
to save the lives of innocents in this way—by limiting their exposure to violent
conflict and fighting—a military intervention by NATO was not necessary. In
the absence of evidence of planned mass or systematic killings of Albanian civilians prior to the NATO attack, it is not possible to establish that the NATO
military intervention in fact saved more innocent lives than it caused deaths.

In spite of this, it is still possible to argue that NATO governments, on the
basis of the previous evidence of mass killings carried out by the Serb forces
in Bosnia-Herzegovina, had good reason to expect a similar policy to be pursued in Kosovo. According to this argument, NATO's military intervention
was intended and carried out to prevent mass killings of the kind which took
place in Bosnia-Herzegovina. The Serb forces that carried out mass killings
in Bosnia-Herzegovina were most often volunteer paramilitaries (often re-
cruited from among persons with criminal records) or special police/military
forces and not ordinary conscripts of the Bosnian Serb military. To prevent
such mass killings in Kosovo, NATO aircraft would have had to attack the
units and their command posts most likely to carry them out. But these units
and their command posts could not have been successfully targeted from the
safe altitude at which NATO aircraft had to fly to avoid anti-aircraft fire. The
initial bombing of Yugoslav army military installations and troops all over
Yugoslavia from this altitude could not have been intended to stop or prevent
mass killings; according to the commanding officer of the NATO operation,[9]
they were not intended to do so. In fact the bombing did nothing to prevent
those mass killings of Albanians, carried out by paramilitaries or special police
units, which followed the air attacks on Yugoslavia. The effective prevention
of the mass killings of innocents would not have been possible under NATO's
partial death minimization strategy in which the highest priority was assigned
to saving the lives of NATO personnel.

NATO's partial death minimization strategy was compatible not with a
military operation that would effectively prevent mass killings of innocents in
Kosovo but with a military operation aimed at securing control over Kosovo
for NATO's ally, the KLA, and its political leaders. In answer to the first question above, then, one can say that the way NATO's military operation was
carried out did not indicate that its overriding aim was to save the lives of innocents; if so, it is doubtful that NATO's primary or overriding intention was
to minimize the death toll of innocents. Even if evaluated only from the point
of view of its intention, NATO's military intervention in Kosovo does not appear to satisfy the Death Minimization condition.

THE NO OTHER OPTION CONDITION

The NATO attack on Yugoslavia was preceded by a series of negotiations aimed at reaching a peaceful settlement between the Yugoslav government and the Kosovo Albanian political parties.[10] Prior to and during the negotiations, NATO government leaders repeatedly and publicly threatened the Yugoslav government with a military action unless it signed a peace agreement prepared and proposed by NATO governments. The attack ensued after the Yugoslav government, and its leader Milosevic, refused to sign this peace agreement. A major reason for their refusal was article 8, which allowed the deployment of NATO forces throughout Yugoslavia without the Yugoslav government's permission.[11] The attack was launched upon the Yugoslav government's refusal to allow the NATO forces to be deployed throughout Yugoslavia.

This indicates that NATO's war against Yugoslavia was not the only option available to NATO governments for preventing the expected mass killings of Kosovo Albanians. Another option, which NATO governments failed to pursue, was a mutually agreed deployment of NATO forces, under the mandate of the UN Security Council, in the province of Kosovo alone. Such a deployment—and the withdrawal of most of the Yugoslav military forces from Kosovo—would have been sufficient to prevent any action by the Serb paramilitary or professional police units against Kosovo Albanian civilians. Since the Yugoslav government agreed to such a deployment, the effective prevention of mass killings of Kosovo Albanians could have been achieved without any war against Yugoslavia. In fact, after 78 days of bombing Yugoslavia, NATO governments accepted a similar arrangement, allowing NATO's deployment of forces in the province of Kosovo alone under the UN Security Council mandate. From this it follows that there were other options apart from waging war and killing innocents: NATO's war against Yugoslavia thus fails to satisfy the No Other Option condition.

THE JUSTIFIABILITY CONDITION

It appears that the US government and its NATO allies started to support the KLA in its armed struggle against the Yugoslav government in early 1998. However, in spite of their help, by mid-1998 the KLA lost large areas it had previously controlled and failed to hold on to any towns. Thus, its attempt to establish itself as an alternative or replacement government of Kosovo had largely failed. Moreover, the probable defeat of the KLA as an effective fighting force would have also ended its political effectiveness as well. It is still an open question whether and to what extent NATO's war against Yugoslavia was used to cover up the failure of its earlier policy of support for the KLA and to prevent its removal as an effective military and political force in Kosovo. If it turns out that NATO governments waged this war to cover up the failure of their earlier policies, its justifiability in terms of the saving of lives would be, as I have argued above, questionable.[12]

CONCLUSIONS

Thus, NATO's war against Yugoslavia fails to satisfy the No Other Option condition and, on the available evidence, it does not appear to satisfy the Death Minimization condition. There is also some room for doubt as to whether it satisfies the Justifiability condition. In short, this war, at least on the available evidence, failed to save more innocent lives than it caused deaths — and those lives that were saved could have been saved by peaceful means, through a UN-supervised withdrawal of the Yugoslav forces and administration from Kosovo.

There are two obvious reasons for this failure. First, the partial Death Minimization strategy aimed at saving the lives of NATO personnel and its allies first, under the conditions of nationalist conflict, led to an increased number of civilian deaths of all national groups. Second, NATO's commitment to the victory of its ally, the KLA, among the warring parties prevented it from pursuing other options at its disposal for stopping or preventing the mass killing of innocents. In short, NATO's political and military goals — the victory of its preferred ally in the nationalist conflict at the lowest possible cost in human lives to its own personnel — were incompatible with the policy of saving innocent lives from all national groups involved in the conflict.

Let us now consider two alternative approaches that NATO could have taken in its military intervention in Kosovo. First, NATO could have taken a neutral stance in this conflict and intervened not in support of the KLA but only to save innocent lives from any national group. As pointed out in the preceding section, such a military intervention in all probability would have satisfied the No Other Options and Justifiability conditions, but it is unlikely that it would have satisfied the Death Minimization condition. NATO military intervention, using primarily air strikes against all warring parties might have led to a greater number of killed innocents than the lives saved; a deployment of its ground troops, if resisted by all sides, would have also led to a substantial number of deaths among its personnel.

The second alternative, a NATO intervention without its partial Death Minimization strategy (aiming to protect the lives of its personnel) would assume that the NATO personnel engaged in it would have a duty to sacrifice their lives in a war waged in order to save the lives of threatened innocents in Kosovo. This raises two interrelated questions: first, are the citizens of NATO countries under any moral obligation to sacrifice their lives for the sake of saving the lives of non-citizens? And, second, would a protracted military operation aiming to save the lives of non-citizens, leading to a large number of deaths among NATO personnel, find electoral support in NATO constituencies?

A full discussion of these questions is beyond the scope of this paper. Here I can only state, without any elaboration, my preferred answers. As for the first question, I do not believe that NATO citizens had any general or special duties to sacrifice their lives for the sake of saving the lives of innocents in Kosovo. I do not believe that there is a general duty of every individual to sacrifice his or her life, if need be, for the sake of the saving lives of others, however those may be threatened. Further, the citizens and governments of NATO states at the time did not have any special duties towards the citizens of Kosovo and of Yugoslavia which could justify such a sacrifice. The citizens and governments of NATO bear no responsibility for the nationalist conflict in Kosovo and had not participated in the decision-making which led to the war between the KLA and the Yugoslav forces in the first place. The responsibility for the conflict is borne, I believe, principally by the national leaders and on their constituencies in that region. Moreover, these leaders and their constituencies were, at the time when NATO attacked Yugoslavia, still in a position to end the conflict and thus to save innocents without sacrificing any lives. If so, NATO citizens were not obliged to sacrifice their lives for the sake of saving the lives of non-citizens which could have been saved without their (or anyone else's) sacrifice.

Thus, NATO electoral constituencies would be right not to support any policies willingly sacrificing their co-citizens' lives for the sake of saving lives which could have been saved without that sacrifice. The partial Death Minimization policy pursued by NATO was, I take it, meant to avoid any sacrifice of NATO personnel's lives. In so far as this was its aim, I believe it was justifiable both by prudent political considerations and by broader considerations of their citizens' duties towards non-citizens.

In short, I have argued, first, that NATO's war against Yugoslavia in 1999 cannot be justified by the saving of innocent lives and, second, that NATO governments had no alternative ways of waging war or of military intervention at their disposal which would be so justified. This suggests—although it does not entail—that one should not attempt to justify a military intervention in a nationalist conflict by reference to the saving of innocent lives. Let us see whether (or how) this suggestion can be resisted.

Saving Lives Regardless of the Three Conditions

The above argument against the humanitarian justification of military interventions in nationalist conflicts is open to a number of objections of which I shall consider only two.

Let us start with an objection which rejects the three (or any other) conditions as necessary for any humanitarian justification of military intervention in nationalist conflicts, including that in Kosovo. The objection could start with the observation that NATO's military action, by removing the Yugoslav administration and the military from Kosovo, stopped the mass killing of Albanians that had been taking place. In this way NATO's military action saved many innocent lives, which would have been lost. The saving of these lives is, by itself, sufficient to justify its military action. No other consideration—such as the number of deaths caused by this operation, what other options there were to stop the killing, and so on—is in this case of any relevance to that simple justification. A lot of lives were saved, and that justifies the action taken to save them. Any attempt to make other considerations look relevant to this justification is ungrateful nitpicking. This was an operation of saving lives *tout court*.

This objection, as it stands, is ambiguous in its implications. Are other considerations, apart from the over-all number ("a lot") of lives saved, irrelevant to all such justifications or only to this one? Had NATO used active nuclear weapons (instead of enriched uranium shells) and caused tens of thousands of (immediate as opposed to delayed) civilian deaths, would this consideration of the deaths caused be irrelevant? Would the fact that many lives were saved in such circumstances be an adequate justification of military operations with such consequences? If this is not the case, and other considerations are irrelevant only in this particular case, one would need to know why they are so.

One reason for their irrelevance may lie in the simple *assumption* that the number of innocent deaths caused by NATO's military intervention was *not* larger than the number of innocent lives saved. In the preceding section I have argued, rather too briefly, that so far there is no evidence that this indeed was the case. Regardless of my or any other argument, this assumption is (so far) unsubstantiated; if the objection rests on this assumption, it is itself unsubstantiated.

However, if the objection makes no such assumption, then one needs to show why NATO's action of saving those lives justifies killing many other innocent people in order to do so. In other words, one would need to show why the number of people killed by NATO's action (or inaction) is irrelevant to this particular justification of their killing. I think that the principle of equal value of human lives—which I endorsed in the beginning of the essay— makes it quite difficult to show this. The principle implies that the value of each individual life saved by NATO's operation is equivalent in value to each individual life it terminated. For the purposes of the argument, we can restrict this to the lives of innocent people. If the number of innocent lives terminated is irrelevant here for the justification of the intervention, this suggests that these lives are not of equal value to the lives which were saved. I do not know how this suggestion can be resisted, and, therefore, I do not know how one could show that the number of innocent people killed is irrelevant without abandoning the principle of the equal value of human lives.

The second objection to be examined here is based on the distinction between willful and inexcusable murder and unintentional and excusable killing. The innocent people killed in NATO's military operation were not intentionally killed: these people were not targeted and every effort was made (short of exposing the lives of NATO's personnel to risk) to avoid killing them. If they were killed, they were, the objection assumes, killed by accident. In contrast, the innocent Albanians in Kosovo were targeted to be killed, on the sole grounds of belonging to a national group, and therefore they were either murdered or in danger of being murdered. They were to be (or were) killed intentionally, premeditatedly, and not by accident. Killing by accident is, by definition, excusable. NATO's killing of innocent civilians, committed by accident, is thus excusable and is not, in any way, to be compared with the murder and planned murder of innocent Albanians. Therefore, saving innocent Albanians from murder is justified, regardless of the number of accidentally killed innocents.

This distinction implies that those who kill by accident are not to be condemned in the same way as those who murder. If NATO killed the innocents only by accident, one cannot condemn it in the same way as one can condemn Milosevic's regime for its mass murder of Albanian innocents. This essay presents no grounds whatsoever to question this conclusion.

Yet this distinction does not absolve those who kill by accident of the blame nor of the responsibility for taking someone else's life: the killer in such a case is not freed from blame nor responsibility. NATO's command was responsible for conducting the bombing in a way that risked killing innocents. They were capable of predicting that some civilians would be killed; their killing was not an unpredictable or unexpected accident. Moreover, the killing of innocents did not result from sheer negligence to take appropriate precautions against killing civilians. While some precautions against this were indeed taken, many bombing raids were conducted with full knowledge of the risk to the lives of civilians. To put it rather crudely, NATO command knew that their bombing campaign would lead to the death of innocent civilians and that knowledge did not stop it from conducting the campaign in the way that they did. If so, their killing of innocents was not an accident that they were not in a position to prevent. In short, NATO's killing of innocents cannot be excused or justified on the grounds that it was an unpreventable or unpredictable accident.

But, if NATO's killing of civilians is not excusable solely on the grounds that it was done by accident, how can one justify it? Let us try this argument: the murder of innocents for self-interested reasons (such as any government's mass murder of its subjects) is incomparably worse than any killing of innocents by accident. In order to prevent or stop the murder, one is justified in committing acts which are not equally bad. Therefore, one is justified in killing innocents by accident in the course of an action aimed at prevention of murder. To put it in a much simpler if not too precise manner, since murder is evil while killing by accident is not, from this follows a simple principle of justification: for the sake of the prevention of evil, one is allowed to use any means that are not equally evil. From this simple principle, it should follow that accidental killing of innocents, regardless of the number of innocents killed, is justified if done for the sake of saving other innocents from evil, that is, from murder.

To challenge this argument one does not need to disagree with the starting premise that murder and accidental killing differ in terms of their moral wrongness. One needs only to point out that sometimes they do not differ in terms of the specific harm they cause. From the point of view of the harm done to the families and, of course, to the victims themselves, it is of little if any consequence whether the action leading to their death was willful but preventable murder by enemy forces or unintentional killing by these forces or their allies that the latter could have prevented. From the point of view of the nationalist ideologies and their mass following, any mass killing of unarmed civilians in such a conflict harms, in various ways, the national group to which these civilians belong. In view of this, it is possible to regard mass killings of innocents performed as unintentional killing on the same scale of harm (but not of moral wrong) as premeditated mass murder. If this is possible, then it is possible to ask how the prevention of harm caused by murder justifies the inflicting of harm by unintentional killing. The above argument and simple principle on which it is based offers no answer to this question.

The above argument implies that even if the number of innocents killed in this preventable but unintentional way is far greater than the number of innocents saved from murder, still the two acts — the latter act of (attempted) murder and the former act of preventable but unintentional killing — are not to be measured on the same scale of moral wrongness. In some cases, however, these two acts can be compared on the same scale of wrongness. Suppose in an operation to rescue a few kidnapped white tourists, a white rescue force killed indiscriminately a large number of colored natives; they did not target the colored natives specifically but fired indiscriminately in the crowds of colored natives in which the kidnappers were hiding. Had the kidnappers been hiding among the white crowd of the same nationality as the rescue force, the latter would not have fired indiscriminately into the crowd. Their action, one can argue, exhibits their unspoken belief that the lives of the colored natives are worth less than those of the white people. But killing people of a certain nationality or race, in the belief that their lives are worth less than the lives of people of other nationalities or races, one may argue, is on the same scale of wrongdoing as murder: as the latter, the former assumes that the lives of certain people are expendable. Indiscriminate killing of this kind may indicate a disregard for, or a breach of, the principle of equality of human lives.

The above two considerations—of the harm caused and of the breach of the principle of equality of human lives—indicate that the simple principle above does not, on its own, justify unintentional killing of (any number of) innocents for the sake of prevention of murder. As in the previous objection from the saving of lives *tout court*, further argument is required to show why either the principle of equality of human lives should be breached or that the principle is not, in fact, breached, in cases in which the number of "excusably" killed innocents is allegedly irrelevant to the justification of actions saving (other) innocents from murder.

Why Do We Justify Killing of Innocents by Reference to the Lives Saved?

There are many circumstances under which killing innocent bystanders can be justified by the attempt to stop a murderer or murderers from committing murders or escaping from justice. The simplest case is the one in which a lawful arrest is resisted by an armed murderer: as he fires at police officers, they return the fire in self-defense and unintentionally and by accident kill an innocent bystander who found herself at the scene. The bystander in this case was not in the line of fire but was killed by a bullet which ricocheted from the wall. The officers could not have predicted this and consequently could not have prevented this event (short of not defending themselves).

But suppose now that the armed murderer hid in a crowd of innocent people and fired from that crowd. In returning his fire, the police officers, using automatic weapons, sprayed the whole crowd with bullets, killing several people. They could have easily predicted and prevented this killing but believed that there was no other way to stop the murderer from continuing on with his murders and that, therefore, the sacrifice of a few innocent lives, randomly terminated, was justified.

Suppose that all of us agree with them that the indiscriminate use of automatic weapons was in this case the only way to stop the murderer getting away. In spite of this, many of us would disagree with them that their killing innocent bystanders was justified; many of us would argue that preventing (further) murder by sacrificing innocent lives in this case is not justified. The extent to which one would accept that their killing innocents was justified would depend, among other things, on the degree of danger that the murderer, hidden in the crowd, presented. If the murderer had access to weapons of mass destruction—for example, to nuclear devices—and the police officers knew that, many more people would share their belief that the sacrifice of a few randomly chosen lives is preferable than a much larger number of potentially lost lives. While this does not demonstrate that, under some circumstances, the sacrifice of innocent lives is justified, it does indicate that the ratio of innocents killed to lives saved is of relevance in a justification of the killing of innocents in the course of prevention of murder.

In this paper, I have attempted to point out the difficulties that this kind of calculation of comparative harm encounters in cases of outside military intervention in a nationalist conflict. First, since the participants in the conflict do not believe that there are any innocents in this conflict, any mass killing of innocents will be perceived as a harm to one warring party, the one to which these innocents belong. However politically neutral the outside intervention may be, if it involves mass killing of any civilians, its effects are going to be perceived to be far from politically neutral. Second, by attempting, rightly, to minimize deaths among the interventionist personnel, the risk of deaths among innocents will be further increased and may threaten to exceed the number of lives saved. Third, in protecting members of one warring party from the other, the interventionist force may enable the protected warring party to kill innocents from their enemy group, thereby further increasing the total number of innocents killed. Fourth, in cases in which the interventionists are a dominant global or regional power supporting one warring party over the other(s), there will be some room for doubt that the interventionist power had no other option ("no other way") to prevent the mass murder of innocents, except by going to war and thus killing other innocent people. Finally, I suggest that these difficulties arise both from the features of nationalist conflict and from the conflicting obligations which the interventionist government has to its own citizens (the partial Death Minimization strategy) and to the noncitizens whose lives are endangered in a nationalist conflict.

While these difficulties may not be insuperable, they suggest that military interventions into nationalist conflicts, if justifiable at all, may require better justifications than those which refer to the saving of innocent lives.

Notes

1. I would like to thank Robert Young of La Trobe University, Melbourne, for very useful suggestions and comments on an earlier version of the paper.

2. For a further discussion of the murder/accidental killing distinction see below, pages 60-63.

3. The estimates of the number of victims of this policy vary from a half to two–and-a-half million. In addition, from 90,000 to 150,000 people — mostly government or party employees and professionals — were executed in the "interrogation" centers. For a survey of the evidence and of the number of victims, see Gary Klintworth, *Vietnam's Intervention in Cambodia in International Law* (Canberra: AGPS Press, 1989) 59-85.

4. Klintworth points out that the Vietnamese did not justify their invasion by references to humanitarian considerations (Klintworth 11) and that their intervention was prompted "by fundamental reasons of security and self-defense" (Klintworth 60).

5. See William Drozdiak, "B-52 Strike Devastates Field Force In Kosovo…" *Washington Post* (9 June 1999): 19.

6. For an account of killing and kidnapping of non-Albanians, see Human Rights Watch Report, "Federal Republic Of Yugoslavia Abuses against Serbs and Roma in the New Kosovo," 11, 10D (August 1999), accessed at <http://www.hrw.org/reports/1999/kosov2/ >, on 20 April 2002. Also, Letter to the President of the UN Security Council from the Deputy Prime Minister of Serbia, Nebojsa Covic, 24 April 2002. For an account of the organized killing of Serbs, see "KLA Units Specialized In Hunting Down Serbs," *Agence France Press*, Pristina (19 September 1999). Also "Kosovo Resurgent," *Economist* (23 September 1999) and "Reconstructing Kosovo," *Economist* (18 March 2000).

7. The debate on the number of Albanians killed by the Serbian forces, prior to NATO's attack on Yugoslavia, is still carried out without any attempt to substantiate the claims that the bodies recovered by the teams of the Hague International Tribunal or other international forensics teams in Kosovo had been buried before the attack. For an example of this kind of polemic see Michael Ignatieff, "Counting Bodies in Kosovo," *The New York Times* (21 November 1999): s4, 15. For an early report outlining the problems of establishing the number of people massacred, see Chris Bird, "Graves put Kosovo death toll in doubt: killings and forensics do not tally," *Guardian* (11 November 1999): 2.

8. The village of Racak, the site of an alleged massacre of Albanian civilians, was the site of intense fighting a day before the bodies of around 40 Albanians (all allegedly civilians) were shown to the OSCE observers as evidence of the alleged massacre. No evidence of this kind — that is, bodies of Albanian civilians allegedly massacred by Serb forces — was presented to international observers or media prior to the NATO attack in March 1999. For a good survey of evidence, including the Serb government sources and the French reports from the village of Racak, see *Slucaj Racak: Zlocin i Kazna* ("The Racak case: the crime and punishment"), *NIN*, special supplement, Belgrade (17 January 2002).

9. In an interview on the US Public Broadcasting Service (PBS), General Wesley Clark told the interviewer, Jim Lehrer, "Jim, we never thought that through air power we could stop these killings on the ground; it's not possible. You can't stop paramilitaries going house

to house with supersonic aircraft flying overhead and dropping bombs; we all knew this...." News Hour with Jim Lehrer, interview with General Wesley Clark, 29 March 1999, accessed at <http://www.pbs.org/newshour/bb/europe/jan-june99/clark_3-29.html> on 3 April 2002.

10. The last in the series was held in February-March 1999 in Rambouillet, France, under the chairmanship of British and French foreign ministers. The accords presented at this negotiation were then further negotiated separately with the Albanian delegates and the Serbian leader Milosevic.

11. For the text, see *Le Monde* (23 April 1999): Appendix B, Article 8. Quoted in A. Pavkovic, *The Fragmentation of Yugoslavia: Nationalism and War in the Balkans* (London: Macmillan, 2000) 237, n. 6.

12. In a later interview, General Wesley Clark described the reasons for waging war against Yugoslavia as follows: "Because what Milosevic never really understood was this wasn't a conflict strictly about Kosovo. It wasn't even a conflict, ultimately, about ethnic cleansing. It was a battle about the future of NATO, about the credibility of the United States as a force in world affairs. And the longer it went on, the more clearly the nations of the West would see those issues." CBS News Interview of General Wesley Clark by David Martin, 15 May 2000, accessed at <http://cbsnews.com/htdocs/pdf/clark.pdf> on 2 April 2002.

4 / Interdependence and Intervention[1]

Ernst-Otto Czempiel

In my contribution I shall deal, first, with the normative aspects of intervention. Second, I shall describe the contemporary socio-political situation in Euro-Atlantic and its meaning for the problem of intervention. I then delineate some operational consequences for a new concept of foreign policy which is applied to the problem of intervention.

Normative Aspects of Intervention

I shall argue not so much from an ethical as from a political-operational point of view. Any ethical obligation presupposes a relationship, either a conceptional or an empirical one. Concepts of mankind, humanity, and religion create general obligations. They are neither weak nor virtual, but they are difficult to implement. What does it mean, practically, to be a member of mankind or of humanity?[2] Of course, this membership demands a certain behavior, but it can be formulated only in very general terms. The membership in a religious community does not go much further. Christianity has been the main belief system all over Europe since the Middle Ages, but it has not kept kings and societies from fighting each other.

The more concrete a relationship becomes, the more specific are the ethical obligations. Neighborhood, community, and citizenship generate a number of responsibilities.[3] Some of them have legal authority, all of them are ethically binding. The closer the relationship, the stronger becomes the obligation. This is the normative basis of the European social state.

What about interstate relationships? They are regulated by legal norms imbedded in international law. In its traditional form, it submits that the state dominates and regulates all relations towards other states. Subjects of law (and politics) in traditional international law are the states only. People do not qualify, at least not yet.

77

There are tendencies in international law to overcome this traditional, outmoded model of the world as a world of states and to use a new model treating people not as objects but as subjects of the state. The American political scientist David Easton[4] has developed such a — democratic — model of a state and its decision-making processes, which convert societal demands into the output by the political system. The lacking dimension of foreign policy has been added in the meantime.[5]

As long as the world of states is accepted as the right and pertinent model, the ethics of intervention are blocked by the concept of sovereignty and its ingredient, the law of non-intervention. As long as the Westfalian Order is accepted as valid, intervention, even if ethically mandated, is legally forbidden. Only the UN Security Council acting under Chapter VII of the UN Charter is entitled to intervene with military power.

Obviously, this situation is not satisfactory.[6] But it cannot — and should not — be improved by the return to the right to war which after so many decades of endeavor finally ended in 1945 with the UN Charter. Progress must be made, not regress. We must not go back to the old concept of just war, but should go forward to a new concept of intervention.

The first step must be to analyze, and to recognize, how the world of the twenty-first century has changed and why. This must be done regionally. The current term "globalization" pretends that our world is a unit showing the same conditions everywhere. This is simply not correct. The regions of our world are in very different stages of development. Therefore, I deal here exclusively with the Euro-Atlantic region, reaching from Vancouver to Vladivostok. In practical terms, it reaches only to the Urals. In this part of Euro-Atlantic, the texture of international politics has changed substantially. In other regions of the world, the conditions have also changed, but not as much as in Euro-Atlantic.

The Socio-Political Situation in Euro-Atlantic

In Euro-Atlantic, two substantial changes have occurred after 1945. First, formerly independent, autonomous, and sovereign states have become functionally dependent on each other and have lost parts of their sovereignty. They are not isolated anymore but are very close to each other. Many of them are already partially integrated, and all of them cooperate in international organizations. Interdependence has many meanings and definitions. Waltz thinks, it is a "relationship costly to break."[7] Keohane and Nye distinguish several degrees of "sensitivity."[8] In my view, both definitions are neither new nor convincing. Already the eighteenth century knew that all states react to domestic developments in other states.[9] For me, interdependence means that an actor can accomplish his goals only if other actors cooperate. No European state today can provide security and economic well-being for its society without the cooperation of other states. And no societal actor can reach his goal if other societal actors do not go along.

Secondly, within the states, an even more dramatic change has occurred. The processes of industrialization and democratization have changed the system of government.[10] Formerly monarchic and/or autocratic, the European-Atlantic states have become democracies. Under the cover of the Cold War many important shifts have occurred. During the "Golden Age" between 1950 and 1973, European societies became rich and the states democratic.[11] Since then, they have left the industrial age and entered the informational age. Mutual dependence has permeated the frontiers. Mobility and the media have transformed the foreigner into the neighbor.

Better informed and better educated, the societies have elevated their position vis-à-vis the government. Democratization is a fact and a tendency. Both processes have created the "societal world," as I call it.[12] It is not a world society, but a European world, where within the states the societies play a much more important, sometimes the crucial role. Societal demands influence, often even direct, the foreign policy of the state. Without the consensus of the society, foreign policy cannot be pursued successfully. Societal actors have escaped the authority of the government and have formed their own systems of interaction.[13] Globalization is the name of this game. And political scientists all over the world wonder what the future of the nation state, the future of the state as such, will look like.

I leave open whether this "societal world" is better or not than the world of states. My point is that it is a different world in many ways:

1. In the pre-industrialized world, where farming had been the source of income and wealth, territorial expansion and war could make sense. Great armies were necessary to enlarge the territory and/or defend it against the expansionist intentions of neighboring countries.

2. In the industrialized, above all in the post-industrialized world, territorial expansion is not useful anymore. War has lost its functional importance. The key to development and wealth are knowledge and innovation. What is needed is not the enlargement of territory and population but access to the market of the world.

3. The position of the state within the international system also has changed.[14] Formerly independent and, therefore, sovereign, the states are now interconnected very closely with each other because of the situation of interdependence. Alone, they are unable to provide security for their society. It can be realized and institutionalized only if and when all other states of an

international system cooperate. Security has become a common good. All states, therefore, must see to it that in all states of an international system the political preconditions for peace do exist. It is this kind of interdependence, which has changed the nature of the international system. It is not anymore the famous "situation hobbésienne" (Raymond Aron), where one state was the enemy of the other. The Euro-Atlantic system is an ensemble of closely interconnected states, some of them already integrated, which depend on each other for their security. From there stems the right to intervene in the domestic concerns of all member states if causes of war do arise there. In this sense the Euro-Atlantic system has become similar to, but not yet identical with, the domestic politics of a nation state.

4. War has changed its character. It is not anymore the classical international war. The dominant type of modern war in the "societal world" is the civil war. There were 36 wars registered in 2000. With the exception of the war between Ethiopia and Eritrea, all of them have been domestic wars. As different as they have been, they had one thing in common: people did not accept, nor tolerate, the kind of government which had been forced upon them. If other means prove to be futile, people use violence.

5. States have lost parts of their sovereignty and power vis-à-vis their own societies. As Secretary-General Kofi Annan has put it: "States must respect the individual sovereignty, the human rights and basic freedoms of each individual."[15] If they do not do that, citizens rebel. They even use arms to topple unwanted governments or to suppress unwanted minorities. At stake in each case of violence are the type of the society and the structure of government.

6. Civil war is totally different from the international war which, in Euro-Atlantic, has nearly vanished. The civil war is not a "little war," as many authors will have it.[16] It is a completely different kind of violence. In civil wars, societies and societal actors fight the government to get rid of its dictatorial or majority rule. In a few cases, societal factions fight each other in order to create a new state. The Balkans are cases in point.

What we have in Europe is, therefore, a transitory situation. Europe is no longer a region of sovereign and independent states. It is at the same time not yet a regional state with a regional government to which all the powers which the individual states have lost have been transferred. The European Union is possibly the nucleus of such a regional state, but its reach is limited, and the final shape of its organization is very much in the shadows of the future.

The crucial question is, what happened to those rights which the nation-states have lost? Did they evaporate? Are they up for grabs for anybody willing and capable to take them? My answer is: they belong to the community of neighbors interconnected by interdependence and organized in an international organization.[17] The community of states in a region, acting together by the consent of a majority, can administer these parts of authority and power which the individual state has lost. The international organization lies midway between the dwindling national state and the emerging regional state. Acting together, the states of the region administer their interdependence.

Acting together they reproduce those parts of legitimacy and legality which the individual state cannot claim any longer. They lift authority and power to the regional level, where some day in the future both will reside. By doing it together, they protect this authority from being conquered by states that have the capability (and the intention) to do so. The consensus of the region constitutes a legitimacy which discourages any deviation. Against the verdict of the neighbors acting within an international organization, no government could justify its violation of human rights. Thus, in my view, the international organization fits exactly the quasi-domestic situation we have in Europe. The international organization is the quasi-government of the region. It respects the states, but requires and organizes their cooperation which, by consent, will administer the treatment of common problems.

The international organization is the body to which belong those competences which the single nation-state because of interdependence has lost. If the majority of the members of such an organization decides that military power must be used to cure the violation of human rights and democracy in a given country, this decision carries legitimacy.

To have acted outside the international organization was the basic fault of the "Operation Allied Force" against Yugoslavia. Being manifestly illegal, it deprived itself of necessary effectiveness. It was perceived in the Balkans and in the world not as an act of authoritative action to stop the atrocities of a civil war, but as a military intervention by a strong alliance for political purposes. Occasionally it has been compared with the operations of the Concert of Europe in the nineteenth century, which, under the pretext of humanitarian intervention, pursued power politics. Of course, the governments of many NATO-states were honestly convinced that they acted in "the sense of the United Nations" and in favor of humanitarian purposes. They tried very hard to persuade their societies accordingly. But in international politics, as in human life, intention must be implemented by appropriate means in order to be successful. The German Secretary of Defense Rudolf Scharping correctly submitted that Western Europe was obliged to react against the atrocities by Serbian troops.[18] However, he failed to recognize that in the transitorial situation in Europe, intervention is appropriate, but not the use of military power without a mandate by an international organization.

The New Concept of Foreign Policy

In the short period between 1990 and 1994, the surprising ending of the Cold War did provoke a new thinking. In November 1990 in Paris, the Charter of a New Europe called for the promotion of democracy, human rights, and market economy as the political basis of the Euro-Atlantic region. The Conference for Security and Cooperation had been elevated to an institutionalized organization with the prime goal to prevent violence, to protect minorities, to foster democratization, and to spread market economies.[19] In other words, what the CSCE and the Charter of Paris proclaimed amounted to a political program of mutual intervention in the domestic affairs of member states to produce the necessary structural changes.

This was a very audacious and modern concept of foreign policy. Born out of practical insights and experience, won during the last phases of the Cold War, the new concept pointed in the right direction, but it lacked a solid conceptual basis. No theoretical-empirical analyses supported the conclusions drawn by the conference of Paris, no Foreign Office started to write the handbook of foreign policy in times of interdependence. Without a systematic follow-up, the progress, made in Paris by correct insights and good intentions, was doomed.

After four years of relative silence, NATO succeeded in regaining the upper hand in the theory and praxis of foreign policy-making in Europe. The Organization for Security and Cooperation in Europe almost disappeared to Vienna. The expansion of NATO won the competition, with the European Union as the main ordering factor in Europe.[20] As a consequence, western policies in Euro-Atlantic returned to old-fashioned patterns:

1. The promotion of democracy in the states of the FSU was scaled down after 1994.

2. NATO, the Western defense alliance, started to expand as if new threats against Western Europe were imminent.

3. Russia, which in 1990 had been accepted as a partner of the West, slowly became excluded from the reordering of Europe.

4. Arms reduction was stopped; arms control lost attention.

5. Military power won back its old attraction as the best tool of foreign policy-making. The bombing of Serbia by NATO in 1999 was consequential.

This restoration of outmoded strategies of power politics was all the more astonishing, since there was no prospect of a new military threat in Europe. As a substantial consequence of the new thinking in Europe after 1990, the East-West situation was completely secure, cooperative, and harmonious. In 1990, the Treaty on Conventional Armed Forces in Europe (CFE) between NATO and the Warsaw Pact was signed; it was implemented in 1992. The treaty reduced weapons all over Europe, particularly in Germany and Russia. As a second step, military personnel also was reduced. In 1999, at the OSCE Summit in Istanbul, the CFE Treaty was adapted to the dissolution of the Warsaw Pact and the Soviet Union. Although not ratified immediately, because of Russian politics in Chechnya, the CFE Treaty is working very well.

Add to this the Treaty on the Open Skies, which has not been ratified but has been working for the last 10 years, and you get the picture that no threat whatsoever exists in the European situation. Together with the so-called Vienna Document of 1994, those treaties provide for an extensive system of mutual information on defense, defense-planning, and armaments. They permit the verification of the reductions agreed upon. They even arrange for on-sight inspections. During the 10 years which have elapsed since 1991, more than 6,000 on-site inspections have occurred. The Vienna Document doubled all this mutual information and added provisions for confidence-building that had no precedent.

As a consequence, there is transparency, mutual trust, confidence, and security all over Europe, from the Atlantic to the Urals, from Norway to Turkey and Greece. No tank can be moved, no barrack can be closed or opened without the knowledge of all partners. In other words, in Europe today there is no danger of war whatsoever; there is not even insecurity.[21]

From our point of view, this system of verification and inspection is sheer intervention. It enters the most sacred secret of the traditional nation-state—its armaments, its military, its defense budgets, even its planning for the future. Before 1990, such an infiltration of the "domaine reservée" had been unthinkable. The military was the cornerstone of sovereignty and the most important provider of security. It was unsuccessful, as so many wars in European history have demonstrated, but it had been protected against all intrusions from the outside.

After 1990, the European states, and above all, the military itself, turned around 180 degrees. They recognized that keeping their military forces apart would strengthen, not eliminate the greatest cause of war: insecurity. In the theory of realism, the feeling of insecurity and uncertainty towards the capabilities and intentions of neighbors is the most important cause of war.[22] To eliminate it, cooperation was the best strategy. In contrast to the realist assumption that cooperation under the condition of anarchy is impossible, liberal theory recommends it. And interdependence demands it. As explained earlier, comprehensive security in Europe can be gained only if all states cooperate. This insight dominated European politics in the early1990s. The European states sacrificed parts of their sovereignty and accepted the intervening on-site inspections and deep-reaching controls by their neighbors in order to create that high degree of security which realists think is impossible.

Comprehensive security is not identical with the capability to defend oneself. This is how the term has been understood traditionally and is being understood again today. NATO tries to enlarge the architecture of security by expanding the defense capabilities of the military alliance.

This understanding is not sufficient. The Warsaw Pact and the Soviet Union were not weak on defenses. On the contrary, during the years of the Cold War, NATO believed that the East was superior. In spite of their military capability, the Warsaw Pact broke down, the communist governments were toppled, and the Soviet Union was dissolved. A look into history gives the same lesson. In nineteenth-century Europe, all states had been able to defend themselves, but this capability did not provide for security but for war, victory and defeat.

The modern interpretation of security points to a situation in which a state is no longer being threatened. If there is no enemy, security does exist. A state is secure if and when it is surrounded by friends and partners only.

Such a situation is not utopian—it does exist in Western Europe. Until 1945 the most war-prone region, Western Europe since then has become a zone of definite and lasting peace. No European state threatens its neighbor. Within the European Community or, later on, the European Union, all states are friends and partners. What has appeared in Western Europe, therefore, must be transferred to other parts of Europe in order to reach the same degree of security.

What is Intervention?

Up to now I have used a rather broad understanding of intervention. Accepted by mutual agreement, this kind of penetration of military sanctuaries by other states does not pose any problem. But if there is no consensus, the law of non-intervention raises its head again.

In order to overcome this obstacle, we have

1. to define intervention more precisely, and
2. to look into the modern strategies of intervention.

In the literature, there is no clear-cut meaning of intervention. Interpretations oscillate between influence and the use of military power.[23]

My proposal is to define intervention via the intended goal. To intervene means to try to change from outside the system of government of a certain state. If there is any "domaine reservée" — any realm belonging exclusively to the right of a society — it is the right to choose its own government, to decide on its particular constitution.[24]

In Europe, however, where interdependence has connected the states towards a quasi-domestic situation, exactly this kind of intervention into the "domaine reservée" is required. Comprehensive security depends mainly on democratic systems of government. Research in international relations worldwide has established that there is a causal relationship between democratic systems of government and peace.[25] All zones of peace in the world of today consist of democracies. Only if all governments within a region are democratic, will comprehensive security and peace be ensured. In a situation of interdependence, the comprehensive security of all depends on the democratic structure of governments in all states. If there are autocratic left-overs, they must be induced to democratize.

Intervention becomes the order of the day of a foreign policy which tries to enlarge and foster the structures of comprehensive security all over Europe. Therefore, the law of non-intervention must be changed into a regime of mutual intervention. This sounds revolutionary, and in a certain sense it *is* revolutionary. But the provocation dwindles when we look into the operative strategies of this intervention.

Intervention as a Strategy

The crucial question now is how to intervene. What kind of strategies of democratization are permitted and effective under the conditions of interdependence? Military power must be applied only in two cases.

1. If a genocide takes place (as in Rwanda and Burundi a couple of years ago when the West abstained), neighbors must intervene immediately and with military power to stop the mass murder.

2. Military power can be used when ordered by an international organization, the UN Security Council or a regional organization as indicated above. Regional organizations for the time being do not have the right to do so, but this part of the UN Charter should be changed. It was inserted in 1945 in favor of controlling interests of the US and other great powers of that time. In Europe, for instance, the OSCE could get that authority. Under the conditions of interdependence within the quasi-domestic situation we have in Europe, the OSCE could take over the authority to legitimize the use of military power against recalcitrant governments if no other means is left over.

Without such a mandate by an international organization to use military power, all interventions must be non-violent. This is decisive ethically, because help must not kill. It is required politically, because only such a mandate le-gitimizes coercive actions. It is obvious under international law, incorporated in the UN Charter. And, finally, non-violence is required pragmatically. To change a system of government can only mean to help the society concerned to change it. This societal consensus is absolutely required. It cannot be en-forced, but must be gained by cooperation and support. Non-violence is the absolute precondition for a successful intervention.

Non-violent means are extremely effective, and they are available. The conditions of interdependence offer a plethora of new possibilities of inter-vention. Dependence invites bargaining and interactions that will influence attitudes and political demands. Both can be used abundantly.

Strategies of Intervention

There are two strategies available, one direct and the other indirect.

DIRECT STRATEGIES OF NON-VIOLENT INTERVENTION

The European Union demands democratization and respect for human rights from all applicants for membership. It is a condition they have to meet. This "conditionality" is a very strong means of intervention. It is useful only in special cases, because democratization cannot be imposed from above, it must grow from the bottom. Eastern Europe is prepared to meet this condition any-way; therefore, "conditionality" will be effective.

Another special situation benefited the European Recovery Program of 1948. Here, too, democratization was required as a precondition for getting aid from the US. Under the special circumstances in Europe and in Germany, this direct strategy worked well.

Somewhat more doubtful is the direct strategy involved in the Stability Pact for the Balkans. With its three tables, the Stability Pact tries to buy de-mocratization and civil rights for economic and industrial aid. It might work, but it also could meet resistance. The chances of failure are very great because the amount of money involved is very small.[26]

Generally speaking, direct intervention into the domestic affairs of a country to turn it into a democracy works only under special circumstances. It should be used very cautiously and only in exceptional cases.

INDIRECT STRATEGIES

Much better, less sensitive, but probably more successful is the use of indirect means of intervention. There are many of them, produced by the new conditions of the "societal world" which exists in Euro-Atlantic. Here, the third wave of democratization (Huntington)[27] has spread the interest in democratization to all societies. Their members long to have more influence on their respective governments, to participate in its decision-making. This situation came into being only after 1945, particularly in the1950s. It appeared publicly when the Cold War ended. This change was the basis of the soft revolution in Eastern Europe at the end of the1980s. This general interest in democratization is the basis for several new strategies.

1. Robert Seeley, the British historian, has explained that the degree of freedom in a country depends on a low degree of pressure from outside. The stronger the pressure, the lower the degree of democratization and vice versa.[28] The result for an indirect strategy is to offer cooperation in détente towards a country in order to strengthen its internal advocates of liberty and democratization. To give just one example, the end of the East-West conflict was very much promoted by the INF Treaty (Intermediate-Range and Shorter-Range Nuclear Forces Treaty) which lowered the tension between East and West substantially.

2. Make use of international organizations to foster cooperation. The main function of international organizations is to reduce the security dilemma by replacing uncertainty with information and confidence. A side effect is to promote cooperation as the prevailing pattern of international relations.[29] It is necessary, therefore, to include all states of a region into its international organization. It is counterproductive to exclude any "state of concern." To give again one example: including China in the World Trade Organization is the right strategy; to isolate the People's Republic is wrong.

3. Make use of dependencies with a tit-for-tat strategy. The best example here is the Final Act of Helsinki 1975, in which the West exchanged the benefits of economic cooperation against more leeway for human rights groups in the East.

4. Use foreign aid only for economic purposes that benefit societies. There should be no military aid whatsoever and no sales of weapons to developing states.

5. Aid should not be given to central governments but to subnational actors, countries, cities, and environmental groups.

6. Investments should be steered toward the civilian infrastructure of a country and the production of consumer goods, thereby benefiting the society and not the government.[30]

The most important indirect strategies make use of the numerous interactions between societal actors which evolve daily. They are known by the wrong comprehensive term "globalization." Much more relevant is the fact that those societal interactions fill the space between neighboring states, connecting societies and strengthening them toward their respective governments.

7. The most modern strategy is to make all those interactions vehicles of intervention, not by politicizing them but by promoting them as a non-political but very effective means of influencing the structures of a society.

8. There is the "twinning" of cities, with the cooperation between political parties, business organizations, churches, and universities.

9. There are numerous NGOs which connect the societies.[31]

They all can be used to transfer the knowledge of the practice of democracy; they all can be used to strengthen the forces of democracy in a given country. Even tourists transfer such messages because they spread the image of democratic societies. The desire to imitate those images will be strengthened accordingly.

Those interactions should be kept outside foreign policy. They are societal in character and should remain so. But foreign policy should support those interactions because of their interventional character. To give one example: "The American Way of Life" has remained outside politics, but its influence worldwide has been tremendous. It has contributed to the spread of democracy more than any direct strategy.

The conditions of interdependence present a great variety of strategies which can be used for non-violent, non-cogent, but highly effective interventions in favor of democracy. They add up to what Joseph P. Nye Jr. calls "soft power."[32]

To use those strategies is easier said than done. Any strategy of intervention is a strategy of prevention. That means it must be used early, when structures are still unfolding. Traditional foreign policy, in contrast, is a policy of reaction, usually starting when it is too late. Serbia is a case in point. Instead of intervening in favor of democratization immediately after the death of Tito, or at least after 1986 with regard to Kosovo, the West waited until the civil war in Kosovo began. Then, at this late stage, the West intervened militarily. It compensated early inactivity with late overreaction.

In its present shape, foreign policy is still geared to the conditions of the world of states. It must be modernized to fit the "societal world" which exists in Euro-Atlantic. In order to make use of interdependence for intervening with "soft power" in favor of democracy, a new paradigm of foreign policy is required. It should rely on prevention and use non-violent strategies in order to change the political structures in a given country. They, in turn, will produce and institutionalize a foreign policy which will be non-aggressive. Comprehensive security — peace — will be the result.

This modernization of foreign policy requires the education of politicians, diplomats, bureaucrats, and the military in favor of a culture of prevention.[33] It requires, above all, the knowledge of the public. The tax-payer should know that politics of preventive intervention are not only more successful than traditional foreign policy, they are much cheaper. The former OSCE High Commissioner on National Minorities, Max van der Stoel, has calculated that the eight years of his activities, which prevented many deadly conflicts, were cheaper than the price of two cruise missiles.[34]

To sum up, to intervene non-violently in the governmental structures of neighboring countries is, under the conditions of interdependence, an ethical and political obligation. Interdependence has provided the appropriate strategies, which can implement such an intervention. The challenging task is to transfer these insights into the realm of practical politics.

Conclusion

Under the conditions of interdependence the problem of intervention presents itself in a new shape. Interdependence has connected formerly isolated states with each other. The situation between them has become similar to (not identical with) domestic politics. From there, two conclusions derive.

First, the domestic situation in a given country is of concern to its neighbors. They have, therefore, the responsibility to act when human rights have deteriorated and the system of rule is autocratic or dictatorial. In the situation of independence which prevailed in the world of states, intervention into the domestic affairs of another country had been prohibited. Under the conditions of interdependence, intervention in favor of democratization has become an ethical and political obligation. There is only one pre-requisite: intervention must be non-violent.

Secondly, the conditions of interdependence have offered new strategies for such kinds of intervention that had not been available in the world of states. The many interactions creating interdependence between states offer numerous possibilities of contributing to the change of governmental structures in a given country. Not only foreign aid but also commercial trade, investments, and even tourism can be used as intervening means. These processes should not become politicized, but foreign policy should understand that these processes by themselves contain intervening strategies.

Foreign policy should realize that "soft power" which intervenes in societal and political structures is more effective and cheaper than the traditional "power politics."

Notes

1. The text is the written version of my presentation to the 4th Annual Meeting of the International Law and Ethics Conference Series, "Ethics of 'Humanitarian Intervention': Grounds for Internationalizing Internal Conflicts," University of Belgrade, 23-25 June 2000.

2. See London School of Economics, "Ethics and International Relations," *Millennium* 27.3 (1998).

3. See Louis Kriesberg, "Coexistence and the Reconciliation of Communal Conflicts," *The Handbook of Interethnic Coexistence*, ed. E. Weiner (New York: Continuum, 1998) 182-98.

4. David Easton, *A Framework for Political Analysis* (Englewood Cliffs, NJ: Prentice-Hall, 1965).

5. See Ernst-Otto Czempiel, *Internationale Politik: Ein Konfliktmodell* (Munich: Paderborn 1981) 15ff.

6. See, e.g., Martin Ortega, *Military Intervention and the European Union*, Chaillot Paper 45 (Paris: Institute for Security Studies, March 2001).

7. Kenneth N. Waltz, "The Myth of National Interdependence," *The International Corporation: A Symposium*, ed. Charles Kindleberger (Cambridge, MA: MIT Press, 1970).

8. Robert O. Keohane and Joseph S. Nye, Jr., *Power and Interdependence: World Politics in Transition* (Boston, MA: Little, Brown, 1977).

9. Gottfried Achenwall, *Geschichte der allgemeineren Europäischen Staatshändel des vorigen und jetzigen Jahrhunderts im Grundrisse als der europäischen Geschichte zweyter Theil* (Göttingen: Vandenhoeck, 1761).

10. See Samuel P. Huntington, *The Third Wave: Democratization in the Late 20th Century* (Norman, OK: University of Oklahoma Press, 1991).

11. Anthony Sutcliffe, *An Economic and Social History of Western Europe Since 1945* (London: Longman, 1996).

12. Ernst-Otto Czempiel, *Weltpolitik im Umbruch, Das internationale System nach dem Ende des Ost-West-Konfliktks* (München: Muenchen, 1993).

13. Peter F. Drucker, "The Global Economy and the Nation-State," *Foreign Affairs* 76.5 (September-October 1997): 159ff.

14. See the profound analysis by James N. Rosenau, *Turbulence in World Politics: A Theory of Change and Continuity* (Princeton, NJ: Princeton University Press, 1990).

15. Kofi Annan, "Annual Report to the UN General Assembly," 20 September 1999; United Nations Press Release SG/SM/7136.

16. Martin Hoch, "Krieg und Politik im 21. Jahrhundert," *Aus Politik und Zeitgeschichte* B 20.2001 (11 May 2001): 17-25.

17. In extenso I have dealt with this problem in my article: "Einmischung als Strategie. Über Interdependenz und Intervention," *Merkur* 54.1 (January 2000): 11-23.

18. Rudolf Scharping, *Wir durften nicht wegsehen: der Kosovo-Krieg und Europa* (Berlin: Ullstein 1999).

19. *Gemeinsame Erklärung von zweiundzwanzig Staaten über die neuen Ost-West-Beziehungen in Europa, am Rande des KSZE-Gipfels in Paris am 19. November 1990 verabschiedet*, in Europa-Archiv 45, 24, 25.12.1990, p. D 654ff. (Common Declaration of 22 states regarding the new East-West Relations in Europe, signed at the CSCE summit, Paris, 19 November 1990.)

20. See Robert W. Rauchhaus (ed.), "Explaining NATO Enlargement," *Contemporary Security Policy* 21.2 (August 2000): passim, especially 173ff.

21. *Schlusdokument der Ersten Konferenz zur Überprüfung der Wirkungsweise des Vertrags über konventionelle Streitkräfte in Europa und der abschliesenden Akte der Verhandlungen über*

Personalstärken vom 15. bis 31. Mai 1996 in Wien. Printed in *Internationale Politik* 51.12 (December 1996): 110ff, 112. (Final Document of the First Conference for Controlling the Effects of the Treaty of Conventional Forces in Europe and the Final Document on Military Manpower, Vienna, 15-31 May 1996.)

22. Kenneth N. Waltz, *Theory of International Politics* (Reading, MA: Addison Wesley, 1979).

23. See, e.g., the contributions in Ernst-Otto Czempiel and Werner Link (eds.), *Interventionsproblematik aus politikwissenschaftlicher, völkerrechtlicher und wirtschaftswissenschaftlicher Sicht* (Strasburg: Engel 1985).

24. See Ernst-Otto Czempiel, "Intervention in den Zeiten der Interdependenz," *HSFK-Report* 2.2000 (Frankfurt: Hessische Stiftung Friedens-und Konfliktforschung, 2000): 4ff.

25. Bruce Russet, *Grasping the Democratic Peace: Principles for a Post-Cold War World* (Princeton, NJ: Princeton University Press, 1993).

26. See Marie-Janine Calic, "Der Stabilitätspakt für Südosteuropa. Eine erste Bilanz," *Aus Politik und Zeitgeschichte* B 13-14.2001 (23 March 2001): 9-16.

27. See note 10.

28. Quoted in Otto Hintze, *Staat und Verfassung: Gesammelte Abhandlungen zur allgemeinen Verfasungsgeschichte*, ed. Gerhard Oestreich (Göttingen: Vandenhoeck and Rupercht, 1962) 411.

29. See Clive Archer, *International Organizations* (London: Routledge, 1983) 163.

30. Larry Diamond, "Beyond Authoritarianism and Totalitarianism: Strategies for Democratization," *The Washington Quarterly* 12.1 (Winter 1989): 148ff.

31. Jessica T. Mathews, "Power Shift," *Foreign Affairs* 76.1 (January/February 1997): 66ff.

32. Joseph P. Nye, Jr., "Soft Power," *Foreign Policy* 80 (Autumn 1990): 153ff.

33. Carnegie Commission on Preventing Deadly Conflict. *Final Report* (New York: Carnegie Corporation, 1997).

34. Max van der Stoel, *Peace and Stability through Human and Minority Rights: Speeches by the OSCE High Commissioner on National Minorities*, ed. Wolfgang Zellner and Falk Lange (Baden-Baden: Nomos, 1999) 22.

5

Biased "Justice": Humanrightsism and the International Criminal Tribunal for the Former Yugoslavia

Robert M. Hayden

> Justice is the right to do whatever we think must
> be done, and therefore justice can be anything.
> —*Mesa Selimovic*, *Death and the Dervish*

Human Rights Watch ("HRW") has hailed the new millennium as "the beginning of a new era for the human rights movement," based on "an evolution in public morality."[1] Its *World Report 2000* trumpets the trumping of state sovereignty by human rights[2] because courts are willing to indict leaders, and organizations, such as NATO, are willing to intervene militarily against regimes that commit crimes against humanity. HRW cites the International Criminal Tribunals for the former Yugoslavia and for Rwanda, the incipient International Criminal Court, prosecutions of assorted Yugoslavs and Rwandans by Austrian, Belgian, French, German and Swiss courts, and a Spanish judge's indictment of former Chilean dictator Augusto Pinochet. It then mentions the NATO military actions against Yugoslavia and the international intervention in East Timor. It concludes that all of this "foretells an era in which the defense of human rights can move from a paradigm of pressure based on international human rights law to one of law enforcement."[3]

The interlinking rhetorics of law, justice, and morality, along with their opposites of crime and injustice, underpin calls for "humanitarian [military] intervention," and the image of justice via international tribunals is dominant. HRW put "significant progress towards an international system of justice" to prosecute crimes against humanity at the head of its discussion of 1999 achievements,[4] and is a strong proponent of the International Criminal Court. The link between tribunals and military intervention is explicit: "like the use of military intervention, the emergence of an international system of justice signals that sovereignty is no longer the barrier it once was to actions against crimes against humanity."[5]

The millennial shift includes a remarkable transformation of the capabilities of "human rights organizations," from persuasion to prosecution:

> Until now … human rights organizations could shame abusive governments. They could galvanize diplomatic and economic pressure. They could invoke international human rights standards. But rarely could they trigger prosecution of tyrants or count on governments to use their police powers to enforce human rights law. Slowly, this appears to be changing.[6]

HRW is not the only human rights organization that calls for governments to use their "police powers" to intervene in other states in the name of morality. Bernard Kouchner, UN Governor of Kosovo after NATO's occupation of the place but otherwise one of the founders of Doctors Without Borders, the organization that won the Nobel Peace prize in 1999, is another: "a new morality can be codified in the 'right to intervention' against abuses of national sovereignty…. In a world aflame after the Cold War, we need to establish a forward-looking right of the world community to actively interfere in the affairs of sovereign nations to prevent an explosion of human rights violations."[7] To Kouchner, this "right to intervene" is not "human rights imperialism" because

> everywhere, human rights are human rights. Freedom is freedom. Suffering is suffering. Oppression is oppression. If a Muslim woman in the Sudan opposes painful clitoral excision, or if a Chinese woman opposes the binding of her feet, her rights are being violated. She needs protection … When a patient is suffering and desires care, he or she has the right to receive it. This principle also holds for human rights.[8]

Chinese foot-binding was last reported in the 1930s, and both the knowledge and the seriousness of a 1999 writer who calls for protection against it might thus seem doubtful. Yet Kouchner's elevation to administrative office indicates that the NATO powers, at least, take him seriously.[9] Certainly his sentiments echo those of Vaclav Havel, that "human beings are more important than the state … the idol of state sovereignty must inevitably dissolve" and that NATO's war against Yugoslavia "places human rights above the rights of the state," thus demonstrating that "human rights are indivisible and that if injustice is done to one, it is done to all."[10]

Assertions of devotion to justice, however, are common in the world—probably every political actor makes public claims to be on the side of justice and to uphold morality. HRW and other human rights organizations that call for military intervention are thus acting as classic political figures, demanding the application of massive violence to those whom they define as immoral. As such, their own actions and the actions of those whom they support should be exposed to the same scrutiny that they claim to apply to others.

This article thus takes a close look at one of the most important of the elements of the new international legal order which human rights activists promote, the International Criminal Tribunal for the Former Yugoslavia (ICTY, or "the Tribunal"). It finds that the ICTY delivers a "justice" that is biased, with prosecutorial decisions based on the national characteristics of the accused rather than on what available evidence indicates that he[11] has done. Evidence of this bias is found in the failure to prosecute NATO personnel for acts that are comparable to those of Yugoslavs already indicted, and of failure to prosecute NATO personnel for *prima facie* war crimes. This pattern of politically driven prosecution is accompanied by the use of the Tribunal as a political tool for those western countries that support it, and especially the United States: put bluntly, the Tribunal prosecutes only those whom the Americans want prosecuted, and the US government threatens prosecution by the supposedly independent ICTY in order to obtain compliance from political actors in the Balkans. Further, judicial decisions by the ICTY render it extremely difficult if not impossible for an accused to obtain a fair trial, while the Tribunal has also shown a lack of interest in the investigation of potential prosecutorial misconduct.

An exposé of the ICTY has its own intrinsic merits, but there is a wider point. The materials that are cited in this paper are almost all from readily accessible sources, and the *facts* discussed should be well known. Yet the arguments made here are not those commonly taken in regard to the ICTY by those who claim to be human rights advocates, which raises the question of why NATO actions that so clearly violate human rights, and Tribunal actions that so clearly violate fundamental fairness towards defendants, are not the subject of much concern by those who profess to support human rights. The answer is found in the transformation of human rights concepts, from protesting the application of state violence on non-violent dissidents to demanding the application of massive violence on states deemed to be inferior. This transformation turns human rights into humanrightsism, with the new ism, like most isms, a repudiation in practice of the principles that it supposedly embodies. The ICTY is a particularly striking manifestation of humanrightsism because of the high principles that are routinely invoked to justify it, which are betrayed in practice.

Selective Prosecution 1: Cluster Bombs and War Crimes

In July 1995, Milan Martic, President of the Republika Srpska Krajina (the self-proclaimed Serb "Republic" in Croatia), was indicted before the ICTY for violations of the laws and customs of war, in that he had ordered a missile attack on the city of Zagreb in retaliation for the successful Croatian offensive of May 1995, which had driven Serbs from Slavonija.[12] What is interesting about this indictment is that what made the bombardment a war crime was that it was carried out by missiles that had been fitted with cluster bomb warheads: "warheads containing 288 bomblets, all of which in turn have 400 small steel balls, which are scattered, along with bomblet fragments, on a lethal radius of ten meters.... It is used for soft targets, that is troops on the ground and vehicles, not for buildings or military installations."[13] Seven civilians were killed and many more wounded, and it was noted in the Rule 61 hearing that one rocket damaged a home for the aged and a children's hospital.[14]

The use of cluster bombs is key to the Martic indictment, and the nature of these bombs was described in detail in the Rule 61 hearing. As the indictment put it, the rocket in question could "be fitted with different warheads to accomplish different tasks: either to destroy military targets or to kill people. When the [missile] is fitted with 'cluster bomb' ... it is an anti-personnel weapon designed only to kill people."[15] With this in mind, it is interesting to see the lack of response by the ICTY Prosecutor to NATO's May 7 attack on the city of Nis, when cluster bombs fell on the market, killing 15 people, and the city's main hospital was also hit.[16] Over the course of the NATO bombings, nine hospitals were damaged or destroyed and over 300 secondary and elementary schools and other educational institutions were damaged.[17] According to the *Philadelphia Inquirer*, the US Defense Department says that "American planes dropped 1,100 cluster bomb canisters, with 220,000 bomblets, over Kosovo," while "British planes dropped about 500 bombs, each with 147 bomblets."[18] British authorities have acknowledged dropping large numbers of cluster bombs, and in August 2000 had to admit that about 60 per cent of those cluster bombs either missed their targets or remained unaccounted for, leaving perhaps 60,000 bomblets unexploded in Yugoslavia and Kosovo.[19]

In light of these statistics, the conclusion of the committee established by the Prosecutor to review the NATO bombing campaign, that there should be no investigation into NATO's use of cluster bombs, is remarkable.[20] The committee's report attempted to distinguish NATO's use of cluster bombs from the culpability asserted in the *Martic* indictment by saying that condemnation of the use of cluster bombs should be limited only to the facts of that case. However, the Tribunal's holding in the Rule 61 proceeding in *Martic* was apparently wider:[21] "weapons, projectiles, and materials and methods of warfare of a nature to cause superfluous injury" are prohibited.[22] Dropping cluster bombs from 30,000 feet "despite evidence from the Gulf War that if this was done they were likely to miss their targets."[23]

Neither will it do to say that NATO was only aiming at military targets and missed; Martic also said that he was aiming at military targets in Zagreb,[24] and it cannot be argued that the US and British commanders did not know that they were risking civilian casualties. Martic's comment to a Western reporter that "I am very sorry if civilian targets were hit because our aim was to hit military targets"[25] may be compared to any of a large number of NATO statements about "collateral damage," including NATO's decision on about May 1 to stop even issuing such apologies.[26] While the Rule 61 hearing on Martic introduced evidence from interviews that showed that Martic targeted cities intentionally, this is also true of NATO generals, including, specifically, American ones, who have openly complained that French politicians did not permit them to attack even more sites in Yugoslav cities.[27]

The reason for the Tribunal's disinterest in NATO's actions is perhaps found in the views expressed by the official NATO spokesman, Dr. Jamie Shea, on May 16 and 17, 1999, when he was questioned during the daily NATO press conferences about the possibility of NATO liability for war crimes before the ICTY. Dr. Shea said on May 16 that "NATO is the friend of the Tribunal ... NATO countries are those that have provided the finances to set up the Tribunal, we are among the majority financiers." He repeated the same message on May 17: NATO countries "have established these tribunals ... fund these tribunals and ... support on a daily basis their activities." Therefore, he was "certain" that the Prosecutor would only indict "people of Yugoslav nationality."[28]

Any remaining doubts on this last point have been put to rest. In the last week of 1999, several major newspapers reported that the ICTY Prosecutor was investigating the conduct of NATO pilots and their commanders during the Kosovo war,[29] including commissioning a preliminary study of NATO's use of cluster bombs by looking at the history of such weapons and at how they have been used in previous wars.[30] While Milan Martic might well wonder why the Prosecutor had not found it necessary to make such a study before indicting him for using cluster warheads, NATO officials clearly had little to fear. Within days of the first reports of prosecutorial interest in NATO, tribunal officials were reported as saying that the study was a preliminary, internal document that was highly unlikely to lead to indictments or even to be published.[31] While the Prosecutor had told the *London Observer* on December 26 that if the confidential report indicated that NATO broke the Geneva conventions she would indict those responsible, on December 30 she issued a press release saying that "NATO is not under investigation by the Office of the Prosecutor. ... There is no formal inquiry into the actions of NATO during the conflict."[32]

This last announcement by the Prosecutor was plainly untrue, as the Committee Report itself indicates that the Committee was working through at least May 2000.[33] It is, of course, possible that this quick retreat and face-saving falsehood by Mrs. Del Ponte was unrelated to US government denunciations of the reported inquiry into NATO's actions.[34]

Selective Prosecution 2: Wanton Destruction of Property

In July 1995, the Prosecutor of the ICTY indicted Radovan Karadzic and Ratko Mladic. One of the sets of acts said to constitute a crime against humanity was "the systematic destruction of Bosnian Muslim and Bosnian Croat homes and businesses. These homes and businesses were singled out and systematically destroyed in areas where hostilities had ceased or had not taken place."[35] They were also indicted for a "grave breach" of the Geneva Conventions because of "extensive destruction of property": that they had

> individually and in concert with others planned instigated, ordered or otherwise aided and abetted in the planning, preparation or execu-
> tion of the extensive, wanton and unlawful destruction of Bosnian Muslim and Bosnian Croat property, not justified by military neces-
> sity, or knew or had reason to know that subordinates were about to destroy or permit others to destroy the property of Bosnian Muslim
> or Bosnian Croat civilians or had done so and failed to take necessary and reasonable measures to prevent this destruction or to punish the
> perpetrators thereof.[36]

With these indictments in mind, the enormous economic destruction of Serbia by NATO is relevant. According to the Group 17 economists (who form the core of the *Savez za Promenu*, the Serbian opposition coalition most favored by the US, and thus who may be presumed to be fairly reliable observers), the economic damage caused by the NATO bombings to infrastructure, economic facilities, and non-economic civil facilities was slightly over four billion dol-lars.[37] According to the BBC, "at least 30% of the adult population [of Serbia] is unemployed. The economic collapse was caused as NATO switched to in-frastructure targets as the war continued"[38] — switched from military targets. In the first month of bombing alone, according to the European movement in Serbia, NATO targets included drug and pharmaceutical plants, tobacco plants and warehouses, printers, and shoe factories,[39] while the G 17 economists listed as well wood, textile, and food industries, among others. There was clearly no "military necessity" for hitting these targets, unless "military necessity" is defined as meaning "anything the destruction of which might have a political impact." Neither can it be said that these were "collateral damage." NATO's generals and politicians made a very purposeful decision to attack non-military infrastructure early in the war.[40] They planned the attacks very carefully, and only one proposed target was ever rejected because of concerns about its relation to the military.[41] But the Yugoslav military was not the target. NATO generals told the *Philadelphia Inquirer* on May 21 that "Just focusing on fielded forces is not enough.... The people have to get to the point that their lights are turned off, their bridges are blocked so they can't get to work." Note that the purpose of destroying these bridges was *not* military, but this was clear when NATO destroyed the bridges in Novi Sad, 500 kilometers from Kosovo, installations that clearly did not make the "effective contribution to military action" in Kosovo that would have rendered them legitimate targets under Art. 52 of Protocol I additional to the 1949 Geneva Conventions.

Aryeh Neier has noted that the UN commission that investigated war crimes in Bosnia concluded that "attacking the civilian population is a war crime."[42] There is no question but that, in attacking "infrastructure," NATO attacked civilians. Judging from the wording of the indictments of Karadzic and Mladic, we should expect indictments against those in NATO who planned and carried out these attacks, and against Bill Clinton and Tony Blair for having failed to take necessary and reasonable measures to prevent this destruction or to punish the perpetrators thereof. However, I would suspect that Jamie Shea's view, as quoted in the last section, is accurate, and that we should not expect to see the FOT (Friends of the Tribunal) indicted.

Selective Prosecution 3: Murder

On May 27, 1999, Slobodan Milosevic, three other Yugoslav politicians, and a Yugoslav Army general were indicted by the Prosecutor of the ICTY for, among other charges, "murder, a violation of the laws and customs of war,"[43] for the deaths of Albanians who were killed by Serb/Yugoslav forces in Kosovo. It would seem, however, that NATO political and military leaders should also be liable for the charge of murder for, at the least, the bombing of the studios of Radio Television Serbia (RTS) on April 22, 1999. There is no question but that the RTS studios were civilian targets: NATO spokesman Jamie Shea had stated as much in an April 12, 1999, letter to the general secretary of the International Federation of Journalists, noting that "television and radio towers are only struck if they are integrated into military facilities."[44] No one has suggested that RTS studios played any military role. Indeed, NATO spokesman David Wilby had stated at NATO's news briefing on April 8, 1999, that RTS would not be bombed if it broadcast Western news broadcasts for six hours per day, which indicates clearly that there was no concern that the studios were integrated into the military. Bombing RTS was an intentional effort to widen the war to civilian targets,[45] which resulted in the deaths of at least 16 civilians.

These statements by NATO's own spokesmen make ridiculous the Committee Report's conclusion that "NATO's targeting of the RTS building for propaganda purposes was an incidental (if complementary) aim of its primary goal of disabling the Serbian military command and control system."[46] Amnesty International, in its report on NATO's operations, calls the attack on RTS a war crime[47] and after the Committee report was issued, challenged that report's findings on this incident.[48] Human Rights Watch agrees that the RTS studios did not constitute a legitimate military target and further states that "NATO failed to provide clear warning of the attacks," as required by the Geneva conventions.[49] Why the deaths of the 16 journalists would not then be murders is not addressed by HRW.

At least, however, HRW recognizes the RTS dead to be journalists, more than can be said for the Committee to Protect Journalists (CPJ), which publishes a list annually of journalists killed on the job worldwide.[50] CPJ's 1999 list intentionally excluded the RTS journalists on the grounds that what RTS broadcast was not journalism but propaganda.[51] Rather ironically, at the moment that the NATO bombs killed 16 RTS people, the station was broadcasting an interview of Yugoslav President Slobodan Milosevic by an American scholar, who did the interview on behalf of a CBS affiliate in Texas. That interview had already been broadcast in the US, so the CPJ presumably would regard CBS headquarters in New York as having been a legitimate NATO target.

In regard to charges of "propaganda," CBS would actually seem as vulnerable as RTS, but from the other side, if only it had had cruise missiles. In a speech to the National Press Club in Washington DC, CBS anchorman Dan Rather referred to American attacks on Yugoslav water and power systems as "our" attacks, something that "we" did; when questioned by a member of the audience on the propriety of a supposedly independent journalist associating himself with one side, Rather responded that:

> I'm an American reporter. Yes I'm a reporter and I want to be accurate. I want to be fair. But I'm an American. I consider the US government my government. So yes I do—when US pilots in US aircrafts turn off the lights, for me, it's "we." And about that I have no apology. ... I'm an American, and I'm an American reporter. And yes, when there's combat involving Americans, [you] can criticize me

if you must. Damn me if you must, but I'm always pulling for us to win. [applause from the audience][52]

Presumably, the CPJ would have protested had Rather been injured in Belgrade (which he was not), and not only because of his status as a CPJ "Benefactor" who had given more than $25,000 to the organization (as did CBS News).[53] But can we say that he was not engaged in "propaganda" when he was "pulling for us to win"?

CPJ was founded in 1981 to "monitor abuses against the press and to promote press freedom around the world," and "accepts no government funding" in order to ensure its independence.[54] Yet this supposedly independent organization "pulled for us to win," adopting NATO's definition of legitimacy: NATO spokesman Wilby had justified attacking RTS by saying that it "is an instrument of propaganda. ... It is therefore a legitimate target in this campaign,"[55] and the CPJ agreed. Thus the CPJ abandoned the principles it was founded to embody, in a striking manifestation of humanrightsism.

Failure to Prosecute *Prima Facie* War Crimes: Depriving A Civilian Population of Water

Art. 54 of the Protocol Additional to the Geneva Conventions of 12 August 1949 is about as unequivocal as humanitarian prohibitions of military targeting get. Entitled "Protection of objects indispensable to the survival of the civilian population," it states (Para. 2) that "it is prohibited to attack, destroy, remove or render useless objects indispensable for the survival of the civilian population, such as ... drinking water installations and supplies ... for the specific purpose of denying them for their sustenance value to the civilian population or to the adverse Party, whatever the motive."

On April 25, a NATO official, who did not wish to be identified, told the *Washington Times* that a new phase of the NATO campaign would aim to destroy electrical systems and water systems in Belgrade and in other major Serbian cities in order to take the war directly to civilians.[56] On May 23, "15 NATO bombs hit water pumps ... in the northwestern town of Sremska Mitrovica for the second night in a row."[57] Attacks on May 24 "slashed water reserves by damaging pumps and cutting electricity to the few pumps that were still operative."[58] Only 30 per cent of Belgrade's two million people had running water, and the city was down to 10 per cent of its water reserves.[59] The fact that these attacks were not aimed at military operations in Kosovo is clear from the remarks attributed by the *Washington Post* to a Pentagon official, who stated that the attacks had been limited to Serbia proper but that "NATO commanders are understood to be planning to extend the attacks to Kosovo."[60] A clearer example of NATO's targeting civilians in Serbia rather than soldiers in Kosovo would be hard to find.

To be sure, NATO responded to criticisms of these attacks by saying that it had not targeted water supplies but only the power system.[61] This was clearly not true in regard to Sremska Mitrovica; in any event, it is irrelevant because what is prohibited is also "rendering useless" a water system, and NATO acknowledged that it was aware that its bombing of electrical stations would do this: "We are aware this will have an impact on civilians," a NATO official told the *New York Times* on 24 May. US Senator Joseph Lieberman was even more direct: "We're not only hitting military targets, otherwise why would we be cutting off the water supply and knocking out the power stations—turning the lights out."[62] Lieberman, it should be noted, spoke of this *prima facie* war crime with approval as a way "to bring the war in Kosovo home to the people, the civilians in Belgrade."[63]

Clearly, NATO committed a *prima facie* war crime and the evidence that it did so knowingly is at least as strong as anything used in the speedy indictment of Milan Martic. However, as a spokesman for the International Relations Committee of the US House of Representatives told the Canadian *National Post*, "You're more likely to see the UN building dismantled brick-by-brick and thrown into the Atlantic than to see NATO pilots go before a UN tribunal."[64]

US Government Direction of Prosecution 1: Milosevic But Not Tudjman

The putative independence and impartiality of the ICTY was utterly compromised by the indictment on May 27 of Yugoslav President Milosevic and four of his political associates. While there may be little question that Milosevic is guilty of war crimes, "justice" that is not impartial cannot be seen as just. The failure of the Prosecutor to indict NATO or its clients would seem to confirm Jamie Shea's message that he who pays the prosecutor determines who is charged. It is particularly noteworthy that while the Prosecutor has been reported unable to indict Croatian generals for the 1995 ethnic cleansing of the Krajina because the US government has refused to provide requested information,[65] she made well publicized visits to American and British officials to gather information with which to indict Milosevic. When a Prosecutor who is a citizen of one NATO country seeks assistance from the governments of other NATO countries in order to indict the president of the country that NATO is attacking, not even the pretence of prosecutorial independence remains. The matter was well described by Nina Bang-Jensen of the Coalition for International Justice in testimony during the Kosovo war before the US

Congress's Commission on Security and Cooperation in Europe: the ICTY prosecutors "have to recognize ... that even though they should make prosecutorial decisions independent of political considerations, and make their decisions in an unbiased legal and just way, they are wholly dependent on the cooperation of states in order to execute their orders. So they can be a little too pristine about their not wanting to acknowledge that they ultimately have to rely on political institutions."[66] In light of these comments, the independence of the ICTY seems compromised by the fact that the President of the Tribunal, Judge Gabrielle Kirk McDonald, had been the guest of honor of Ms. Bang-Jensen's organization a month before the testimony quoted, and referred on that occasion to US Secretary of State Albright as "the mother of the Tribunal."[67]

US Government Direction of Prosecution 2: Threats against Vuk Draskovic

In July 1999, I was surprised when a close advisor to Vuk Draskovic told me that the US was threatening Draskovic with indictment by the ICTY. If the Prosecutor's office were truly independent, such a threat could not be plausible. However, the *New York Times* has also reported that "Washington has threatened Mr. Draskovic with indictment by the international war crimes tribunal in the Hague for the activities of his short-lived Serbian Guard, a paramilitary group, in Croatia in 1991."[68] Since contacts in Washington inform me that a major task of the US government's interdepartmental Balkans Task Force is now to support the Prosecutor's office, that Washington feels free to threaten indictments seems highly plausible.

Denial of a Fair Trial 1: Judicial Deference to Prosecutor

Politicization of the ICTY Prosecutor's Office is especially troubling in light of the extraordinary deference that the *judges* of the Tribunal afford the prosecutor. This deference was first shown in regard to a truly outstanding scandal in the first case tried before the ICTY, that of Bosnian Serb Dusko Tadic.[69] In that case, no witness had testified to having seen Tadic personally commit an atrocity, such as murder or rape. However, the Prosecutor's final witness testified that not only had he seen Tadic rape and murder, but he had also been forced by Tadic to rape and murder as well. The witness was a Bosnian Serb who had been captured by the Muslims, convicted by them of genocide, and then presented to the ICTY Prosecutor as a witness against Tadic.

The witness testified under complete anonymity, his identity having been kept a secret even from the defense under a "protection order" meant to allay the fears of witnesses that they or members of their families would suffer retribution if they testified before the Tribunal. In permitting such protection orders, the ICTY adopted one of the less admired procedures of the Spanish Inquisition, which also concealed the identities of witnesses from the accused,[70] and so it is interesting that such American human rights advocates as the Jacob Blaustein Institute for the Advancement of Human Rights of the American Jewish Committee, the Center for Constitutional Rights, the Women's Human Rights Law Clinic of the City University of New York, and the Women Refugees Project of the Harvard Immigration and Refugee Law Program supported prosecution witness anonymity in a joint *Amicus* brief filed with the Tribunal.[71]

As it happened, the Defense was able to show that the witness, "Witness L," had lied.[72] The man had said that his father was dead and that he had no brothers, but a member of the defense team was able to discover that, in fact, he had a brother and that his father was not dead, and arranged to confront the witness with his father and brother by bringing them to the Hague. At that point the witness not only confessed to lying about his family, but also claimed to have been forced by the Muslims, while he was in their custody, to agree to lie against Tadic and then trained by them in the testimony he was to give in the ICTY. Confronted with these lies, the Prosecutor in *Tadic* informed the court that it did not regard his testimony as reliable and invited the court to disregard it, and the identity of the witness, one Dragan Opacic, was revealed.

At this point, the obvious questions would seem to have been why the witness lied and whether in fact he was trained to do so by the Bosnian government, which had made him available to the Tribunal. Indeed, the Trial Chamber did order the Prosecutor's office to investigate the matter in order to determine whether charges of perjury should be brought against the witness. However, at this point, the Trial Chamber gave both the Prosecutor and the Bosnian government extraordinary deference.

On December 2, 1996, the Prosecutor sent a letter to Alija Izetbegovic, President of the Presidency of Bosnia and Herzegovina, thanking him for his cooperation in investigating the Witness L matter and exonerating his government of wrongdoing.[73] Tadic's defense lawyers, who had gone to Sarajevo to investigate the matter themselves but who had been given the "cold shoulder" by the Izetbegovic government,[74] first heard of this letter several weeks later when I asked them for a copy of it.[75] The Trial Chamber accepted this action by the Prosecutor without questioning why the Prosecutor had never shown greater zeal in determining the truth of the witness's story before the defense challenged basic facts about it, an especially interesting question since the Prosecutor knew the identity of the witness, and the defense, by virtue of the protection order, did not.[76] Since some parts of the witness's story seemed to indicate that the Prosecutor's office might also have been involved in training him to give false testimony, the Tribunal in effect asked the Prosecutor to investigate possible wrongdoing by her own office, while offering no support to the defense in its own efforts to investigate the matter.

To make matters even odder, neither the judges nor the Prosecutor showed any interest in determining whether the witness had, in fact, been threatened by the Bosnian government or whether he would be mistreated were he to be sent back to that government. Opacic, who said that he had been tortured into making a confession to genocide in Sarajevo, asked not to be returned to the Bosnian government, requesting asylum in Holland.[77] However, even though Opacic had an attorney to represent him on these issues, he was returned to the Muslims without prior notice being given to his attorney.[78] Opacic's fears seemed not unreasonable—in at least one case similar to his, two supposed victims of a Serb who confessed to murdering them and was thereupon convicted of genocide were found alive, but the Bosnian government's courts refused a new trial.[79] Yet immediately after this false case received world-wide publicity, Opacic was returned to the control of the Bosnian government, where he now is serving a 10-year sentence for "genocide" following a conviction based solely on his own confession, which he says was extracted from him by torture.[80]

When the Dutch *Argos* journalists asked the Tribunal for an explanation of this failure to investigate the Opacic matter more thoroughly, or to consider his request for asylum, a Tribunal spokesperson said that

> Defense Counsel Vladimirof [sic] did not prove that all of Dragan Opacic's story was untrue. The only point that was established is that Opacic lied about his family members. His father wasn't at all dead, as he had claimed. And that is the basis upon which the prosecutor decided that Opacic was not a reliable witness. ... Why Opacic lied and whether the rest of his story was correct was not relevant to the Tadic case. He was no longer any use as a witness, and that is why we sent him back to Bosnia.[81]

Of course, Wladimiroff had not proven more about Opacic because his cross examination of him was stopped as being in violation of the protection order,[82] and the Prosecutor had also objected even to the evidence about Opacic's identity but was overruled.[83]

The questions of why Opacic lied and especially of whether the Bosnian government and even the Prosecutor's office trained him to do so were basic to determining whether other witnesses might also have been trained to commit perjury. The Tadic defense did try to raise this question on appeal, in regard to the testimony of another witness who had been presented by the Bosnian government, but the Appeals Chamber did not accept this claim because the "circumstances" of the two witnesses were "different. Mr. Opacic was made known to the Prosecution while he was still in the custody of the Bosnian authorities, while [the other witness's] introduction was made through the Bosnian embassy in Brussels."[84] Why this particular difference might matter was not explained by the Appeals Chamber, which also failed to notice that while Opacic was in the custody of the Bosnian government because he was captured as a soldier in the Bosnian Serb Army, the second witness's name (Nihad Seferovic) indicated that he was a Muslim and thus perhaps not as in need of persuasion to lie at the behest of the Muslim government as Opacic had been.

In the Witness L matter, then, the judges of the ICTY afforded very great deference to the Prosecutor and an equally great indifference to the causes of the perjury of a prosecution witness who had been found by the Bosnian government, or of the implications of the possible causes of the perjury for defendant Tadic and for the witness himself (who claimed, apparently with justification, to have been the victim of mistreatment by the Bosnian government), or for future defendants who might be victimized by what may have been collusion by the Prosecutor and the Bosnian government.

Denial of a Fair Trial 2:
Changing the Trial Rules after the Trial is Over

In its decision on a preliminary question before the start of the *Tadic* trial, the ICTY Appeals Chamber stated that charges under Art. 2 of the Statute of the Tribunal (covering "grave breaches" of the Geneva Conventions) apply only to persons or objects "to the extent that they are caught up in an international armed conflict."[85] The same interlocutory decision concluded "that the conflicts in the former Yugoslavia have both internal and international elements."[86] It argued that, had the Security Council considered the conflict international and bound the Tribunal to that position, an "absurd" conclusion would result:

> Since it cannot be contended that the Bosnian Serbs constitute a State, arguably the classification just referred to would be based on the implicit assumption that the Bosnian Serbs are acting not as a rebellious entity but as organs or agents of another State, the Federal Republic of Yugoslavia (Serbia-Montenegro). As a consequence, serious infringements of international humanitarian law committed by

the government army of Bosnia-Herzegovina against Bosnian Serb civilians in their power would not be regarded as "grave breaches," because such civilians, having the nationality of Bosnia-Herzegovina, would not be regarded as "protected persons" under Article 4, paragraph 1 of Geneva Convention IV. By contrast, atrocities committed by Bosnian Serbs against Bosnian civilians in their hands would be regarded as "grave breaches," because such civilians would be "protected persons" under the Convention, in that the Bosnian Serbs would be acting as organs or agents of another State, the Federal Republic of Yugoslavia (Serbia-Montenegro) of which the Bosnians would not possess the nationality. This would be, of course, an absurd outcome, in that it would place the Bosnian Serbs at a substantial legal disadvantage *vis-à-vis* the central authorities of Bosnia-Herzegovina. This absurdity bears out the fallacy of the argument advanced by the Prosecutor.[87]

In accordance with these decisions, the Prosecutor was required in the *Tadic* trial to prove that the conflict was, in fact, international. The Trial Chamber viewed the matter as controlled by the International Court of Justice's decision in the *Nicaragua* case,[88] that external support to a party in an internal conflict would only internationalize that conflict if the external party had "effective control" over the forces in question. The Trial Chamber, over the dissent of the presiding judge, found that the evidence showed only a coordination between the Bosnian Serb Army and the Yugoslav Army, not control of the latter by the former, and thus held that "on the evidence presented to it, after 19 May 1992, the armed forces of the *Republika Srpska* could not be considered as de facto organs or agents of the Government of the Federal Republic of Yugoslavia (Serbia and Montenegro)."[89] Accordingly, the Trial Chamber found Tadic not guilty of charges under Article 2 of the Statute.[90]

The Prosecutor appealed that decision and won: the Appeals Chamber held that the Bosnian Serb forces were acting as "*de facto* organs" of the Federal Republic of Yugoslavia.[91] In doing so, the Appeals Chamber reached precisely the conclusion in the *Tadic* appeal that it had itself pronounced "absurd" in the interlocutory appeal in the same case. The fairness of a Tribunal that sets explicit rules before a trial and then changes them after it is over is certainly dubious, but that is what the ICTY has done.

Also dubious is the reasoning of the *Tadic* appeal. At trial, of course, the burden of proof rested with the Prosecutor to prove that the events in question took place in the context of an international conflict, and the Trial Chamber concluded that this had not been proved. The Appeals Chamber, however, noted that the Trial Chamber had not said what the nature of the conflict was after May 19, 1992. Since the burden was on the prosecutor to show that it *was* international, there was no burden on the defense to show that it was *not* international. Yet the Appeals Chamber phrases the question as whether the conflict "became ... *exclusively* internal" after that date.[92] Since the *Tadic* interlocutory judgment had concluded that the conflict had *both* internal and international elements, this could not have been the question that the defense had been required to counter, or, for that matter, that the Trial Chamber was required to determine.

Indeed, the Appeals Chamber itself recognized that the conflict was *"prima facie* internal," because it set up the legal question involved as determining "the legal criteria for establishing when, in an armed conflict which is *prima facie* internal, armed forces may be regarded as acting on behalf of a foreign power, thereby rendering the conflict international."[93] The Trial Chamber had undertaken a serious review of the facts in Bosnia in 1992 and had concluded that while the Bosnian Serb forces were allied to those of the Federal Republic of Yugoslavia, "there is no evidence on which this Trial Chamber can conclude that the Federal Republic of Yugoslavia ... and the [Yugoslav Army] ever directed ... the actual military operations of the [Bosnian Serb Army], or to influence those operations beyond that which would have flowed naturally from the coordination of military objectives and activities" by the two armies.[94] The Trial Chamber based this conclusion in part on the fact that the Republika Srpska political leaders were popularly elected by the Bosnian Serb people and that these elected political leaders played a role in the activities of the Bosnian Serb Army.[95]

The Appeals Chamber, on the other hand, paid no attention to the activities of Bosnian Serbs as political or military actors in their own right. Instead, it concluded that since the Bosnian Serb Army had received some financing and equipment from the Yugoslav Army, "participation in the planning and supervision of military activities" would constitute "overall control" by the Yugoslav Army, thus rendering the conflict "international." This reasoning, of course, negates the meaning of the term *control* by conflating it with *participation*. At this point, the Appeals Chamber's earlier acknowledgment that the conflict had both internal and international elements vanishes, and the *Tadic* appeal judgment reaches precisely the conclusion that the *Tadic* interlocutory judgment had rendered "absurd" and that even though both the Bosnian Serbs and their victims were nationals of Bosnia and Herzegovina, the victims were "protected persons" because "they found themselves in the hands of armed forces of a State of which they were not nationals."[96]

The Appeals Chamber, perhaps aware that it was rejecting its own earlier conclusion even if unwilling to admit it, justified its new holding on the "object and purpose" of Article 4 of Geneva Convention IV, as "the protection of civilians to the maximum extent possible."[97] If this justification is valid, the distinction between "internal" and "international" conflicts that the Appeals Chamber affirmed in the *Tadic* interlocutory judgment is invalid—*but for* Tadic, *it is the interlocutory standard that must apply.* In any event, the *Tadic* appeals judgment then makes an extraordinary statement, that the applicability of the Geneva Conventions is not "dependent on formal bonds and purely legal relations."[98] The same judgment had already said, approvingly, that international law concerning State responsibility "is based on a realistic concept of accountability, *which disregards legal formalities.*"[99] But legal formalities protect an *accused*—prosecutors, after all, need no protection, but the rest of us may benefit by the bounds put on prosecutorial zeal. The ICTY Appeals Chamber has thus clearly indicated that fairness of the proceedings for defendants is not high in its concerns.

In yet another striking lapse from both fundamental fairness and the principles of fair trials, the Appeals Chamber, apparently on its own initiative, introduced and discussed what it saw as evidence of FRY control over the Bosnian Serbs in 1995 as evidence that the FRY controlled the Bosnian Serb Army in 1992.[100] Since the same Appeals Chamber judges had refused to permit the *Tadic* defense to introduce additional evidence after the conclusion of the trial,[101] this is grossly unfair. However, "legal formalities" in regard to evidence do not seem to have been among the stronger points of this Appeals Chamber, which refers in the *Tadic* appeal to findings of the international character of the conflict in "three Rule 61 Decisions" in other ICTY cases.[102] Rule 61 proceedings are reviews of evidence in cases in which the defendant is not in custody, which "permit the charges in the indictment and the supporting material to be publicly and solemnly exposed."[103] Rule 61 proceedings are uncontested; in one, the Trial Chamber noted that powers of attorney had been lodged successfully by one defendant but refused the attorney access to the courtroom or any role in the proceedings.[104] Judicial presentation of the Prosecutor's uncontested allegations in cases other than the one at trial as being evidence on key issues in the latter seems grossly unfair.

For the Appeals Chamber, however, it would seem that justice is indeed the right to do whatever they think must be done, and therefore justice can be anything.

Problems for America? State Responsibility

The dissenting Trial Chamber judge in *Tadic* was an American; by far the greatest number of staff working in the Prosecutor's office were American, and it is likely that the US government supported the Appeals Chamber's reversal of its own interlocutory decision in regard to the nature of the conflict.

Yet if such a thing as international law ever does come into existence, in the sense of a legal order binding all international actors, the US might regret elements of the appellate decision in *Tadic*. The view that the imposition on states of responsibility of "*de facto* agents" should disregard "legal formalities" would not only hold the US responsible for the actions of the *Contras* in Nicaragua, but also for those of the Croatian Army in its 1995 offensives against Serbs in Croatia and Bosnia. It is no secret that the US government arranged for the "private" firm Military Professional Resources, Inc. (MPRI) to train the Croatian Army, beginning in September 1994,[105] activity that is attributable to the US government under the *Tadic* appeal judgment. That the American-trained and American-equipped Croatian forces were committing war crimes was known to the US government; witness Richard Holbrooke's reference to the "harsh behavior of Federation troops during the [Sept. 1995] offensive," which would have produced "forced evictions and random murders" of Serbs had Banja Luka been taken — yet Holbrooke told the Croatian Defense Minister that "Nothing that we said today should be construed to mean that we want you to stop the rest of the offensive, other than Banja Luka.... We can't say so publicly, but please take Sanski Most, Prijedor and Bosanski Novi."[106] Indeed, Holbrooke himself admits telling Croatian President Tudjman that the actions of Croatian forces could be viewed "as a milder form of ethnic cleansing."[107] Yet he urged that the offensive continue. Of course, as one of Holbrooke's colleagues had put it when the offensive started, "We 'hired' these guys [the Croatian Army] to be our junkyard dogs because we were desperate. We need to try to 'control' them. But this is no time to get squeamish about things."[108] In addition to Holbrooke, then-US Ambassador to Croatia Peter Galbraith has been reported to have "attended meetings when Croats planned war."[109]

In the unlikely event that the ICTY ever takes its mandate as a charge to render impartial justice and follows the principles announced by its Appellate Chamber in the *Tadic* appeal, American political actors who trained, armed, and helped in the planning of Croatian offensives in which war crimes were committed should expect to be indicted and the US as a state should be charged with responsibility for the actions of its junkyard dogs and *de facto* agents, the Croatian Army. I do not expect this to happen, however. As Jamie Shea said, after all, the US is the friend of the Tribunal, and the US is the major financier of the Tribunal.

What, then, does this politicization of the ICTY say about the chances of ever creating a regime of international law? We might ponder the view of a leading human rights advocate, that the ICTY "was a significant advance over the tribunals at Nuremberg and Tokyo, because it had a mandate to prosecute and punish malefactors from all sides ... and has carried out its charge.

Accordingly, unlike its predecessors, it is not susceptible to accusations of victor's justice."[110] It is clear, however, that the ICTY is no more impartial than were these earlier tribunals. Instead of being victor's justice after the conflict, it is a tool meant to ensure victory during it.

"Human Rights Peccadilloes" and Humanitarian War Crimes

To its credit, HRW has recognized that NATO's actions in its war against Yugoslavia signaled "a disturbing disregard for the principles of humanitarianism that should guide any such action"[111] and criticized in particular NATO's use of cluster bombs. Its report on "Civilian Deaths in the NATO Air Campaign" did say that civilian deaths resulted from nine "attacks on non-military targets that Human Rights Watch believes were illegitimate,"[112] and noted that "the use of cluster bombs was a decisive factor in civilian deaths in at least three incidents."[113] HRW also concluded that "NATO violated international humanitarian law," although it prefaced this conclusion with the interesting distinction that it had "found no evidence of war crimes."[114] However, HRW has not called for investigation of NATO actions with the goal of prosecuting those in NATO who have violated human rights. One must wonder why this is so. At the least, we should expect to see HRW issue a demand for an independent investigation that could facilitate prosecution of those in NATO who have committed the crimes that HRW says that NATO committed in Yugoslavia, comparable to HRW's December 1999 request that the UN Security Council appoint an independent commission of inquiry to investigate war crimes by Russian forces in Chechnya.[115] Instead, HRW demanded, in its report on civilian deaths, only that "*NATO and its individual member states*" "establish an independent and impartial commission ... that would investigate violations of international humanitarian law and the extent of these violations, and would consider the need to alter targeting and bombing doctrine" and otherwise engage in "investigations."[116]

The HRW distinction between "war crimes" and (mere?) "violations of international humanitarian law" is specious in this context (genocide, after all, is not a war crime), because the ICTY has jurisdiction over both kinds of delict.[117] Indeed, in convicting Croatian general Tihomir Blaskic, the presiding judge specified that the "extremely serious crimes" he committed included "acts of war carried out with disregard for international humanitarian law."[118] One might wonder whether the HRW call for an "independent and impartial commission" might be an acknowledgement of the truth of the Jamie Shea position that he who finances the Tribunal determines the prosecutions and thus imply that a really independent and impartial body should replace the ICTY, were HRW not explicitly calling for NATO to investigate, independently and impartially, itself.

The difference in standards applied to NATO and to Russia might be explained by a distinction in a 1998 *Washington Post* op-ed piece by HRW executive director Kenneth Roth.[119] Trying to assuage US government concerns that new international judicial institutions could be used to accuse Americans of war crimes, Roth states that "clearly it is not US policy" to commit genocide, war crimes, or crimes against humanity and that "there is no prospect" of harassment of "democratic leaders who have at worst a few human rights peccadilloes to their record." Of course, Roth made this distinction before NATO committed what HRW identifies as violations of the Geneva conventions, but the distinction, perhaps, still holds: NATO, after all, is by definition democratic, so presumably its war crimes are peccadilloes, not worthy of prosecution. The consequences of indictments of NATO personnel for war crimes for the new international judicial institutions that HRW wishes to promote were made clear by Senator Jesse Helms in his January 2000 speech to the UN Security Council:

> any attempt to indict NATO commanders would be the death knell for the International Criminal Court. But the very fact that [the ICTY Prosecutor] explored this possibility at all brings to light all that is wrong with this brave new world of global justice, which proposes a system in which independent prosecutors and judges, answerable to no state or institution, have unfettered power to sit in judgment of the foreign policy decisions of Western democracies.[120]

Since HRW's executive director says that Western democracies commit human rights peccadilloes rather than war crimes, and the US clearly controls the ICTY, Senator Helms's concerns are, clearly, baseless.

Another explanation might be said to lie in the extremity of the situation to which NATO responded in Kosovo: that "it took NATO's controversial bombing campaign before Belgrade would acquiesce in the deployment of international troops to stop widespread ethnic slaughter and forced displacement," and that the inspiration for "NATO's action was fundamentally humanitarian ... the desire to stop crimes against humanity was a major goal."[121] HRW's recounting of the events leading up to NATO's attacks closely tracks that of Bill Clinton, who asserted that NATO "had to act" when Yugoslav forces "began an offensive" against the Albanians of Kosovo.[122] Assuming that he read the reports of his own State Department, the President must have known that his account was inaccurate: in a report issued two weeks before the President published his article in the *New York Times*, the State Department said that until the NATO attacks were under way, Serb forces were engaged in "the selective targeting of towns and regions suspected of [Kosovo Liberation Army] activities," not a general offensive against the Albanian population.[123] This pattern of Serbian actions before NATO's offensive is confirmed by the OSCE in its massive report on events in Kosovo, which shows that Serbian forces, until NATO attacked, were fighting the KLA and not engaged in systematic ethnic cleansing.[124] HRW might have tacitly recognized this uncomfortable fact when it stated that "before using military force to stop crimes against humanity, planners at a minimum should be confident that intervention will not make matters worse by provoking a wider war or setting in motion a string of new atrocities."[125] Yet applying this criterion to NATO's actions would delegitimate them, which HRW clearly does not want to do.

The more fundamental problem in any event is HRW's assertion that war can be seen as humanitarian. Attacks against civilians are probably inevitable in any supposedly humanitarian intervention. Every nation has the right to defend itself, and at the level of practical politics, a nation that is attacked will try to resist the attacker. Winning the war thus requires defeating not only the army, but the nation—the civilian population. Thus the decision to attack a sovereign state is, logically, a decision to attack the civilian population of that state, not just the military. NATO's targeting of the civilian infrastructure of Serbia (and earlier, of Iraq), is thus logical, and the constant repetition that "NATO never targets civilians" was hypocritical, presumably meant to obscure the uncomfortable fact that humanitarian intervention requires the committing of humanitarian war crimes. At this point, the greatest triumph of the human rights movement, "humanitarian intervention," is revealed as its greatest defeat, because it transforms what had been a moral critique against violence into a moral crusade for massive violence. Of course, HRW could escape this trap by demanding the indictment of NATO leaders, but it would then precede the UN in being dismantled brick by brick and thrown into the Atlantic. While speaking truth to power is admirable, telling power what it wants to hear tends to bring more tangible rewards.

Humanrightsism

A month after NATO began its attacks on Yugoslavia, Vaclav Havel gave what seems to be a principled justification for the war:

> this is probably the first war that has not been waged in the name of "national interests," but rather in the name of principles and values.... This war places human rights above the rights of the state. The Federal Republic of Yugoslavia was attacked by the alliance

without a direct mandate from the UN. This did not happen irresponsibly, as an act of aggression or out of disrespect for international law. It happened, on the contrary, out of respect for the law, for the law that ranks higher than the law which protects the sovereignty of states. The alliance has acted out of respect for human rights.[126]

Havel then states that human rights "are as powerful as they are because, under certain circumstances, people accept them without compulsion and are willing to die for them."[127]

Havel sounds great but, in fact, even as he gave the speech quoted (April 29, 1999) he must have known that he lied. Few indeed were willing to die for human rights, particularly in the Czech Republic,[128] but rather NATO was engaged in killing for human rights. As Havel spoke, the alliance was targeting civilian "infrastructure" because attacking Yugoslav military targets would have exposed NATO pilots to danger. In the five days before his speech, NATO repeatedly bombed oil refineries in Novi Sad, causing massive pollution of the air and of the river Danube; bombed civilian targets in central Belgrade; and bombed a Serbian town on the Bulgarian border, destroying houses and killing civilians.[129] All but the last were intentional targeting, so damage to the environment and civilian deaths were not "collateral damage." Havel's speech is thus either politically cunning, as befits the elected president of a sovereign nation-state, or else evasive, avoiding the truth that Havel could not, as a long-term supporter of human rights, admit.

But the difference between Havel the advocate of human rights and Havel the War President embodies the difference between human rights as a principle for criticism of the actions of governments and humanrightsism as a justification for government actions that violate human rights. By humanrightsism, I mean what the *New York Times* has described as the "elevation" of human rights to a "military priority,"[130] since military priorities are by definition based on the threat and use of force. This "elevation" is actually a striking inversion of the principles that have guided the growth of human rights organizations. For example, Amnesty International long required that its "prisoners of conscience" not be advocates or practitioners of violence.[131] Humanrightsism, however, itself calls for violence.

I am aware, of course, of the revival of "just war" arguments, by political philosophers[132] and politicians.[133] In regard to the latter, however, surely even Vaclav Havel realizes that all politicians justify wars by reference to "principles and values," and justification for attacks that are not based on self-defense are often less than reliable assessments. After all, were governments that apply force always candid in their reasons for doing so, HRW and other human rights organizations would not have been in business in the first place.

The question then, remains: why have human rights advocates ignored the actions by NATO and by the ICTY that they would condemn were they performed by, say, China, or Russia, or India?

This question is addressed directly in a brilliant and brave article by Dimitrina Petrovna, Executive Director of the European Roma Rights Center in Budapest.[134] Petrovna acknowledges that she herself was in favor of NATO intervention in Kosovo until she saw, soon after the bombing began, that it was escalating the human rights catastrophe for everyone in the Federal Republic of Yugoslavia, inside Kosovo and in Serbia, and that "from a campaign to defend the lives and rights of Kosovo Albanians, [the war] metamorphosed into something else: the monster of an escalated war."[135] While Petrovna herself then called for an immediate end to the bombing and a negotiated peace, few others in the human rights community did so. She notes that for east European human rights workers, their very status and funding could have been jeopardized by criticism of NATO and especially of the US—NATO countries are, after all, the major financiers of more than just the ICTY. In the Western countries themselves, however, the reasons are more troubling. There, she notes, "human rights are becoming indistinguishable from official political ideology," producing "a gradual usurpation of the human-rights culture by the dominant powers, and the very argument for human rights is turning into an apologia for the global status quo, all in the interests of these very powers."[136]

From the evidence of NATO's actions in Kosovo and the ICTY's treatment of defendants, this transformation of human rights inverts the concept, from one premised on the protection of people from the violence of states, to one justifying the application of violence by the world's most powerful states against weaker ones. With this transformation, the concept of human rights betrays its own premises and thus becomes its own travesty: humanrightsism.

Notes

1. Human Rights Watch, *World Report 2000: Introduction* <http://www.hrw.org/wr2k/Front.htm>.

2. Human Rights Watch, "Human Rights Trump Sovereignty in 1999," press release, 9 December 1999.

3. Human Rights Watch, *World Report 2000*.

4. Human Rights Watch, *World Report 2000*.

5. Human Rights Watch, *World Report 2000*, 6.

6. Human Rights Watch, *World Report 2000*, 1.

7. Bernard Kouchner, "Establish a Right to Intervene Against War," *Los Angeles Times* (18 October 1999): 7.

8. Kouchner.

9. Kouchner's former organization, Doctors Without Borders, though, may not take him so seriously. In August 2000, the organization withdrew from Kosovo, blaming Kouchner's administration of the province as ineffective and failing to protect minorities there. "UN has Failed Kosovo Minorities," *The Independent* (17 August 2000): 1.

10. Vaclav Havel, "Kosovo and the End of the Nation-State," *New York Review of Books* (10 June 1999): 4, 6. The idea that "people" have rights superior to those of states is extended by John Rawls to mean that "liberal and decent peoples," not states, should be the true actors in international society. John Rawls, "The Law of Peoples," *Critical Inquiry* (Autumn 1993). Since each such "people" has a government (23) and a territory which it has the right to protect (29), it is very difficult to see how his distinction is meaningful—what, after all, is a state but a government united with a territory?

11. The gendered pronoun is intentional—no women have yet been charged by the ICTY.

12. *Prosecutor of the Tribunal v. Milan Martic*, Indictment, 25 July 1995 (hereinafter, Martic Indictment). Note: unless otherwise specified, references to ICTY documents are to versions on the Tribunal's web page: <http://www.un.org/icty/>.

13. *Prosecutor of the Tribunal*, ICTY case no. IT-96-11-R61; Rule 61 Evidentiary Review (27 February 1996) at 5 <http://www.un.org/icty/transe11/960227IT.txt> (hereinafter Martic Rule 61 hearing).

14. *Prosecutor of the Tribunal*, ICTY case no. IT-96-11-R61, 19.

15. Martic Indictment, ¶ 7.

16. See report, May 7 1999 <http://www.bbc.co.uk/>.

17. "Milosevic at Bay in Shell of his 'Victory,'" *Sunday Times* (13 June 1999): 4.

18. *Philadelphia Inquirer* (21 November 1999): 1.

19. Richard Norton-Taylor, "MoD Leak Reveals Kosovo Failure," *The Guardian* (15 August 2000): 2.

20. "Final Report to the Prosecutor by the Committee Established to Review the NATO Bombing Campaign against the Federal Republic of Yugoslavia," ¶ 27 <http://www.un.org/icty/pressreal/nato061300.htm> (hereinafter, Committee Report).

21. I say "apparently" because the ICTY has not published the Decision in the Rule 61 hearing in *Martic* in its entirety, even though it did publish the transcript of the 1996 Rule 61 hearing itself. The only available quotes from the Decision are in the *Bulletin* of the Tribunal.

22. ICTY *Bulletin* #2 (1996).

23. Norton-Taylor 2.

24. Martic Rule 61 hearing 20.

25. Martic Rule 61 hearing 21.

26. "At NATO, a crash course in spin" (1 May 1999), <http://www.MSNBC.com/news/default2sp?cp1=1>.

27. Annie Gardner, "US General Condemns French 'Red Card'" (22 October 1999), <http://www.bbc.co.uk/>.

28. "NATO's Role in Kosovo" (last updated 16 May 1999) <http://www.nato.int/kosovo/press/p990516b.htm>; "NATO's Role in Kosovo" (last updated 17 May 1999) <http://www.nato.int/kosovo/press/p990517b.htm>.

29. Emma Daly, "Dossier of NATO 'Crimes' Lands in Prosecutor's Lap," *The Observer* (26 December 1999): 15; "UN to Review NATO in Kosovo," *New York Times* (29 December 1999): A5.

30. Stephen Erlanger, "UN Tribunal Plays Down Its Scrutiny of NATO," *New York Times* (30 December 1999): 2.

31. Erlanger.

32. ICTY Press Release PR/ P.I.S./ 459-e (30 December 1999).

33. Committee Report, ¶ 12 <http://www.un.org/octu/pressred1/nato061300.htm>.

34. Rowan Scarborough, "UN Denounces UN Probe of NATO Bombing," *Washington Times* (30 December 1999): A1; Steven Lee Myers, "Kosovo Inquiry Confirms US Fears of War Crimes Court," *New York Times* (3 January 2000): A7.

35. *Prosecutor v. Karadžic and Mladic*, Indictment, ¶ 29, July 25, 1999 (hereinafter, Karadzic/ Mladic indictment).

36. Karadzic/Mladic indictment ¶ 41.

37. Grupa 17, *Zavrsni Racun: Ekonomske Posledice NATO Bomabardovanja* (Beograd: Stubovi Kulture, 1999) 9.

38. "Kosovo War Cost £30bn" (15 October 1999) <http://news6.thdo.bbc.uk/hi/english/world/europe/newsid%5F476000/476134.stm>.

39. <http://www.msnbc.com/news> (visited on 26 April 1999).

40. See, e.g., *Wall Street Journal* (27 April 1999) 1; "Kosovo War Cost £30bn."

41. *Washington Post* (20 September 1999): 1.

42. Aryeh Neier, *War Crimes* (New York: Times Books, 1998) 192.

43. "The Prosecutor of the Tribunal against Slobodan Milosevic et al." (27 May 1999), <http://jurist.law.pitt.edu/indict.htm>.

44. Jamie Shea, "Letter to the General Secretary of the International Federation of Journalists," <http://www.ifj.org/hrights/natoreply.html>.

45. *Wall Street Journal* (27 April 1999).

46. Committee Report, ¶ 76.

47. Amnesty International, "Collateral Damage or Unlawful Killings? Violations of the Laws of War by NATO During Operation Allied Force," <http://www.amnesty.org/ailib/aipub/2000/SUM/47001800.htm>.

48. "Amnesty International's Initial Comments on the Review by the International Criminal Tribunal for the Former Yugoslavia of NATO's Operation Allied Force" (13 June 2000) <http://www.amnesty.org/news/2000/47002900.htm>.

49. Human Rights Watch, "Civilian Deaths in the NATO Air Campaign" 14-15.

50. That the dead were simply employees of RTS—editors, technicians, mixers, make-up artists—see Steven Erlanger, "An Ordinary Serb, Lost in Air Attack, is Buried," *New York Times* (2 May 1999): 13. I confess a personal connection: an old friend who worked at RTS as a night-shift translator had, fortunately, just left the building when it was hit. Had he not left he, too, would have been among the CPJ's propagandists even though, ironically enough, his past 20 years had been spent in the employ of the US government, first in the Fulbright office, later in the embassy until it closed at the start of the war. Note that the RTS victims were not even "collateral damage," as NATO meant to hit them.

51. C. Glass, "When It's OK to Kill a Hack," *The Spectator* (5 February 2000).

52. Sam Husseini, "Accuracy in Media," <http://www.sam@accuracy.org>.

53. Benefactors and other major donors listed on <http://www.cpj.org>.

54. <http://www.cpj.org>.

55. NATO news Briefing, 8 April 1999.

56. *Washington Times* (25 April 1999): C9.

57. *Washington Post* (24 May 1999) World Wide Web Edition.

58. *Washington Post* (25 May 1999): A1.

59. *New York Times* (25 May 1999): A1.

60. *Washington Post* (25 May 1999): A1.

61. BBC News Online, 24 May 1999. "NATO Denies Targeting Water Supplies," http://news6.thdo.bbc.co.uk/hi/english/world/europe/newsid%5F351000/352780.stm.

62. "Fox News Sunday," Fox News Television Broadcast (23 May 1999).

63. "Fox News Sunday."

64. *National Post* (22 May 1999).

65. *New York Times* (21 March 1999).

66. "Accountability for War Crimes: Progress and Prospects" Hearing before the Commission on Security and Cooperation in Europe," 106th Cong. 25 (1999).

67. "Remarks at the US Supreme Court by Gabrielle Kirk McDonald on the Occasion of Receiving the ABA CEELI Award" (visited on 5 April 1999), <http://www.un.org/icty/pressreal/SPUSSC.htm>.

68. *New York Times* (15 October 1999): A8.

69. Candor requires me to state that I was actually the very first *defense* witness to appear before the ICTY, in the *Tadic* case, on the question of the character of the conflict (national or international), a question discussed in the next section. My testimony was limited to constitutional and political issues in Yugoslavia and in Bosnia through 1992 (a précis of the testimony is found in my article in *The Fletcher Forum of World Affairs* 22.1 [1998] 45-64). Apart from one very brief meeting with Tadic in May 1996, at the request of his defense counsel, I had and have no personal acquaintance with Tadic or knowledge of the crimes for which he was accused.

70. H. Kamen, *The Spanish Inquisition* (Hartford, CT: Yale University Press, 1997) 182, 194-95.

71. *Prosecutor v. Dusko Tadic*, "Decision on the Prosecutor's Motion Requesting Protective Measures for Victims and Witnesses" (10 August 1995): ¶¶ 10, 11.

72. The basic story of "Witness L" can be found in news accounts: e.g., Internet Nasa Borba (28 October 1996), Reuters (25 October 1996), Associated Press (25 October 1996). Copies of an interrogation of "Witness L" by Tadic's defense attorney, Michail Wladimiroff, and of an October 25, 1995 statement by ICTY Prosecutor's investigator Robert Reid concerning Witness L's lies and accusations against the Bosnian government are in this author's files. The most detailed account of the "Witness L" matter was broadcast on Dutch VPRO Radio's "Argos" program on 10 September 1999, a transcript of which (in English) is available at <http://www.domovina.net/opacice.html> (hereinafter, Argos).

73. Institute for War and Peace Reporting, *Tribunal Update* 6 (2-6 December 1996).

74. Letter from Michail Wladimiroff to Alija Izetbegovic (11 November 1996).

75. Fax letter from author to Michail Wladimiroff (30 December 1997); fax letter to author from Michail Wladimiroff (7 January 1997).

76. It is in fact likely that the defense was in violation of the protection order when it questioned people who, the defense thought, might have been related to the anonymous witness. Had they followed the rules, however, the defendant could not have had a fair trial.

77. *ICTY: Tadic Case: Update* (2 June 1997).

78. Argos.

79. *New York Times* (1 March 1997): 3; *Washington Post* (15 March 1997): A17; *New York Times* (15 June 1997): 10.

80. Argos.

81. Argos.

82. Fax letter to author from Michail Wladimiroff (30 October 1997).

83. Fax letter to author from Michail Wladimiroff (30 October 1997).

84. *Prosecutor v Dusko Tadic*, Judgment (15 July 1999) ¶ 65 (hereinafter *Tadic* Appeal Judgment).

85. *Prosecutor v Dusko Tadic*, Decision on the Defense Motion for Interlocutory Appeal on Jurisdiction (2 October 1995) ¶ 81 (hereinafter "Tadic Interlocutory").

86. "Tadic Interlocutory" ¶ 77.

87. "Tadic Interlocutory" ¶ 76.

88. *Case Concerning Military and Paramilitary Activities in and Against Nicaragua*, 1986 ICJ Reports 14. Ironically, the defendant in Nicaragua was the United States, so that the US in *Tadic* was urging the abandonment of the position that had protected it in Nicaragua.

89. *Prosecutor v Dusko Tadic*, Opinion and Judgment, ¶ 607 (7 May 1997) (hereinafter, *Tadic* Trial Judgment). The 19 May 1992 date was important because the Bosnian Serb Army was formally separated from the Yugoslav Peoples Army on or before that date, and the only evidence presented on the chain of command between the two armies after that date was that of a witness who said that "there was no real chain of command" between them, and evidence that the Bosnian Serb Army used secure communications links that ran through Yugoslav Peoples Army headquarters in Belgrade for its own internal communications. *Tadic* Trial Judgment¶ 598.

90. *Tadic* Trial Judgment ¶ 608.

91. *Tadic* Appeal Judgment ¶ 167.

92. *Tadic* Appeal Judgment ¶ 86.

93. *Tadic* Appeal Judgment § IV.B.3 (heading).

94. *Tadic* Trial Judgment ¶ 605.

95. *Tadic* Trial Judgment ¶ 599.

96. *Tadic* Appeals Judgment ¶ 167.

97. *Tadic* Appeals Judgment ¶ 168.

98. *Tadic* Appeals Judgment

99. *Tadic* Appeals Judgment ¶ 121.

100. *Tadic* Appeals Judgment ¶¶ 157-60.

101. *Tadic* Appeals Judgment ¶ 16.

102. *Tadic* Appeals Judgment n.107.

103. *Prosecutor v Radovan Karadžic and Ratko Mladic*, Review of the Indictments Pursuant to Rule 61 of the Rules of Procedure and Evidence (11 July 1996), ¶ 3 (hereinafter Karadzic and Mladic, Rule 61 proceeding).

104. Karadzic and Mladic, Rule 61 proceeding ¶ 4. Interestingly, the Trial Chamber described its actions in this uncontested Rule 61 proceeding as being in pursuit of the "mission" of "international criminal justice" of "revealing the truth about the acts perpetrated." Karadzic and Mladic, Rule 61 proceeding ¶ 3. Truth, apparently, can be found reliably in the uncontested allegations of the Prosecutor.

105. *Globus* (20 October 1995).

106. Richard Holbrooke, *To End a War* (New York: Random House, 1998) 166.

107. Holbrooke 160.

108. Holbrooke 73.

109. *New York Times* (30 May 1996): A7.

110. Neier 259.

111. Human Rights Watch, *World Report 2000* 5.

112. Human Rights Watch, *Civilian Deaths in the NATO Air Campaign*, February 2000, <http://www.hrw.org/reports/2000/nato>, "Summary."

113. Human Rights Watch, *Civilian Deaths*.

114. Human Rights Watch, *Civilian Deaths*, "International Humanitarian Law and Accountability."

115. See <http://www.hrw.org/campaigns/russia/chechnya>.

116. Human Rights Watch, *Civilian Deaths*, "Summary," 7-8.

117. The Statute of the ICTY grants it jurisdiction over Grave Breaches of the Geneva Conventions of 1949 (Art. 2), Violations of the Laws and Customs of War (Art. 3), Genocide (Art. 4) and Crimes Against Humanity (Art. 5).

118. ICTY Press Release JL/P.I.S./474-E (3 March 2000) <http://www.un.org/icty/pressreal/ p474-e.htm>.

119. Kenneth Roth, "Justice for Tyrants," *Washington Post* (26 November 1998): A31.

120. <http://www.usis.it/wireless/wfa00120/A0012011.htm>.

121. Human Rights Watch, *World Report 2000* 1, 5.

122. *New York Times* (23 May 1999): § 4, p.17.

123. US State Department, *Erasing History: Ethnic Cleansing in Kosovo* (May 1999).

124. OSCE, "Kosovo/Kosova As Seen, As Told: The Human Rights Findings of the OSCE Verification Mission" <http://www.osce.org/kosovo/reports/hr/part1>, Part II, Chapter 3.

125. Human Rights Watch, *World Report 2000* 6.

126. Vaclav Havel, "Kosovo and the End of the Nation-State," *New York Review of Books* (10 June 1999): 6.

127. Havel.

128. See M. Znoj, "Czech Attitudes Toward the War," *Eastern European Constitutional Review* 8.3 (1999): 47.

129. UN Environment Programme and UN Centre for Human Settlements, *The Kosovo Conflict: Consequences for the Environment* (1999) 17.

130. Michael Wines, Editorial, "The World: Double Vision: Two Views of Inhumanity Split the World, Even in Victory," *New York Times* (13 June 1999): §4, p.1.

131. See, e.g., Amnesty International, *Yugoslavia: Prisoners of Conscience* (1985) 9-10:

> [T]he following violations of human rights in Yugoslavia are of concern to Amnesty International: the arrest and imprisonment of people for their non-violent exercise of internationally recognized human rights ... the vague formulation of certain legal provisions which enables them to be applied so as to penalize people for the non-violent exercise of their human rights.

132. E.g., Michael Walzer, *Just and Unjust Wars*, 2nd ed. (New York: Basic Books, 1992), and John Rawls, *The Law of Peoples* (Cambridge, MA: Harvard University Press, 1999) Rawls's assertion that "If the political conception of political liberalism is sound ... then liberal and decent peoples have the right ... not to tolerate outlaw states," seems, remarkably but as yet unremarked, a call for liberal *jihad*. Rawls 81.

133. E.g., William Clinton, "A Just and Necessary War," *New York Times* (23 May 1999): 4-17.

134. Dimitrina Petrovna, "The War and the Human Rights Community," *Eastern European Constitutional Review* 8.3 (1999): 97.

135. Petrovna 99.

136. Petrovna 101.

6

The Myth of Humanitarian
Intervention in Kosovo[1]

Marjorie Cohn

"First, do no harm." — The Hippocratic Oath

NATO's 11-week bombardment of Yugoslavia has been widely characterized as a "humanitarian intervention." NATO's humanitarian bombs killed between 500 and 1800 civilians and wounded thousands more.[2] They hit not only military forces and facilities, but also destroyed Yugoslavia's entire public *infrastructure*, inflicting an estimated $4 billion of damage on bridges, highways, railroads, civilian airports, oil refineries, factories, construction equipment, media centers, hospitals, schools, apartment buildings, houses, buses, electrical plants, and hundreds of acres of forest.

Javier Solana, former Secretary General of NATO, claimed the goal of the bombing was to "stop further humanitarian catastrophe." US-NATO Commanding General Wesley Clark, however, outlined NATO's strategy to disrupt, degrade, devastate, and destroy the infrastructure of the country. In describing the aerial bombardment, Clark once rose from his seat, slapped the table and exclaimed, "I've got to get the maximum violence out of this campaign—now!"[3] This is the campaign that has been labeled "humanitarian."

NATO aircraft flew more than 38,000 sorties in "surgical strikes" 15,000 feet above the ground to protect its airplanes and pilots. In a report issued in July 2000, Amnesty International concluded that this practice "made full adherence to international humanitarian law virtually impossible."[4] Moreover, NATO's bombing campaign was undertaken in direct violation of international law, most notably the UN Charter.

The primary motivation for the bombardment was not humanitarian. It was the US's desire to maintain its status as sole superpower in the world. Control of Europe, through the strengthening of US-led NATO, will ensure hegemony over the transportation of rich oil deposits from the Caspian Sea, as well as control of European markets. The American military bases in the

Balkans—including Camp Bondsteel in Kosovo, the largest US base constructed since the Vietnam War—provide a counterweight to Russian dominance.

To justify the bombing of Yugoslavia, American officials demonized not only Slobodan Milosevic, but the Serbian people as well. For example, US Senator Joseph Biden, speaking on CNN in August, 1993, characterized Serbs as "illiterates, degenerates, baby killers and rapists."[5]

The dehumanization of the Serbian people enabled NATO to present Milosevic with an ultimatum at Rambouillet. George Kenney, formerly of the US State Department's Yugoslavia desk, reported that a senior State Department official said at Rambouillet the US "deliberately set the bar higher than the Serbs could accept." The official stated the Serbs needed a little bombing to see reason.[6]

The precipitating excuse to launch NATO's armed intervention against Yugoslavia was the "Racak massacre" on January 15, 1999. Now widely perceived as staged by the US to galvanize public opinion against the Serbs, reports were made that Serb forces had massacred Albanian civilians at Racak. "Racak transformed the West's Balkan policy as singular events seldom do," wrote *Washington Post* correspondent Barton Gellman.[7]

NATO's bombs terrorized the entire population. They gave rise to stepped-up killings in Kosovo, due to the withdrawal of the unarmed Organization for Security and Cooperation in Europe (OSCE) Kosovo Verification Mission (KVM), which had served as at least a partial deterrent to the worst atrocities. When it responded to the Rambouillet ultimatum, the Serb National Assembly actually condemned the withdrawal of the OSCE monitors.[8]

The bombing also caused the largest refugee flow in Europe since World War II. In its Foreign Affairs Fourth Report in June 2000, the British House of Commons admitted, "a very serious misjudgement was made when it was assumed that the bombing would not lead to the dramatic escalation in the displacement and expulsion of the Kosovo Albanian population."[9]

British General Sir Michael Rose, former commander of UN troops in Bosnia, wrote in a letter to the *Times* (London): "After 11 weeks of one of the most intensive air campaigns in the history of warfare, it is clear that NATO tragically failed to accomplish its objective of preventing further violence against Kosovo's ethnic Albanians."[10]

Why did the US and other NATO countries spend billions of dollars to bomb this small eastern European country, killing its people, destroying its infrastructure, and creating one of the largest flights of refugees in the twentieth century?

The Head of an Empire

The history of NATO holds the answer. NATO was created during the Cold War to protect Western Europe from a perceived threat from the Soviet Union, because after World War II, the countries of Western Europe were not capable of defending themselves. Although they now have the resources to provide for their own security, NATO, nevertheless, has expanded eastward, adding Hungary, Poland, and the Czech Republic, and has redefined its strategic purpose.[11]

A 1992 draft of the Pentagon Defense Planning Guidance on post-Cold War Strategy, advocated continued US leadership in NATO by discouraging the advanced industrialized nations "from challenging our leadership." It said, "We must maintain the mechanism for deterring potential competitors from even aspiring to a larger regional or global role." One of the authors of the draft called the function of the US "adult supervision." The French journalist J.J. Servan Schreiber, in 1950, had said of the US role in Europe: "When a nation bears the responsibility" for the military security and the economic stability of a geographic zone, "that nation is in fact—whether it wants it or not—the head of an empire." The Pentagon paper sought to ensure that the US, through NATO, would be the predominant force in Europe, stating, "we must seek to prevent the emergence of European-only security arrangements which would undermine NATO."[12]

By reincarnating and expanding NATO and moving its influence eastward, the US maintains its role as the "head of an empire." The Pentagon Defense Planning Guidance draft emphasized that "Our first objective is to prevent the re-emergence of a new rival, either on the territory of the former Soviet Union or elsewhere." "Our overall objective," states the document, "is to remain the predominant outside power in [the Middle East and Southwest Asia to] preserve US and Western access to the region's oil."[13]

In 1996, the *New York Times* reported, "Now, in the years after the Cold War, the United States is again establishing suzerainty over the empire of a former foe. The disintegration of the Soviet Union has prompted the United States to expand its zone of military hegemony into Eastern Europe (through NATO) and into formerly neutral Yugoslavia. And—most important of all—the end of the cold war has permitted America to deepen its involvement in the Middle East."[14]

The United States Keeps its Thumb on Iraq

The key to this analysis is the role the US has played in the Middle East. In order to keep any country from becoming too powerful on the western shore of the Persian Gulf, to ensure its access to Middle East oil, the US played Iraq off against Iran. After the US-friendly shah was toppled by his people, the US quietly encouraged Saddam Hussein to invade Iran. But the US overlooked the fact that when Iraq won, Saddam would act to consolidate his victory.

Thinking the US was still his ally, Saddam informed its ambassador to Iraq that he was about to invade Kuwait. He received no protest from the ambassador, but the US, not wanting Iraq to dominate the western shore of Persian Gulf, reacted by re-invading Kuwait.[15]

The US did not wish to destroy Iraq; it still wanted Iraq as a counter-weight to Iran. But it underestimated Saddam's ability to maintain his position of control over the Kurds and the Shiites—both politically and through the use of terror. The survival of Saddam, like Milosevic, represents a severe limitation on American political power. Having worked to convince Americans that Saddam is the reincarnation of Hitler, the US cannot be seen negotiating with him.

By mid-2000, the US had dropped 88,000 tons of bombs over Iraq, killing many civilians, in clear violation of the Geneva Conventions. Napalm, cluster bombs, and depleted uranium were used, in what the *Los Angeles Times* described as a "massacre" and a "massive slaughter."[16]

Utilizing the same strategy it later used in Yugoslavia, the US attacked the infrastructure of Iraq. It bombed electrical, water, and sewage plants, as well as agricultural, food, and medical production facilities. The destruction of electrical generators—many of which were used for water purification and sewage treatment—has led to hundreds of thousands of Iraqi deaths from disease caused by unclean water since 1991. Current estimates are between 4000 and 5000 children killed per month in Iraq as a result of US bombing. When asked on national television in 1996 for her reaction to these deaths, former Secretary of State Madeleine Albright said, "we think the price is worth it."[17]

After Operation Desert Storm in 1991, the US and its allies created a "no-fly zone" in the airspace over Iraq's own territory, without Security Council authorization. During Operation Desert Fox in 1998, the US bombed Iraq after Saddam refused to let UN inspectors into his country, on the grounds they were spying for the CIA. It turns out they were indeed CIA spies.[18]

American and British aircraft continue surgical strikes against Iraq in order to maintain moderate but steady pressure on that country and, in turn, to neutralize its power in the Persian Gulf. The *Washington Post* reported in June 2000 that about 300 Iraqis had been killed and more than 800 wounded in the preceding 18 months.[19]

Caspian Sea Oil

Why does the US desire control over Eastern Europe? Because of the instability in the Persian Gulf, the US feels the need to control an alternate source of oil. The Caspian Sea region may promise oil and gas resources equal to those in the Middle East. Caspian oil deposits were estimated at four trillion dollars by *US News and World Report*. The Washington-based American Petroleum Institute, voice of the major American oil companies, called the Caspian Sea region, "the area of greatest resource potential outside of the Middle East."[20]

In May 2000, a consortium of Western oil companies found a vast petroleum reserve off the coast of Kazakhstan in the northern Caspian Sea. The *Washington Post* quoted US officials and industry sources as saying this might be the largest oil discovery in the last 20 years.[21]

Since the breakup of the Soviet Union, there has been an ongoing competition between Russia and the richest US oil companies for access to Caspian oil. According to retired Navy Admiral T. Joseph Lopez, who until recently oversaw all US naval forces in Europe, including the Caspian area, "within the next decade, the Caspian and Black Sea area will become the next Persian Gulf, with the same enormous potential for positive engagement as well as trouble." The US Trade and Development Agency published a report in May 2000, which said Caspian oil would "provide American companies with a key role in developing the vital east-west corridor, advance the privatisation aspirations of the US government in the region and facilitate rapid integration of the Balkans with western Europe."[22]

How does Caspian oil relate to the bombing of Yugoslavia? Russia and the US each want to control the flow of Caspian oil to world markets. The Caspian Sea is landlocked between Russia and a group of former Soviet republics (including Azerbaijan, Georgia, and Kazakhstan). Russia wants Caspian oil pipelines to run through its territory to the Black Sea. The US, conversely, wants those pipelines routed through its ally, Turkey. In 1998, Russian President Boris Yeltsin told a newspaper interviewer, "Some seek to exclude Russia from the game and undermine its interests. The so-called 'pipeline war' in the [Caspian Sea] region is part of this game."[23]

Bombs dropped by NATO warplanes played a direct role in the pipeline war described by Yeltsin. The April 1999 bombings of bridges at Novi Sad and other points on the Danube River blocked international cargo traffic to the Black Sea. The Danube crosses from Yugoslavia into Romania just east of Belgrade. Until April, tankers carried Caspian oil on the Danube from the Black Sea directly into Europe. NATO's bombs halted this flow of oil along the route favorable to Russia. The bombing established US military dominance at the choke point for direct access of Caspian oil from the Black Sea into Europe.[24]

The bombing is part of a strategy of containment, to keep the region stable for the Trans-Balkan oil pipeline that will transport Caspian oil though Macedonia and Albania. The pipeline is slated to carry 750,000 barrels a day, worth about $600 million a month at current prices.[25] Cooperation of the Albanians with the pipeline project was likely contingent on the US helping them wrest control of Kosovo from the Serbs. The US seeks to contain Macedonia, as well, supporting both sides in the conflagration there. Military Professional Resources International, a mercenary company on contract to the Pentagon, has trained both the Kosovo Liberation Army and the Macedonian army. MPRI also supplied and trained the Croatian Army in the 1990s, before the Croats brutally cleansed more than 200,000 unarmed Serb civilians from the Krajina region.[26]

US control of Caspian Sea oil became a Clinton priority seven years ago. Former US National Security Adviser Zbigniew Brzezinski, sent by Clinton as an emissary to Azerbaijan, said "Clinton became rather directly involved" at that time. Clinton's energy secretary, Bill Richardson noted in 1998 that the extraction and transport of Caspian oil "is about America's energy security. It's also about preventing strategic inroads by those who don't share our values." He explained, "We're trying to move these newly independent countries toward the west. We would like to see them reliant on western commercial and political interests rather than going the other way. We've made a substantial political investment in the Caspian, and it's very important to us that both the pipeline map and the politics come out right."[27]

Clinton created an ambassadorial position in the State Department to deal with Caspian projects. Richard Morningstar, Clinton's Caspian energy advisor, was a keynote speaker at "The US Caspian Ambassadors' Tour," held in New Orleans in May 1999. He outlined Clinton's Caspian region goals of providing commercial opportunities to US firms, mitigating regional conflicts among Caspian nations, and promoting energy security for the US and its allies. He said, "For these countries to be independent, the resources have to be able to get out freely without undue influence from competitive countries." Morningstar was well aware of the significance of what was characterized in the *Washington Post* as "the Caspian oil rush."[28]

Interestingly, former US Secretaries of State Alexander Haig and James Baker, as well as Brzezinski, have earned large consulting fees for oil companies working in the Caspian region. Brzezinski, in an op-ed in *The Wall Street Journal*, strongly advocated stationing ground troops in Yugoslavia, notwithstanding disagreement within NATO: "To end the Kosovo campaign in a manner that not only redeems its original purpose but also safeguards the vitality of NATO, the alliance will have to take some risks." He was concerned that "a setback for NATO" might also discredit "America's global standing."[29]

Economic Hegemony

The US and other NATO countries are committed to privatization and the promotion of a global free market economy. When Slobodan Milosevic's socialist government committed the unpardonable sin of trying to stop the market reforms imposed by the International Monetary Fund and the World Bank in the early 1990s, the US Congress cut off all aid, credits, and loans from the US to Yugoslavia, and the CIA predicted the eventual disintegration of the federation of Yugoslavia.[30] According to Alex N. Dajkovic:

> The policies implemented by USAID in the Balkan countries, then, will assure that they don't undergo independent economic development but function as service zones to the developed economies, providing raw materials and cheap labor, as well as serving as markets for production surpluses from the developed West.[31]

In addition, Yugoslavia—and especially Kosovo—is also rich in mineral wealth. The Trepca mines, owned by Serbia, contain gold, silver, zinc, lead, cadmium, and bismuth. Stari Trg is "one of the richest mines in Europe," accounting for 40 to 50 per cent of the mining production. The mine's director, Novak Bjelic, was quoted in the *New York Times* as saying: "The war in Kosovo is about the mines, nothing else. This is Serbia's Kuwait—the heart of Kosovo." The Trepca mining complex is "the most valuable piece of real estate in the Balkans," which is "worth at least $5 billion"[32] and the value of the minerals beneath the ground is incalculable.

NATO control of the valuable Trepca mines is also part of its European investment plan. On July 25, 1999, Bernard Kouchner, head of the Kosovo UN peacekeeping force, issued a decree that the "UNMIK [United Nations Interim Administration Mission in Kosovo] shall administer movable or immovable property, including monetary accounts, and other property of, or registered in the name of, the Federal Republic of Yugoslavia or the Republic of Serbia or any of its organs, which is in the territory of Kosovo." In November 1999, the International Crisis Group followed up on Kouchner's directive, and recommended that "UNMIK and KFOR [Kosovo peacekeeping force] should implement a rapid and categorical takeover of the Trepca complex." After assuming complete control over the Trepca complex, NATO turned it over to a consortium of private mining companies from the US, France, and

Switzerland, "[proving] once again that NATO is the military arm to insure primarily US corporate control" of Europe.[33]

Russia's Concerns

Russia has been particularly threatened by the new NATO expansion and especially the air war in Yugoslavia. Viktor Chernomyrdin, former prime minister of Russia and President Boris Yeltsin's special envoy for Kosovo, wrote in the *Washington Post*, "the new NATO strategy, the first practical instance of which we are witnessing in Yugoslavia, has led to a serious deterioration in Russian-US contacts. I will be so bold as to say it has set them back by several decades." According to Chernomyrdin, "The world has never in this decade been so close as now to the brink of nuclear war."[34]

Russians are concerned that NATO could use Kosovo as a precedent to intervene in Russia's breakaway province of Chechnya, also a hot spot along proposed routes for oil pipelines from the Caspian Sea. NATO, in its eastward expansion, has incorporated the former Soviet nations that border the Caspian Sea, into its surrogate group, Partnership for Peace. Thus, Russia is very worried about the expansion of NATO. Although NATO Secretary-General George Robertson has denied that "NATO expansion is an expansion of a hostile military bloc eager to surround Russia on all sides," Russian Defense Minister Sergei B. Ivanov is not convinced. In May 2001, he said, "NATO constantly is stating that this military-political organization poses no threat to Russia. But then the question naturally arises: If there is no threat coming from Russia, then for what reason does this organization need to enlarge itself?"[35]

President Vladimir V. Putin has called for the disbanding of NATO, or alternatively, the admission of Russia as a NATO member. Concerned about NATO's expansion to Russia's borders, as well as President George W. Bush's attempts to abrogate the Anti-Ballistic Missile Treaty by developing and proliferating a "Star Wars" missile defense system, Russia has joined with China in signing a friendship treaty. The new pact was described by a Russian commentator as "an act of friendship against America."[36]

The US also seeks to ensure dominance over Russia by maintaining military bases in the Balkans. Control over Eastern European raw materials and labor markets provide Western investment opportunities and export markets. Even though the Soviet Union has dissolved and Russia is weakened by internal economic and political problems, the US is vying to maintain its status as sole superpower in the world.

Exercising "Adult Supervision" Over Europe

Western European countries are also concerned about the US exercising "adult supervision" over them. According to Gerald Segal, director of studies at the International Institute for Strategic Studies, "Despite years of grumbling about the need to enhance the defense capacity of Europe, the reality is that Europeans are even more dependent on the US than during the Cold War." Leaders of the European Union, alarmed by their "dependence on the United States in NATO's military campaign against Serbia," met in Germany in 1999 and determined to develop a strong common military policy. A new, "more assertive Europe," decided to vitalize the European Union and turn it into a military power no longer reliant on the US. During the NATO bombing, French President Jacques Chirac spoke of the need to counter American "hegemony."[37]

The European Strategic Defense Initiative is organizing itself to respond when the US decides not to get involved in various European conflicts, but Washington is concerned that Europe may act independently of US-run NATO.[38]

The Rambouillet Ultimatum

The substance of the ultimate peace pact that ended the bombing corroborates the true purpose for the bombardment. NATO backed down on three major issues, enabling Milosevic to sign an agreement he would have signed before the Rambouillet ultimatum, which triggered the bombing.[39]

First, under the Rambouillet Plan, NATO—not the UN—would lead the foreign occupation of Yugoslavia, a direct threat to the sovereignty of that country. The *New York Times* reported that "just before the bombing, when [the Serbian parliament] rejected NATO troops in Kosovo, it also supported the idea of a United Nations force to monitor a political settlement there." The peace agreement that stopped the bombing provided for UN—not NATO—supervision of the peacekeeping force. The British House of Commons admitted, "NATO was guilty of a serious blunder in allowing a status of forces agreement into the [Rambouillet] package which would never have been acceptable to the Yugoslav side, since it was a significant infringement of its sovereignty."[40]

An annex to the Rambouillet agreement, which would have given NATO troops free reign to occupy all of Yugoslavia without accountability, was dropped from the pact. Under the peace agreement, there is no requirement of a referendum on Kosovo's independence, slated to occur in three years' time under the Rambouillet ultimatum. Milosevic came out of the peace agreement with Serbian sovereignty. But to justify its bombing campaign, NATO claimed that he capitulated.

The Serb National Assembly Resolution of March 23, 1999, called on the UN and OSCE to broker a diplomatic settlement with negotiations "toward the reaching of a political agreement on a wide-ranging autonomy for [Kosovo], with the securing of a full equality of all citizens and ethnic communities, and with respect for the sovereignty and territorial integrity of the Republic of Serbia and the Federal Republic of Yugoslavia." It suggested the possibility of an "international presence" whose "size and character" would be formulated to carry out the "political accord on the self-rule agreed and accepted by the representatives of all national communities living in [Kosovo]."[41] This resolution was largely blacked out of the mainstream media, which focused instead on preparing us for NATO's invasion of Yugoslavia by discussing Milosevic's alleged intransigence.

US-led NATO flexed its muscle—thousands of lives, a million refugees, and billions of dollars later. Raytheon Company, one of the "Big Three" weapons dealers, estimated that replacing munitions used in the Balkans could result in about $1 billion in new contracts. White House strategists have conceded, according to the *New York Times*, that protecting the Kosovo Albanians "was never really a practical goal. Bombing could neither protect the Kosovars, the officials said, nor could it force out the Yugoslav armed forces."[42]

The day before the bombing began, Clinton sought to justify the air strikes, declaring: "If we're going to have a strong economic relationship that includes our ability to sell around the world, Europe has got to be a key ... That's what this Kosovo thing is all about." Commanding General Clark admitted one month into the bombing campaign that it "was not designed as a means of blocking Serb ethnic cleansing."[43]

Let there be no doubt. The bombing was about oil and world domination, not ethnic cleansing.

NATO's Bombing Violated International Law

NATO's 11-week aerial bombardment of Yugoslavia was executed in direct violation of international law. The bombing violated the United Nations Charter, the NATO Treaty, the Nuremberg Tribunal, the International Criminal Tribunal for the Former Yugoslavia, and many other provisions of international law.

THE UNITED NATIONS CHARTER

The Charter of the United Nations provides a complete system for international peacekeeping and response to international conflicts. It is based on a very specific procedure that was circumvented by NATO.[44]

Article 2(4) provides that all members shall settle their international disputes by peaceful means and shall refrain from threat or use of force against the territorial integrity of any state, and article 2(7) prohibits states from intervening in domestic matters of other states, unless authorized by the Security Council. NATO's aerial bombing assault on the resources, properties, economic, social, cultural, medical, diplomatic, and religious facilities of Yugoslavia was undertaken without Security Council approval, and violated Article 2 of the UN Charter. [45]

Article 33 provides: Parties to a dispute that is likely to endanger international peace and security shall, "first of all," seek a solution by negotiation, settlement, or resort to regional agencies. The peace plan submitted to Yugoslavia at Rambouillet was really an ultimatum, impossible for Milosevic to accept, and a conscious set-up to justify the bombing.[46]

Article 37 of the UN Charter provides: Should the parties to a dispute likely to endanger the maintenance of international peace and security fail to settle it by negotiation or peaceful means, they shall refer it to the Security Council. The Security Council shall then decide what action to take in accordance with specific procedures outlined in Articles 36 to 42. It is up to the Security Council—not NATO—to decide what measures to take when there is a threat to the peace or an act of aggression (under Article 39).

The interventions in Somalia, Bosnia, and Rwanda (by France) were authorized by the Security Council. NATO did not, however, go to the Security Council before bombing Yugoslavia. The *New York Times* described the Clinton administration's position "that NATO should be able to act independently of the United Nations." And Richard Haas, of the Brookings Institute and formerly an official in the first George Bush administration, said: "To require the Security Council's blessing would essentially hand them a veto over [US] policy."[47] NATO purposely bypassed the UN and, in so doing, violated the UN Charter.

Article 51 provides: Nothing in the Charter shall impair the inherent right of individual or collective self-defense if an armed attack occurs against a Member of the UN. All NATO countries are members of UN, and none was attacked. They did not therefore have the right to self-defense under the UN Charter. The use of force by bombing the territory of another country is a violation of its territorial integrity regardless of the motivation.[48]

Article 85 provides: Making the civilian population or individual civilians the object of attack or launching an indiscriminate attack affecting the civilian population is a grave breach of the NATO Protocol.[49]

THE NUREMBERG PRINCIPLES

Principle VI of the Nuremberg Tribunal prohibits the planning, preparation, initiation, or waging of a *war of aggression* or war in violation of international treaties, agreements, or assurances. NATO launched a war of aggression against Yugoslavia, targeting civilians and the infrastructure of the country, in violation of several international treaties and agreements. Walter Rockler, former prosecutor at the Nuremberg War Crimes Tribunal, said the Nuremberg court found that "to initiate a war of aggression [as the US has done in Yugoslavia] is not only an international crime, it is the supreme international crime."[50]

This principle also prohibits *war crimes*, including the wanton destruction of cities, towns, or villages, or devastation not justified by military necessity. The attacks on transportation, educational, religious, medical, and media facilities, as well as utilities and homes, devastated Yugoslavia. These attacks were not justified by military necessity.[51]

INTERNATIONAL CRIMINAL TRIBUNAL FOR THE FORMER YUGOSLAVIA

In 1993, the UN Security Council — with significant prodding and financial aid from the leading NATO countries — set up the International Criminal Tribunal for the Former Yugoslavia, or ICTY. It has jurisdiction over grave breaches of the Geneva Conventions, violations of the laws or customs of war, and genocide and crimes against humanity committed in the former Yugoslavia since 1991. The tribunal indicted President Slobodan Milosevic and other Yugoslav officials for war crimes,[52] but there have been no indictments against NATO leaders for war crimes they committed during the 11-week aerial bombardment of Yugoslavia.

Article 3 of the ICTY Statute prohibits "devastation not justified by military necessity." NATO bombs killed between 500 and 1800 civilians and injured thousands more. Laser-guided weapons hit numerous civil targets.

In February 2000, Human Rights Watch reported, "All too often, NATO targeting subjected the civilian population to unacceptable risks." It reported 33 incidents that resulted in civilian deaths took place in densely populated urban areas, including six in Belgrade. Civilians were killed in 90 separate incidents. NATO failed to minimize civilian casualties by (1) using cluster bombs in populated areas; (2) attacking populated areas during the day; (3)

attacking mobile targets without ensuring they were military in nature; and (4) striking targets of little or no military use, such as Serb radio and TV headquarters in Belgrade. More than half the deaths resulted from "attacks on illegitimate or questionable targets." Kenneth Roth, executive director of Human Rights Watch, said, "In each case that we considered illegitimate, we looked very closely at the circumstances and either found that there was no military value at all or that the marginal military value was outweighed by the civilian cost."[53]

A report released in July 2000, "Collateral Damage: or Unlawful Killings? Violations of the Laws of War by NATO during Operation Allied Force," by Amnesty International, found the April 23, 1999, NATO bombing of the headquarters of Serbian state radio and television, which killed 16 civilians, "was a deliberate attack on a civilian object and as such constitutes a war crime." Amnesty International also criticized several other attacks on civilians or civilian objects. It noted, "NATO forces failed to suspend their attack after it was evident that they had struck civilians."[54]

Mary Robinson, UN High Commissioner for Human Rights, had warned NATO it might be held accountable for war crimes after two buses in Kosovo were bombed, killing more than 50 civilians. She said, "People are not collateral damage. They are people who are killed, injured, whose lives are destroyed."[55]

Also prohibited by Article 3 of the ICTY Statute is the "employment of poisonous weapons or other weapons calculated to cause unnecessary suffering." NATO used cluster bombs banned by international conventions. Children (i.e., "soft targets," according to the manufacturer) are still being mutilated and killed when unexploded bomblets blow up in their hands. One Yugoslav orthopedist described the damage from these weapons: "Neither I nor my colleagues have ever seen such horrific wounds as those caused by cluster bombs.... The limbs are so crushed that the only remaining option is amputation. It's awful, awful."[56]

In May 2000, the *New York Times* reported that 40 per cent of the refugees who had returned to Kosovo since last June had been victims of cluster bombs. In July 2000, one of the top UN officials in Kosovo criticized NATO for refusing to reveal the location of unexploded cluster bombs.[57]

Equally troubling is NATO's use of depleted uranium weapons, condemned in a 1991 US Nuclear Defense Agency report as a "serious health threat." One speck of DU dust lodged in a lung upon impact or ingestion can cause cancer. Doctors in Kosovo estimate that birth defects have increased by 250 per cent over 1998 figures. Dr. Aleksandra Veljovic, of the Cancer Foundation in Yugoslavia, described "a doubling of incidence of cancer" one year after the bombing ended.[58]

This deadly compound, first used on a large-scale by the US during the Gulf War, has been linked to Gulf War Syndrome and high levels of stillbirths, birth defects, and leukemia among Iraqi children. In February 2000, NATO finally admitted it used 10 tons of depleted uranium munitions in Kosovo and Serbia, but, for seven months, it refused to disclose the 112 locations of contamination. In January 2001, NATO finally posted warning signs at the sites.[59]

On April 18, 1999, NATO bombed three major industrial plants in Pancevo, a city near Belgrade. Levels of the carcinogen vinyl-chloride monomer (VHM) released into the air reached 10,600 times more than accepted safety levels. This has poisoned the air, the land, the crops, and the Danube River. Teams from the UN Environmental Program and the UN Center for Human Settlements in Yugoslavia warned of the dangers of "miscarriages, birth defects as well as incurable diseases of the nervous system and liver."[60]

Physicians in Pancevo recommended privately that all women who were present in the town the night of the bombing avoid pregnancy for the next two years. They also advised women less than nine months pregnant to obtain abortions. Most reportedly complied. Dr. Slobodan Tosovic, chief ecotoxicologist at Belgrade's Public Institute of Health, said, "It's enough to make me believe the Americans and NATO were making a biochemical experiment with us."[61]

The US was well aware of the consequences of bombing the petrochemical complex. "The Americans built that factory, so they knew precisely what was inside when they bombed it," said Pancevo Mayor Mikovic.[62] Michel Chossudovsky, professor of economics at the University of Ottawa, has documented that NATO willfully and methodically blew up containers of toxic chemicals with the intention of creating an ecological disaster. NATO's "state of the art" aerial surveillance and satellite thermal image detection distinguished between full and empty containers. Professor Chossudovsky claims that NATO intentionally targeted containers full of poison in order to create an environmental catastrophe.[63]

Chemical, petrochemical, oil, and gas refineries, storage, and transmission facilities were also purposely targeted in the vicinity of Novi Sad, Nis, and other major cities, exposing huge populations to dangerous and noxious pollution.[64]

The ICTY Refuses to Indict NATO

In 1999, a group of Canadian lawyers and professors as well as the American Association of Jurists lodged a complaint with the ICTY. It asked Prosecutor Louise Arbour to "immediately investigate and indict for serious crimes against international humanitarian law" the 67 named heads of state, ministers, and NATO officials.[65]

Article 18 of the ICTY Statute requires the Prosecutor to "initiate investigations" ex-officio or "on the basis of information obtained from *any source*, particularly from Governments, United Nations organs, intergovernmental and non-governmental organizations." Upon determining that a *prima facie* case exists, the Prosecutor shall prepare an indictment.

Carla Del Ponte, the current ICTY Prosecutor, after conducting only an "informal survey," declined to file charges against NATO. The ICTY report admits that when NATO was requested "to answer specific questions about specific incidents, the NATO reply was couched in general terms and failed to address the specific incidents." The report also notes that the "committee has not spoken to those involved in directing or carrying out the bombing campaign." Instead, the committee "tended to assume that the NATO and NATO countries' press statements are generally reliable and that explanations have been honestly given." Nevertheless, the committee concluded, and the Prosecutor agreed, that "neither an in-depth investigation related to the bombing campaign as a whole nor investigations related to specific incidents are justified." The Prosecutor's decision not to hold NATO accountable for its war crimes in Yugoslavia, which was criticized by Amnesty International, violates the ICTY statute.[66]

War Crimes Tribunals Find NATO Guilty of War Crimes

The day after the ICTY prosecutor declined to open a formal inquiry into possible NATO war crimes, a European tribunal in Berlin, convened by non-governmental organizations, unanimously convicted NATO leaders of committing serious violations of international law by their aggression during the bombing. After several public hearings and analysis of international law, the tribunal found violations of the categorical prohibition of the use of force, the territorial integrity of a state and the prohibition against aggression. It further determined that the pre-bombing situation in Kosovo did not amount to a "humanitarian catastrophe."[67] "Humanitarian intervention," the tribunal found, "is not recognized as an institution, legitimating an exemption from the absolute prohibition of the use of force." Even if humanitarian intervention were a legitimate exemption from the absolute prohibition of the use of force, wrote the tribunal, NATO not only failed in its goal to re-establish acceptable conditions for human rights, but it "dramatically deteriorated the already precarious situation." The tribunal was not convinced that the heavy damage of civilian objects was only unintentional "collateral damage," and it condemned the use of depleted uranium and cluster bombs, which represented "a grave violation of humanitarian international law as prescribed by the Additional Protocol to the Geneva Conventions."

Moreover, on June 10, 2000, in New York, the International Tribunal on US/NATO War Crimes Against the People of Yugoslavia found US and NATO political and military leaders guilty of war crimes. The panel of 16 judges from 11 countries heard testimony from eyewitnesses, researchers who visited Yugoslavia, renowned political and economics analysts, historians, physicists, biologists, military experts, journalists, and lay researchers. Proof was established beyond a reasonable doubt that NATO committed *crimes against the peace* by rigging the "Racak massacre" and using the Rambouillet ultimatum to provoke the war; *war crimes* for using illegal weapons, targeting civilians, and destroying the environment and the civilian infrastructure; and *crimes against humanity* for the expulsion of hundreds of thousands of people from Kosovo and Metohija.[68]

Former US Attorney General Ramsey Clark, the lead prosecutor at the people's tribunal, urged a sentence of organizing a campaign to abolish the NATO military pact. The members of the tribunal called for the immediate revocation of all embargoes, sanctions, and penalties against Yugoslavia (a continuing *crime against humanity*); an immediate end to the NATO occupation of all Yugoslav territory; the removal of all NATO and US bases and forces from the Balkans; the cessation of overt and covert operations, including the ICTY, aimed at overthrowing the government of Yugoslavia; and full reparations to be paid to the Federal Republic of Yugoslavia for death, injury, economic, and environmental damage resulting from the NATO bombing, economic sanctions, and blockades.

The 11-week NATO bombing coupled with ten years of sanctions resulted in $30 billion in damage, according to Yugoslav President Vojislav Kostunica. The economy is in shambles, one million people live below the poverty level, half the population is unemployed, and the country has an annual inflation rate of 150 per cent and a foreign debt of $12 billion.[69]

The International Court of Justice (World Court)

Because of the bombing, Yugoslavia sued the NATO countries in the International Court of Justice. The ICJ dismissed several of the cases on jurisdictional grounds; other claims are still pending. The International Court of Justice said: "The Court is profoundly concerned with the use of force in Yugoslavia ... under the present circumstances such use raises very serious issues of international law."[70]

In ruling against the US intervention in Nicaragua, the ICJ had stated that although the US might form its own appraisal of respect for human rights in

Nicaragua, the use of force could not be the appropriate means to ensure such respect. The protection of human rights, a strictly humanitarian objective, said the ICJ, cannot be compatible with the mining of ports, the destruction of oil installations, or the training, arming, and equipping of the Contras.[71] Likewise, the devastation of the infrastructure of Yugoslavia belies NATO's claim to humanitarian motives.

The Illegality of Humanitarian Intervention

"The NATO bombing transformed a humanitarian crisis into a 'humanitarian catastrophe.'" — Sergei V. Lavrov, Russia's representative during the Security Council's adoption of S.C. res. 1244.[72]

In *Yugoslavia v. Belgium*, the ICJ expressed concern about humanitarian law as well as the use of force: "The Court deems it necessary to emphasize that all parties appearing before it must act in conformity with their obligations under the United Nations Charter and other rules of international law, including humanitarian law."[73]

The phrase "humanitarian intervention" was coined in 1992 by the Carnegie Endowment for International Peace, in a book called *Self-Determination in the New World Order*:

As of mid-1992, neither the United States nor the world community has reached a point where humanitarian calamities resulting from self-determination claims or internal repression automatically trigger collective military intervention to accomplish strictly humanitarian objectives. But *humanitarian intervention* will become increasingly unavoidable.[74]

Most scholars believe unilateral intervention — that which is not sanctioned by the Security Council — violates the UN Charter. Many think that "humanitarian intervention" is a violation of a state's territorial integrity and political independence, and runs afoul of Article 2 of the UN Charter, even if it lasts a short time and is effected for a good purpose. None of the major human rights treaties recognize the right of a state to use force in response to violations of rights contained in them. Three Cold War resolutions of the UN General Assembly define armed intervention by states as violations of fundamental human rights and self-determination; they do not affect the Security Council's powers under Chapters VI, VII, or VIII of the UN Charter.[75]

The general notion of humanitarian intervention is the use of force or threat of force by third countries, individually or collectively, to protect people from a government which continuously and arbitrarily subjects people living in its own territory to inhumane treatment.[76]

A danger exists, however, that humanitarian intervention can easily be employed as a pretext for aggression. "Pretextual intervention" is "a nation's use of military force in a different state for the nation's own gain, not for the protection of human rights."[77] Three early examples of how the doctrine of humanitarian intervention can be abused by asserting it as an excuse to warrant aggression are Japan's attack on Manchuria, Mussolini's invasion of Ethiopia, and Hitler's occupation of Czechoslovakia. All were justified on humanitarian grounds.

The British House of Commons concluded that NATO's military action in Yugoslavia was "of dubious legality," observing that "the doctrine of humanitarian intervention has a tenuous basis in current international customary law." That, said the House of Commons, "renders the NATO action legally questionable." According to British General Sir Michael Rose, "Allied bombing accounted for three times as many civilian deaths as Serbian military personnel, and it's likely that we were in breach of the Geneva Convention."[78]

Even assuming that humanitarian intervention might be legally justified in some circumstances, NATO's bombing of Yugoslavia does not qualify. The following criteria were developed by scholars Ved Nanda, Richard Lillich, John Norton Moore and Tom Farer, for judging the legality of humanitarian intervention:[79]

1. *There must be an immediate and extensive threat to fundamental human rights.* The US media consistently claimed that 10,000 to 11,000 Albanians had been killed by Serbs. Reuters and other news services reported that these bodies have not been found in places they were reported to have been buried. The FBI and other forensic teams worked diligently, following up leads of the Albanians. But instead of bodies in the thousands, about 1000 have been found as of two years after the bombing. Although any deaths are horrible, this falls far short of the "genocide" label and comparisons with Nazi Germany which have been bandied about.[80]

2. *All other remedies for the protection of those rights must have been exhausted.* As explained above, the Rambouillet ultimatum was not a true negotiation.

3. *An attempt must have been made to secure the approval of appropriate authorities in the target state.* This was not done.

4. *The intervention must not be used to impose or preserve a preferred regime.* Evidence now indicates that NATO supported the Kosovo Liberation Army, in spite of the United State's prior characterization of the KLA as a "terrorist" group. The KLA is responsible for the oppression and killing of Serbs since the bombing stopped and KFOR began its occupation of Kosovo.[81]

5. *The minimum requisite force must be employed, and/or the intervention must not be likely to cause greater injury to innocent persons and their property than would result if the threatened violation occurred.* This is the concept of *proportionality*. It is undisputed that the bombing exacerbated the killing and refugee crisis. A UN report said the 11 weeks of NATO air strikes had "a devastating impact" on the environment, industry, employment, essential services, and agriculture of Yugoslavia.[82]

6. *The intervention must be of limited duration and a report of the intervention must be filed immediately with the Security Council, and when relevant, with regional organizations.* Recent reports predict a protracted occupation of Kosovo.[83]

"The notion that humanitarian violations can be redressed with random destruction and killing by advanced technological means is inherently suspect," Nuremberg prosecutor Rockler wrote in an op-ed in the *Chicago Tribune*. "This is mere pretext for our arrogant assertion of dominance and power in defiance of international law."[84]

NATO's bombing of Yugoslavia was not a humanitarian intervention. As Noam Chomsky has observed, "the right of humanitarian intervention, if it exists, is premised on the good faith of those intervening." Their actions, says Chomsky, speak louder than their words.[85] The NATO action, which devastated Yugoslavia, was a pretense for the US to maintain economic and political dominance in Western and Eastern Europe.

The Non-Humanitarian Motives

US support for Croat soldiers in their 1995 ethnic cleansing of 200,000 Serbs from the Krajina region during Operation Storm belies US humanitarian motives in Kosovo. The *New York Times* quoted Canadian military officers present during the offensive, who told ICTY investigators that "indiscriminate" and "unnecessary" shelling of civilians took place in Krajina.[86]

There is proof positive that the US's motive for bombing Yugoslavia was access to oil and geopolitical hegemony, not ethnic cleansing. That proof is in the critical role the US would give Turkey in delivering Caspian Sea oil to the Mediterranean. If the US were truly concerned about ethnic cleansing, it would intervene in Turkey. In recent years, Turkey has prosecuted its own ethnic-cleansing campaign, killing tens of thousands of Kurds and burning more than 3,000 Kurdish villages. Human Rights Watch reported in 1995 that the US "becoming complicit in a scorched earth campaign [in Turkey] violates the fundamental tenets of international law."[87]

The US remains undaunted by Turkey's vile campaign. That country is not only the favored US route for Caspian oil pipelines, but is also one of the main recipients of US financial aid. Turkish personnel piloted several US aircraft that bombed Serbia in 1999. In March 2000, the prime minister of Turkey announced plans to give Albania $80 million during the next four years to modernize its armed forces.[88]

The US has been equally silent about the Indonesian genocide against the East Timorese, where more than a quarter of the population was decimated. Noam Chomsky has characterized East Timor as "the site of the worst slaughter relative to population since the Holocaust." Nevertheless, the US armed the Indonesian government for years, with full knowledge of its repression of the East Timorese.[89]

Likewise, the US helped to engineer the human rights tragedy in Somalia in the early 1990s. Inside CIA sources estimate the US military may have killed between 7,000 and 10,000 Somalis.[90]

Historically, the US has used its military force for intervention to protect its own economic and political interests. It has a long history of supporting brutal totalitarian regimes in countries such as Vietnam, Guatemala, El Salvador, Nicaragua, Chile, Iran, and Indonesia, and of using humanitarian justifications as pretexts for politically–motivated incursions in nations like Vietnam, Grenada, and Haiti. Yet no US leader has ever been tried for war crimes, genocide, or crimes against humanity.[91] One week before he left office, President Bill Clinton signed the ICC statute on December 31, 2000, the deadline for signing the treaty without being compelled to ratify it. A signature enables a country to have input into the development of the Court. Clinton urged incoming President George W. Bush to refrain from submitting the treaty to the Senate for ratification because it would make US leaders vulnerable to indictment. Bush has indicated he has no intention of asking the Senate to ratify the treaty.[92]

NATO's intervention in Kosovo "was, and always will be, about containment. It is about the Americans controlling Macedonia, holding down Albanian expansionism, and building themselves a huge tactical military base out of which they can operate in the Balkans," said a former official of the International Committee of the Red Cross, who worked in Kosovo, Albania, and Serbia before, during and after the bombing.[93]

Conclusion

During the Vietnam War, an American infantry officer once said, "It was necessary to destroy the village in order to save it." Indeed, "[a]s many Serb civilians died under NATO bombs as ethnic Albanians had died during the preceding year," according to Doug Bandow of the CATO Institute. "And it was allied bombing that sparked the mass expulsions from Kosovo," he added. Robert Hayden, director of the Center for Russian and East European Studies at the University of Pittsburgh, noted, "the casualties among Serb civilians in the first three weeks of the war [were] higher than all of the casualties on both sides in Kosovo in the three months that led up to this war." However, he said, "those three months were supposed to be a humanitarian catastrophe."[94] Indeed, all but 43 deaths attributed to Milosevic in the ICTY indictment pending against him occurred after the NATO bombing began.

During the bombing campaign, NATO officials bragged about being able to turn the lights off whenever they wanted, a reference to the attack on Yugoslavia's infrastructure. The bombs, the sanctions, the foreign occupation and the ICTY have devastated and continue to devastate this country. Yet the US persists in waging a propaganda war. After the bombing, Madeleine Albright said, "To turn an old phrase rightside up, lights are going on all over the Balkans."[95] In fact, the US-led NATO bombing has cast a pall of darkness over this region. The devastation wrought by NATO on the people of Yugoslavia can hardly be characterized "humanitarian intervention." It is a crime against humanity.

Notes

1. Portions of this article were published in the *International Journal for the Semiotics of Law*. Reprinted with permission from Kluwer Law International.

2. "New Figures on Civilian Deaths in Kosovo War," Human Rights Watch, World Report 2000 (7 February 2000), <http://www.hrw.org/hrw/press/2000/02/nato207.htm>; "Yugoslavia A Year Later: Turning a Blind Eye to NATO War Crimes" (22 May 2000), <www.counterpunch.com>.

3. Transcript of Press Conference by Secretary General, Dr. Javier Solana, and SACEUR, Gen. Wesley Clark (25 March 1999), <http://www.nato.int/kosovo/press/p990325a.htm>. Robert H. Reid, "NATO Bombs Yugoslavia for 2nd Night," *Aponline* (25 March 1999). For the quote from Clark, see Dana Priest, "The Battle Inside Headquarters; Tension Grew With Divide Over Strategy," *Washington Post* (21 September 1999): 1.

4. Stratfor.com, "Kosovo: One Year Later," <http://www.stratfor.com/CIS/special reports/special26.htm>. A *Wall Street Journal* article described an American B-2 pilot who took off in the morning from a Missouri Air Force Base, dropped tons of bombs on Yugoslavia, and returned that evening to his home. After mowing the lawn, "we ordered out for Pizza Hut, because it was a special occasion." Thomas E. Ricks, "For These B-2 Pilots, Bombs Away Means Really Far, Far Away," *Wall Street Journal* (19 April 1999): A1. "NATO violations of the laws of war during Operation Allied Force must be investigated," Amnesty International (25 July 2000), <http://www.amnesty.org/news/2000/4/002500.htm>.

5. Richard B. Bilder, "Kosovo and the 'New Interventionism': Promise or Peril?," *Journal of Transnational Law and Policy* 9 (1999): 153, 169. The quote from Biden is found in William Dorich, "Defending Democracy in the Balkans," *Washington Times* (19 July1998): B5.

6. George Kenney, "Rolling Thunder: the Rerun (Review)," *Nation* (14 June 1999): 48.

7. Noam Chomsky, *The New Military Humanism* (Monroe, ME: Common Courage Press, 1999) 40-48; Mary Mostert, "Is Another Outbreak of War Looming in Kosovo? The Battle of Mitrovica is Not About Visiting Cousins—It's About the Trepca Mines" (24 February 2000), <www.originalsources.com>. See also, Michael McAuliffe, "The Road to Racak," CBC Radio News (22 May 2000). After Racak, the European Union hired a Finnish team of forensic pathologists to investigate the deaths. Its report, kept secret for two years, said that Finnish investigators could not establish the victims were civilians, only one body showed traces of an execution-style killing, and there was no evidence the bodies had been mutilated—*Berliner Zeitung* (16 January 2001). Indeed, the 46 Racak deaths are the only pre-bombing casualties listed in the indictment, in the International Criminal Tribunal for the Former Yugoslavia, against ex-Yugoslav President Slobodan Milosevic. Barton Gellman, "The Path to Crisis: How the United States and Its Allies Went to War; The Battle for Kosovo, A Defining Atrocity Set Wheels in Motion," *Washington Post* (18 April 1999): A1.

8. John J. Merriam, "Kosovo and the Law of Humanitarian Intervention," *Case Western Reserve Journal of International Law* 33 (2000): 111, nn. 127-29 and accompanying text. US Representative Saxton, a Republican Congressman from New Jersey, said, "I know when the ethnic cleansing started, I know when the refugees started to move.... It was when we started bombing." James Dao, "Back From Belgrade, Congressman Says NATO Is Worsening Refugee Crisis," *New York Times* (23 April 1999): B5. See also, Jared Israel, "Why Albanians Fled During NATO Bombing: An Interview With Cedda Pralinchevich," (7 December 2000), <www.emperors-clothes.com>. Stephen Zunes, "Bombing Serbia Not the Answer," *Progressive Response* 2.10 (23 March 1999); Jonathan I. Charney, "Anticipatory Humanitarian Intervention in Kosovo," *Vanderbilt Journal of Transnational Law* 32 (1999): 1231, 1245-46. The US Department of State's press releases acknowledged that while the KVM was present, violence by the Federal Republic of Yugoslavia was limited, focused on suppressing the insurrectionist Kosovo Liberation Army. See, US Department of State, "Kosovo Update" (2 March 1999), <http://www.state.gov/www/regions/eur/rpt_990302_kdom.html>; US Department of State, "Kosovo Update" (12 March 1999), <http://www.state.gov/www/regions/eur/rpt_790312_kdom.html>; US Department of State, "Kosovo Humanitarian Situation Report" (31 March 1999). See also, Charney 1248, n. 44. General Clark said it was "entirely predictable" that terror and violence by the Serbs would worsen after the bombing; "Nato attacks," London *Sunday Times* (28 March 1999): 3. Special Envoy Richard Holbrooke admitted that "our greatest fear by far, by far," was that NATO's air attack would push the Serbs to more vicious "ethnic cleansing"; see, Blaine Harden, "A Long Struggle That Led Serb Leader to Back Down," *New York Times* (6 June 1999): A16. BBC Summary of World Broadcasts (25 March 1999), Thursday Section: Part 2, "Central Europe, the Balkans; Federal Republic of Yugoslavia; Servia; EE/D3492/A," citing the Tanjung (Yugoslav state) news agency.

9. "In Focus: Bombs Away—A Call for the Unconditional Ending of the Bombing Campaign," *Foreign Policy in Focus* 4.13 (May 1999), <http://www.foreignpolicy-infocus.org /briefs/vol4/v4n13koso.html>. Also, British House of Commons Select Committee on Foreign Affairs Report (2 June 2000), <http://www.publicationsparliament.uk/pa/cm19990/cmselect/cmfatt/28/2803.html>. Noam Chomsky reports that US intelligence warned the bombing would lead to "a virtual explosion of refugees" and an ethnic cleansing campaign. Noam Chomsky, "In Retrospect—A Review of NATO's war over Kosovo, Part I." *Z Magazine* (April 2000): 19, 23. In fact, since the bombing, an astronomical number of Serbs have been cleansed from Kosovo. Jan Oberg, Director of the Transnational Foundation for Peace and Future Research in Sweden, reported in October, 1999, "[w]ith perhaps 90%

of all non-Albanians now driven out, the Kosovo-Albanian leadership is responsible for the proportionately largest ethnic cleansing in the Balkans since the wars started in 1991." See, Jan Oberg, "Misleading UN Report on Kosovo (Part A)" (3 October 1999), <http://www.transnational.org>.

10. General Sir Michael Rose, "Nato's 'Failure' to Achieve its Aims," London *Times* (14 July 1999): 1.

11. NATO is also eyeing Estonia, Latvia, and Lithuania for NATO membership. See, "NATO'S Uncertain Role," *Los Angeles Times* (22 July 2001): M4. After the Cold War ended, it was said in Washington, "NATO must either go out of area, or out of business." Diana Johnstone, "Deception and Self-Deception: The Mixed Motives behind NATO's War against Yugoslavia," <www.emperors-clothes.com/articles/Johnstone/balk.htm>. The expansion of NATO also meant new markets for US military contractors. For this reason, the US Committee to Expand NATO, a powerful lobby run by Lockheed's chief executive, overcame US Congressional reluctance to endorse NATO expansion. "NATO is the military arm of an unjust, undemocratic and destructive economic globalization," <www.emperors-clothes.com/articles/Johnstone/balk.htm>.

12. Patrick E. Tyler, "US Strategy Plan Calls For Insuring No Rivals Develop," *New York Times* (8 March 1992): 1. Benjamin Schwarz and Christopher Layne, "NATO: At 50, It's Time to Quit — US Leadership and Aid Are No Longer Needed in Europe. Why Are We Still There?" *Nation* (10 May 1999): 15, 17. Paul Starobin, "The New Great Game," *Foreign Policy* (13 March 1999); Tyler.

13. "Pentagon's New World View," *Washington Post* (24 May 1992): A23. The leaked Pentagon document led to "reverberations around the world among our allies," according to then Defense Secretary Richard Cheney. See, Barton Gellman, "Pentagon Abandons Goal of Thwarting US Rivals; 6-Year Plan Softens Earlier Tone on Allies," *Washington Post* (24 May 1992): A1. In response, the Bush administration sought to control the damage by backing down from the sole superpower goal, even though that goal had been mirrored in Cheney's public statements and testimony. See Patrick E. Tyler, "Senior US Officials Assail Lone-Superpower Policy," *New York Times* (11 March 1992): A6.

14. Jacob Heilbrunn and Michael Lind, "The Third American Empire," *New York Times* (2 January 1996).

15. "Global Intelligence Update," Stratfor.com (30 August 1999), <http://www.stratforcom.com>.

16. Robert Jensen, "Perspective on Warfare — The Gulf War Brought Out the Worst in Us — Foreign Policy: Demonizing one general diverts us from assessing responsibility for the slaughter," *Los Angeles Times* (22 May 2000): B7.

17. Chomsky, *The New Military Humanism* 67.

18. Barton Gellman, "Annan Suspicious of UNSCOM Role; UN Official Believes Evidence Shows Inspectors Helped US Eavesdrop on Iraq," *Washington Post* (6 January 1999): A1.

19. Edward Cody, "Under Iraqi Skies, a Canvas of Death; Tour of Villages Reveals Human Cost of US-Led Sorties in 'No-Fly' Zones," *Washington Post* (16 June 2000): A1.

20. Mortimer B. Zuckerman, "The big game gets bigger — Russia will gain wealth and influence if it controls Caspian Sea oil," *US News and World Report* 126 (10 May 1999): 7576. Marjorie Cohn, "Cheney's Black Gold: Oil Interests May Drive US Foreign Policy," *Chicago Tribune* (10 August 2000).

21. David B. Ottaway, "Vast Caspian Oil Field Found; Discovery May Spur US-Russia Pipeline Rivals," *Washington Post* (16 May 2000): A1.

22. James Kitfield, "Stars and Stripes on the Silk Route," *Foreign Policy* (13 March 1999). George Monbiot, "A discreet deal in the pipeline: Nato mocked those who claimed there was a plan for Caspian oil—Special report: the petrol war," *Guardian* (15 February 2001).

23. Stephen Kinzer, "A New Big-Power Race Starts on a Sea of Crude," *New York Times* (24 January 1999).

24. Nick Elliott, "NATO bombings paralyze traffic up and down Danube," *Journal of Commerce* (14 April 1999): 10A. Kosovo itself is also sitting on rich oil deposits. "There is every reason to believe that in the near future Kosovo will become one of Europe's largest oil-bearing regions." Pyotr Iskenderov, "Will Kosovo Become a 'Balkan Kuwait?'" *Voice of Russia* (18 May 2000). The US Amoco oil company has evidently verified a massive layer of lignite beneath Pristina, Dragosa, and Araholos. "The experience of Kuwait and other Persian Gulf countries shows that oil and the American military presence always go hand in hand," Iskenderov.

25. Monbiot. See also, Michel Chossudovsky, "America at War in Macedonia" (14 June 2001), <http://www.transnational.org/forum/meet/2001/Chossudov_AMBOMacedonia.html>; Daniel McAdams, "Anti-Western Feeling—No Surprise" (26 June 2001), <http://www.bhhrg.org>, and "What is it all about?," Komiti.Com, <http://www.komiti.com/default.asp?page_id=4>. On June 29, 2001, I received an e-mail from Gligor Tashkovich, Executive Vice-President of the US-British consortium AMBO, which is sponsoring the Trans-Balkan Oil Pipeline project. Mr. Tashkovich denied that NATO's bombing was related to his project and stated that the Republic of Albania has supported the project since 1992. But an Executive Summary he sent me says, "An additional branch [of the pipeline] connecting Macedonia and the Panchevo [sic] Refinery near Belgrade is a future possibility." Pancevo and other sites in Belgrade were NATO bombing targets. The Executive Summary also states that the feasibility study for the pipeline was conducted by Brown & Root, a division of Halliburton that was headed by Richard Cheney before he was chosen vice-president of the US.

26. David H. Hackworth, "Wanted: Guns For Hire," *South Florida Sun-Sentinel* (12 July 2001): 21A; Michel Chossudovsky, "Washington Finances Ethnic Warfare in the Balkans" (3 April 2001), <http://emperors-clothes.com/articles/choss/fin.htm>; Karen Talbot, "Former Yugoslavia: The name of the game is oil," *People's Weekly World* (May 2001), <http://www.ecadre.net/pages/news/stories/990917752.shtml>; Christian Jennings, "Nato tanks move in as conflict spreads," *Scotland on Sunday* (18 March 2001): 19; Marjorie Cohn, "Pacification for a Pipeline: Explaining US Military Presence in the Balkans," *Jurist: The Legal Education Network* (27 April 2001), <http://jurist.law.pitt.edu/forumnew__.htm>; Rebecca Sumner, "A New World Order," *London Daily* (5 August 2000). Macedonia has lost faith in NATO and accused it of siding with the Albanian insurgents. "Macedonia Accuses NATO of Siding With Militants," *Stratfor—The Global Intelligence Company* (30 July 2001), <http://www.stratfor.com>. "Either through intent or mismanagement, NATO has helped prepare the ground for civil war," *Stratfor*.

27. Starobin; Monbiot.

28. John M. Biers, "Caspian Region is Filled With Give and Take—Presentation Spotlights Area," *New Orleans Times-Picayune* (2 May 1999): F1. Nora Boustany, "Diplomatic Dispatches—The Room's Not Big Enough for the Two of Them," *Washington Post* (28 April 1999): A17. For summaries of the interests of the major US oil companies in the Caspian region, see, Patrick B. Pexton, "The Hunt for Oil and Gas," *Foreign Policy* (13 March 1999).

29. Jonathan Power, "Russia, US playing new Great Game for Caspian oil," *New Straits Times* (13 February 1999): 8. Vice-President Richard Cheney, ex-CEO of Halliburton, the biggest oil-services company in the world, told a gaggle of oil industry executives in 1998, "I

can't think of a time when we've had a region emerge as suddenly to become as strategically significant as the Caspian." In 1999, Halliburton's Brown & Root Division was awarded a $180 million-a-year contract to supply US forces in the Balkans. Brown & Root built Camp Bondsteel in southern Kosovo, the largest American foreign military base constructed since Vietnam (see Cohn, Cheney's Black Gold), at a cost to the US government of $36.6 million. See, Pierre Briand, "Americans build huge camp in Kosovo to house peacekeepers for winter," *Agence France-Press* (12 October 1999). Zbigniew Brzezinski, "Compromise Over Kosovo Means Defeat," *Wall Street Journal* (24 May 1999): A30.

30. Karen Talbot, "Backing up Globalization with Military Might," *Covert Action Quarterly*, <http://www.covertaction.org/full_text_68_03a.htm>. In 1992, the US pushed the UN Security Council to impose economic sanctions—a total blockade—on Yugoslavia. See, S.C. Res. 713, UN SCOR, 46th Sess., 3009th meeting, 42, U.N. Doc. S/INF/47 (1993). The sanctions aimed to facilitate the secession of Slovenia, Croatia, and later Bosnia and Kosovo from Yugoslavia. The US Navy and its NATO allies enforced the blockade by patrolling the Adriatic Sea and the Danube River and stopping all vessels possibly bound for Yugoslavia. See, Marjorie Cohn, "Milosevic Empowered by Punishment Politics," *Jurist: The Legal Education Network* (31 July 2000), <http://jurist.law.pitt.edu/forumnew12.htm>. In April 1992, after Bosnia-Herzegovina, Croatia, and Slovenia were admitted as members of the UN, Serbia-Montenegro proclaimed the dissolution of the former Socialist Federal Republic of Yugoslavia; Sean Murphy, *Humanitarian Intervention: The United Nations in an Evolving World Order* (Philadelphia: University of Pennsylvania Press, 1996) 201. See also, Michel Chossudovsky and Jared Israel, "The US Moves to Impose a Puppet Regime in Yugoslavia," (5 October 2000), <www.tenc.net>.

31. Alex N. Dajkovic, "A 'Model' for the Balkans," *Z Magazine* (January 2001): 25, 28. Serbia, with 11 million people, should be "an attractive market," according to the *New York Times*. "The Danube, one of Europe's major rivers, runs through it. It is the overland bridge between Western Europe and Greece and Turkey." See, Joseph Kahn, "The Sanctions—Easing of Some Restrictions By West Could Happen Soon," *New York Times* (8 October 2000): Y13.

32. Chris Hedges, "Kosovo War's Glittering Prize Rests Underground," *New York Times* (8 July 1998).

33. "South Balkans—Trepca: Making Sense of the Labyrinth," International Crisis Group (26 November 1999), <http://www.crisisweb.org/projects/sbalkans/reports>. See also, Diana Johnstone, "Taking over the Trepca mines: Plans and Propaganda" (3 March 2000), <www.serbia-info.com/news>. Sara Flounders, "NATO Troops Seize Mining Complex," *Workers World* (24 August 2000), <www.iacenter.org>.

34. Viktor Chernomyrdin, "Impossible to Talk Peace With Bombs Falling," *Washington Post* (27 May 1999): A39.

35. John Daniszewski, "NATO Get-Together in Baltics Has Russia Miffed, Staying Away—Military: Venue for meeting of lawmakers raises hackles in Kremlin, which opposes plans for an expansion into ex-Soviet Union," *Los Angeles Times* (29 April 2001): A4. See also, Michael Wines, "The Russians—Muscovites Savor a Caper After Being Down So Long," *New York Times* (16 June 1999): A15.

36. John Daniszewski, "Putin Urges Russian Role in New NATO—Security: In first big press conference, president calls for a complete overhaul of Europe's treaty system, with equal membership for Moscow," *Los Angeles Times* (19 July 2001): A3. See also, Timothy Garton Ash, "Russia's Eventual Place in NATO," *New York Times* (22 July 2001): WK13. US House of Representatives Minority Leader Richard A. Gephardt has outlined an eventual goal to "extend to Russia the prospect of NATO membership." See Thom Shanker, "Gephardt Launches

an Attack on Bush's Foreign Policy," *New York Times* (3 August 2001): A6. Patrick E. Tyler, "Russia and China Sign 'Friendship' Pact: Join to Oppose Missile Shield for the US," *New York Times* (17 July 2001): A1. In the same article, Russia President Vladimir V. Putin is quoted as telling an Italian newspaper, "[W]hen NATO enlarges, division doesn't disappear, it simply moves toward our borders."

37. Gerald Segal, "Europe Needs US Might to Beat the Serbs," London, *Evening Standard* (2 June 1999). Roger Cohen, "Page Crisis in the Balkans: The Continent—Europe's Aim: Parity," *New York Times* (15 June 1999): A1.

38. Steve Erlanger, "Fresh Air," National Public Radio (13 November 2000). See also, Michael R. Gordon, "Armies of Europe Failing to Meet Goals, Sapping NATO," *New York Times* (7 June 2001): A6; Henry Kissinger, "The questionable future of NATO," *San Diego Union-Tribune* (28 January 2001): G6.

39. Associated Press, "Text of Kosovo Military Agreement" (9 June 1999). See also, <www.un.org>. Roger Cohen, "In Secret Belgrade Talks, London Financier Seems to Have Helped Milosevic Accept Accord," *New York Times* (15 June 1999): A15.

40. "Rambouillet Agreement—Interim Agreement for Peace and Self-Government in Kosovo," <http://www.state.gov/www/regions/eur/ Ksvo rambouillet text.html>. Steve Erlanger, "Milosevic's New Version of Reality Will Be Harder for NATO to Dismiss," *New York Times* (8 April 1999). British House of Commons, Select Committee on Foreign Affairs Report.

41. Noam Chomsky, "In Retrospect: A review of NATO's war over Kosovo, Part II," *Z Magazine* (May 2000): 23.

42. Blaine Harden, "Serb Miscalculation: Persistence and Resources Can Compel Victory," *New York Times* (5 June 1999): A6. Also, Tom Kirchofer, Associated Press, "War Means Business for Arms Clients" (8 June 1999). From 1994, until 5 January 2001, Lynne V. Cheney, wife of Vice-President Richard Cheney, sat on the board of directors of Lockheed Martin, the world's largest defense contractor. Manufacturers of the high-tech weapons used to bomb both Iraq and Yugoslavia received an "advertising dividend" as tiny video cameras enabled hundreds of millions of television viewers to "experience vicariously" the missile attacks. See, "Disarmament: UN Calls for New Partnership with Arms Industry," Inter Press Service (9 July 1999), quoting Jaynatha Dhanapala, UN Under-Secretary-General for Disarmament Affairs.

43. Benjamin Schwarz and Christopher Layne, "The Case Against Intervention in Kosovo," *Nation* (19 April 1999); BBC (19 April 1999).

44. Charter of the United Nations, June 26, 1945, 59 Stat. 1031, T.S. No. 993, 3 Bevans 1153; entered into force 24 October 1945. Ann Fagan Ginger, "What Should We Do About the Next Kosovo?" *Guild Practice* 57 (2000) 65.

45. "There is broad agreement that this prohibition of the unauthorized use of force is at the heart of the Charter and contemporary international law and is one of the most significant legal advances in human history." Bilder 156-57. Apologists for the bombing campaign point to the Security Council's March 26, 1999, defeat of a Russian, Belarus, and India-proposed resolution which would have condemned the NATO bombing attacks as a threat to international peace and a flagrant violation of the UN Charter. UN SCOR, 54th Sess., 3989th meeting 3, 5; UN Doc. S/PV.3989. "But a vote after the fact, particularly after the stepped up ethnic cleansing that the bombing had set off, on a resolution that crassly included no condemnation of that accelerated ethnic cleansing, is not the same as prior Security Council authorization for the bombing." Stephen R. Shalom, "Reflections on NATO and Kosovo," *New Politics* (Summer 1999), <http://www.zmag.org/crisescurevts/shalomnp.htm>.

46. The terms of the peace agreement between NATO and Serbia—which were very different from the Rambouillet Ultimatum were embodied in Security Council Resolution 1244. S/RES/1244 (1999). The Rambouillet plan also violated Articles 51 and 52 of the 1980 Vienna Convention on the Law of Treaties, which forbids coercion and force to compel any state to sign a treaty or agreement.

47. Murphy 206-07, 257. The US refused to participate in the humanitarian intervention or the UN peacekeeping operation in Rwanda, because no US international interests were at stake, notwithstanding the undeniable genocide occurring in that country; Murphy 258. An estimated 500,000 to 800,000 people were slaughtered in eight weeks as the US, Belgium, France, and other NATO countries stood by and watched. See, Bilder 163. Jane Perlez, "Trickiest Divides Are Among Big Powers at Kosovo Talks," *New York Times* (11 February 1999): A3. Haas quoted by Jonathan Landay, "How a NATO strike on Serbs could set precedent," *Christian Science Monitor* (21 January 1999).

48. Charney 1231, 1234, citing *Corfu Channel*, 1949 ICJ 32-22. In the *Corfu Channel* case, the International Court of Justice did not accept Great Britain's claim that its intervention in Albanian territorial waters was justified to vindicate British rights.

NATO's bombing of Yugoslavia violated the NATO treaty as well:

> Article 1: The parties, as set forth in the UN Charter, undertake to settle any international dispute by peaceful means ... and they are to refrain from the threat or use of force in any manner inconsistent with the UN. The NATO bombing was not a peaceful settlement and bypassed the UN. It therefore violated this provision of the NATO Treaty.
>
> Article 51: Protection of the civilian population. This article provides that civil population and individual civilians shall be protected against dangers from military operations. They shall not be the object of attack; indiscriminate attacks are prohibited (those not directed at a specific military objective); and they must not be of a nature to strike military objectives and civilians without distinction. Several NATO bombs hit civil targets, including bombings of 50 bridges, 12 railroad lines, 5 civilian airports, 50 hospitals and clinics, 190 educational institutions, 16 medieval monasteries and shrines, and several factories, power plants, water mains, major roadways, media stations, libraries, and homes. An estimated 500 to 2000 civilians were killed as a result of the bombing.

49. See <http://home.wanadoo.nl/tcc/nato/treaty.html>.

50. UN Doc. A/1316, 2 YBILC 374 (1950). Walter J. Rockler, "War Crimes Law Applies to US Too," *Chicago Tribune* (23 May 1999).

51. In addition, Article 54 of Protocol I of the Geneva Conventions of 1949 prohibits attacking, destroying, or rendering useless "objects indispensable to the survival of the civilian population," including water supplies.

52. Christopher Black, "An Impartial Tribunal? Really?" (June 2000), <www.emperors-clothes.com/analysis/Impartial.htm>. Statute of the International Criminal Tribunal For the Former Yugoslavia, adopted May 25, 1993, SC Res. 827, <http://www.un.org/icty/basic/statut/stat2000_con.htm>. See also <http://www.un.org/icty/indictment/english/mil-ii990524e.htm>.

53. "Pentagon Report Whitewashes Civilian Deaths in Yugoslavia," *Human Rights Watch* (8 February 2000), <http://www.hrw.org/hrw/press/2000/02/nato208.htm>. Spanish Captain Adolfo Luis Martin de la Hoz, who participated in the NATO bombing, reported that NATO consciously chose nonmilitary targets and "every single" mission was planned by high US

military authorities. See, Jose Luis Morales, "Spanish Fighter Pilots Admit NATO Purposely Attacks Civilian Targets," *Z Magazine* (14 June 1999). NATO also violated the 1949 Geneva Convention Relative to the Protection of Civilian Persons in Time of War, the 1977 Geneva Convention, and the 1899 and 1907 Hague Conventions, which specify that military operations should not target and kill civilians. Norman Kempster, "Report Blames NATO for 500 Civilian Deaths," *Los Angeles Times*, (7 February 2000): A6.

54. "NATO violations of the laws of war during Operation Allied Force must be investigated" (6 July 2000): <http://www.web.amnesty.org/ai.nsf/index/EUR70025200>.

55. Steven Boggan, "War In The Balkans: Nato warned on war crimes—Civilians," London, *The Independent* (5 May 1999): 4.

56. Each cluster bomb contains up to 200 bomblets the size of a tennis ball canister. It opens at about 2,000 feet and unleashes a hail of bomblets that cover an area the size of four football pitches with lethal shrapnel. Each bomb can penetrate five inches of steel. See, Jonathan Steele, "Death Lurks in the Fields," London, *Guardian* (14 March 2000). See also, Carlotta Gall, "UN Aide in Kosovo Faults NATO on Unexploded Bombs," *New York Times* (23 May 2000): A3. Paul Watson, "Unexploded Weapons Pose Deadly Threat on the Ground," *Los Angeles Times* (28 April 1999): 5.

57. Carlotta Gall, "NATO Blamed For Delay in Cluster Bomb Cleanup," *New York Times* (23 May 2000). The use of cluster bombs violates the Ottawa Convention on the prohibition of the use of anti-personnel mines. But the United States, party to only a handful of international human rights treaties, has refused to sign the Ottawa Convention.

58. Tony Wesolowsky, "Collateral Damage," *In These Times* (8 August 1999), <http://www.inthesetimes.com/wesolowski2317.html>. Torcuil Crichton and Felicity Arbuthnot, "Global spread of DU reaches food chain," *Sunday Herald Scotland* (15 April 2001).

59. Wesolowsky; Dan Fahey, "Depleted Uranium: America's Military 'Gift' That Keeps on Giving," *Los Angeles Times* (18 February 2001): M2. Depleted uranium, which remains radioactive for four-and-a-half billion years, has penetrated the food chain and has been found in the urine of all civilians tested in Kosovo and Bosnia. Crichton and Arbuthnot.

60. Mark Fineman, "Yugoslav City Battling Toxic Enemies—Balkans: NATO strikes on chemical sites have left environmental nightmare," *Los Angeles Times* (6 July 2000): A1; Wesolowsky; Milenko Vasovic, "Hiding under the black rain—Ecologists say the authorities in Serbia are concealing the extent of the ecological and health threats caused by NATO bombing," <http://www.ddh.nl/fy/Kosova/opinions/1999/black_rain3006.html>.

61. Fineman.

62. Fineman.

63. Michel Chossudovsky, "NATO Willfully Triggered An Environmental Catastrophe in Yugoslavia" (June 2000): <http://emperors-clothes.com/articles/chuss/willful.htm>.

64. The release of these toxic chemicals also violated several other provisions of international law, including the Nuremberg Principle VI; Hague Articles 22 and 23, Protocol for the Prohibition of the Use in War of Asphyxiating, Poisonous and Other Gases; Geneva 1925 (Poisonous Substances Protocol); Geneva 1977, Protocol I Additional, Articles 48, 51, 56; Stockholm Declaration of the UN Conference on the Human Environment 1972; and Principles I, II of UN Conference on Human Environment.

65. See, <http://www.flamemag.dircon.co.uk/lawyers_indict_of_nato.htm>.

66. Final Report to the Prosecutor by the Committee Established to Review the NATO Bombing Campaign Against the Federal Republic of Yugoslavia, <http://www.un.org/icty/pressreal/nato061300.htm>. "Amnesty International's initial comments on the review by the International Criminal Tribunal for the Former Yugoslavia of NATO's Operation

Allied Force," AI Index Eur 70/029/2000, News Service 116 (13 June 2000). These comments noted that NATO refused to answer specific questions about specific incidents, and the ICTY committee had "not spoken to those involved in directing or carrying out the bombing campaign." It concluded, "Amnesty International regrets the lack of full cooperation by NATO in responding to ICTY's inquiries." Diana Johnstone, "The Berlin Tribunal" (21 June 2000), <http://emperors-clothes.com/articles/Johnstone/berlin.htm>, said, "It was hardly conceivable that the ICTY would allow itself to get too interested in crimes committed by the NATO powers who provide it with funding, equipment and investigators ... not to mention its basic political agenda, which is to justify the diplomatic isolation of Serbian leaders by labeling them as 'indicted war criminals.'"

67. Members of the tribunal were jurists, lawyers and activists from Germany, Austria, Poland, Macedonia, Italy, Switzerland, Hungary, Finland, Czech Republic, France, Bulgaria, and Russia. The tribunal included more than 60 peace, civic, and human rights organizations and was independent of all governments involved in the 1999 war; see Johnstone. Also, "Concerning the NATO War against Yugoslavia — Verdict" (3 June 2000), <http://www.berlin.de/home/MeineStadt/Anmeldung>. The tribunal cited UN Charter, Art. 2 Nr. 4; the Principles of the Declaration of Peaceful Coexistence of States; and UN General Assembly Resolution 3314, UN GAOR, 29th Sess. Supp. No. 31, at 142, UN Doc. A19631 (1975). The tribunal also found Article 51 of the UN Charter, which is the only basis that could warrant a "so-called humanitarian intervention," was inapplicable in this case.

68. For former US Attorney General Ramsey Clark's complaint against NATO, see <http://www.iacenter.org/warcrime/indictmt.htm>. Also "US/NATO found guilty of war crimes in Yugoslavia," International Action Center (13 Jun 2000), <www.iacenter.org>.

69. Robin Wright, "US Aid Hinges on Cooperation, Yugoslavia Told — Diplomacy: Kostunica promises Bush he'll create a framework for extraditing Milosevic," *Los Angeles Times* (10 May 2001): A3. Yugoslavia desperately needed the $1.28 billion held ransom by the US in exchange for the deportation of Milosevic. See, Marjorie Cohn, "The Deportation of Slobodan Milosevic," *Jurist: The Legal Education Network* (2 July 2001), <http://jurist.law.pitt.edu/forumnew25.htm>. Also in July 2001, the US government's Overseas Private Investment Corporation signed a deal to increase private investment in Yugoslavia. Peter Watson, OPIC president and CEO said, "Today's agreement not only signals the green light for the US investors but indeed is a signal to the entire international investment community that Yugoslavia is open for business." See, Reuters, "Deal Lets US Investors Back Into Yugo" (21 July 2001), <http://news.excite.com/news/r/010721/13/business-economy-yugoslavia-usa-dc>.

70. Case Concerning Legality of Use of Force (*Yugslavia. v. Belgium*), Request for the Indication of Provisional Measures, (2 June 1999), General List 105, <http://www.ijccij.org/icjwww/idocket/iybe/iybe/iybeframe/htm>, para. 17.

71. Military and Paramilitary Activities (*Nicaragua v. US*), 1986 ICJ 14, para. 268 (June 27).

72. Judith Miller, "Security Council Backs Peace Plan and a NATO-Led Force,"*New York Times* (22 June 1999): A12.

73. Case Concerning Legality of Use of Force.

74. Morton Halperin and David Scheffer, *Self-Determination in the New World Order* (Washington, DC: Carnegie Endowment for International Peace, 1992), emphasis added. Halperin was head of US State Department policy planning under Secretary of State Madeleine Albright, and David Scheffer was Albright's special envoy for war crimes issues. Carnegie Endowment member Morton Abramowitz was an advisor to the Kosovo Albanian

delegation at Rambouillet. The group that developed the concept of "humanitarian intervention" included Albright, Richard Holbrooke, and Leon Feurth, foreign policy advisor to then Vice-President Al Gore. See Johnstone.

75. See Murphy 136, n. 183, for a listing of articles which analyze unilateral humanitarian intervention as a violation of the UN Charter. Also, Murphy 137, n. 185, for references to articles by scholars who view humanitarian intervention as lawful in some circumstances. See also, Aaron Schwabach, "The Legality of the NATO Bombing Operation in the Federal Republic of Yugoslavia," *Pace International Law Review* 11: 405, 416. Murphy 72, 121-22 comments further on the violation of the UN Charter. For UN resolutions, see Declaration on the Inadmissibility of Intervention in the Domestic Affairs of States and Their Independence and Sovereignty, GA Res. 2131, UN GAOR, 20th Sess., Supp. 14, 11 and para. 8, UN Doc. A/6014 (1966); Declaration on Principles of International Law Concerning Friendly Relations and Cooperation Among States in Accordance with the Charter of the United Nations, GA Res. 2625, UN GAOR, 25th Sess., Supp. 28, 121 (Annex) and para. 3, UN Doc. A/8028 (1971); and Definition of Aggression, GA Res. 3314, UN GAOR, 29th Sess., Supp. 31, 142 (Annex) and pmbl., UN Doc. A/9631 (1975). See also, Pacific Settlement of Disputes, Articles 33-38; Action With Respect to Threats to the Peace, Breaches of the Peace, and Acts of Aggression, Articles 39-51;Regional Arrangements, Articles 52-54. Some have justified NATO's action as a regional arrangement. But such arrangements must operate consistently with the purposes and principles of the UN Charter and cannot undertake enforcement action without authorization from the Security Council. UN Charter art. 53, para. 1.

76. Kenji Urata, "Criticism of 'Humanitarian Intervention': The Perspective of the Japanese Constitution," *Guild Practice* 58 (2001). Professor Urata maintains, "Were 'peace' to be the pre-eminent value to be considered when a conflict develops between 'human rights' and 'self-determination,' rather than the colonialism-tinged concept of 'humanitarian intervention,' 'non-violent humanitarian commitment' can become the basis for realizing, on an international scale, the goals set forth in the Japanese Peace Constitution."

77. Barry M. Benjamin, Note, "Unilateral Humanitarian Intervention: Legalizing the Use of Force to Prevent Human Rights Abuses," *Fordham International Law Journal* 16 (1992-93): 120, 122; Murphy 60-62.

78. British House of Commons, Select Committee on Foreign Affairs Report. Will Self, "TV Review: The fog of war gets thicker and thicker," London, *The Independent* (26 March 2000): 14.

79. Frank Newman and David Weissbrodt, *International Human Rights: Law, Policy, and Process*, 2nd ed. (Cincinnati, OH: Anderson, 1006) 244-45.

80. Michael Parenti, "Where Are All the Bodies Buried? NATO commits acts of aggression," *Z Magazine* (June 2000): 35-36; Carlotta Gall, "Serbia Finds Where Bodies Are Buried, and Investigates," *New York Times* (31 July 2001): A3. "The police have three aims," said Dusan Mihajlovic, Serbia's interior minister, "to find all the mass graves in Yugoslavia, to find who gave the orders to bury them there and to establish if these bodies were victims of war crimes, or of war, or of the NATO bombing against Yugoslavia." See also, Daniel Pearl and Robert Block, "Body Count: War in Kosovo Was Cruel, Bitter, Savage: Genocide It Wasn't— Tales of Mass Atrocity Arose And Were Passed Along, Often With Little Proof— No Corpses in the Mine Shaft," *Wall Street Journal* (31 December 1999): A1.

81. Bob Richardson, Princeton University, "Princeton speakers criticize US policy, war coverage, biases," *U-Wire* (18 November 1999); Christian Jennings, "Terrorism hits world support for Kosovo," London *Daily Telegraph* (22 February 2001). "It is senseless to end one

kind of oppression only to replace it with another," London, *The Independent* (6 June 2000): 3.

82. Ruth E. Gordon, "Intervention by the United Nations: Iraq, Somalia, and Haiti," *Texas International Law Journal* 31 (1996): 43, 45. "Damage to Yugoslav Environment 'Immense' UN Team Reports" (29 June 1999), <http:ens.lycos.com/ens/jun99/1999L-06-29-02.html>.

83. David E. Sanger, "Bush, in Kosovo, Tells US Troops Role is Essential: Reversal From Campaign—He Wants to Hasten the Day Soldiers Can Go Home, but Says; It Isn't Likely Soon," *New York Times* (25 July 2001): A1. "Well-informed diplomatic sources of Brussels" said, "American administration wants to hire certain military bases and buildings for 99 years, including 'Bondsteel' KFOR military base in Kosovo"—Beta news agency, "The USA will hire military bases in Serbia" (30 July 2001), <www.blic.co.yu>. Former Defense Secretary William S. Cohen estimated it would cost about $1.5 billion to $2 billion a year for the US to remain in Kosovo. See, Serge Schmemann, "Page Crisis in the Balkans: The White House—From President, Victory Speech And a Warning," *New York Times* (11 June 1999): A1.

84. Rockler.

85. Chomsky, "In Retrospect: A review of NATO's war over Kosovo, Part II" 74. The Southern Summit of the Group of 77, comprised of 133 of the world's poorest countries, met in Havana in April 2000. The Group decried "the right of humanitarian intervention" certain superpowers take upon themselves to attack small states without UN authorization.

86. Carlotta Gall and Marlise Simons, "Croatia in Turmoil After Agreeing to Send Two to Tribunal," *New York Times* (9 July 2001): A3. In July 2001, the Croatian government sent two of its leaders to The Hague to answer ICTY indictments for this incident. See also, Peter Beaumont and Ed Vulliamy, "Guns secret set to haunt US—War crimes hunt turns heat on Croatia's ally," *Observer* (8 July 2001).

87. Human Rights Watch, "Weapons Transfers and Violations of the Laws of War in Turkey" (November 1995), <http://www.hrw.org/reports/1995/Turkey.htm>. Colum Lynch, "Peril seen in supporting Kosovo independence," *Boston Globe* (1 April 1999): A26.

88. "Turkey to double military aid to Albania," *Jane's Defense Weekly* (8 March 2000).

89. Chomsky, "In Retrospect: A review of NATO's war over Kosovo, Part II" 42. Associated Press, "US Seeks to Keep Lid on Far East Purge Role," *Los Angeles Times* (28 July 2001): A19, detailing US financial and intelligence assistance which enabled the slaughter of between 100,000 and 1,000,000 Indonesian communists in the 1960s and efforts to keep the US role secret. See, <http://www.nsarchive.org>.

90. Chomsky, "In Retrospect: A review of NATO's war over Kosovo, Part II" 69.

91. Bilder 163. In 1998, 120 countries adopted the Statute of the International Criminal Court as a multilateral treaty. UN Doc. A/CONF.183/9 (17 July 1998). Established under the aegis of the United Nations, the ICC will be the first permanent international body to try suspected war criminals. Its jurisdiction extends to genocide, crimes against humanity, war crimes and the crime of aggression. Seven countries—including Libya, Iraq, China, India, Sudan, Israel, and the US—voted against the establishment of the ICC. The US is seeking to ensure the legal processes of the ICC do not jeopardize its role as global superpower, insulating its soldiers and policy-makers from becoming defendants in war crimes prosecutions. The US is fully aware that its actions in Yugoslavia could subject it to prosecution under the Rome Statute for intentionally directing attacks against civilians and non-military objects.

92. Marjorie Cohn, "The Crime of Aggression: What is It and Why Doesn't the US Want the International Criminal Court to Punish It?" *Jurist: The Legal Education Network* (22 March 2001) <http://jurist.law.pitt.edu/forumnew18.htm>; Marjorie Cohn, "No 'Victor's Justice'

in Yugoslavia: NATO Must be Held Accountable for Its War Crimes," *Guild Practice* 56 (1999): 146, and *Jurist: The Legal Education Network* (27 March 2000), <http://jurist.law.pitt.edu/forumnew4.htm>; and Abraham D. Sofaer, "International Law and Kosovo," *Stanford Journal of International Law* 36 (2000) 1, 21, n. 88 (2000).

93. Christian Jennings, *Irish Times* (22 March 2000): 12.

94. Richard B. Bilder, "Rethinking International Human Rights: Some Basic Questions," *Wisconsin Law Review* (1969) 171, 202. Doug Bandow, "NATO's Disastrous Victory in Kosovo" (10 March 2000), <http://cato.org/danys/03-10-00.html>. Interview with Doug Henwood, WBAI, 15 April 1999. Edited version in Henwood's *Left Business Observer* 89 (27 April 1999).

95. See, <http:secretary.state.gov/www/statements/2000/000307.html>.

7

Humanitarian Intervention and the (De)Nazification Thesis as a Functional Simulacrum

Milan Brdar

In this article I intend to deal with the problem given in the title, in three steps. First I will reconstruct the discursive genesis of the image Serbs = Nazis as a way of internationalizing existing internal conflicts and paving the way for the moral justification of military intervention. Second, after a review of the functions of the terminological identification with the "Nazis," I will elaborate two moral positions depending on the readiness to intervene in the name of morality. In its third part the analysis will conclude that moral justification unavoidably provides a moral image required for political gains and promotion of amoral interests. All this will be demonstrated with the example of Serbs and the NATO assault on Yugoslavia.

If we agree that intervention cannot take place without some sort of justification, intense motivation exists to reach out for a justification of the strongest kind, presumably a moral justification. During the last decade a great number of writers from various disciplines displayed an uncanny enthusiasm for observing events surrounding the civil wars in Yugoslavia. Their other common feature was their readiness to promote prospective military action against Serbs whom they designated as universal culprits responsible for what was happening to former Yugoslavia. Let us to begin with two remarks:

1. In morally condemning Serbs during the last nine years, various intellectuals, not to mention politicians, have found themselves on the same job. Professor Habermas, former guard of the now bankrupted "emancipatory reason," argued—but not with enthusiasm—that intervention by the NATO military is morally justified. A postmodernist, Andre Glucksmann, who in 1992-93 had loudly demanded bombing of Serbia, screamed in March 1999: "O, at last! It was time!" Susan Sontag, the well-known activist and intellectual, was very happy to see the end of "Serbian crimes" and the outpouring of protection for helpless Albanians.[1] Together with NATO officials, these intel-

lectuals are ready to promote the moral justification of intervention, to call it humanitarian beyond any doubt, and to make remarkable contributions to inventing various strictly moral reasons for it. This is more than enough for us to consider the topic seriously.

2. Let us consider two more items. First, the story that in 1992-93, 250,000 Muslims were expelled by the Serbian military from their homeland of Bosnia and Herzegovina. At the same time, as the story continues, about 30,000 Serbian troops raped over 500,000 Muslim women (according to the testimony of Susan Sontag). This sophistry, together with similar stories, provided sufficient ground to label Serbs collectively as modern-day Nazis.

Second, from 1991 to 1995, 600,000 Serbs were expelled from Croatia and Bosnia, and thousands were killed and imprisoned. Last year, after the end of NATO bombing and UN Resolution 1244 was passed, 350,000 Serbs were expelled from Kosovo and Metohia. This was done by an Albanian para-military, supported by the US—i.e., by the NATO command in Kosmet, named KFOR. This was done in order to create an ethnically clean mini-state with only Albanian inhabitants under American protection, all in the name of a desire to support a "multiethnic community."

Where are the voices in mainstream Western media to tell us that those are Nazi-like crimes? Quite on the contrary: we are told that Albanians "must be understood, after years of Serbian repression," to be engaged in "revenge killings," and "reversed ethnic cleansing," which is understandable, but will not last long, etc. In other words, we are told not to ask too much and not to cause superficial problems.

"Serbs" as a Multi-Functional Symbol: The Logic of Internationalizing an Internal Conflict

How did the Serbs become such colossal criminals, even "Nazis"? Starting in 1991, symbols of Hitler and our president appeared together on the walls of buildings in Paris, and similar accusations were repeated frequently until they became "commonplace," the newly designed anti-Serbian discourse. I analyze this case as follows.

The discursive universe carries primary reality in force. Everything essential is in the language—that holds the frontiers of the world—and it reveals itself on its surface. The symbolic power of discursive media must be recognized as a real force or power medium[2] that dictates the very sense of reality in the ordinary meaning of the concept. The idea of an autonomous referential object that obliges, and gives epistemic value to, a given meaning remains a fairy tale for undergraduate philosophical seminars. The main principle invested in the analysis, therefore, is:

> *Nihil est in intellectu nec in sensum quod non prius habeatur in signo* — *there is nothing in the intellect or in perception that beforehand was not given in the sign.*

The term "Serbs" as a sign[3] in the Western discursive media (press and electronic) is operating with five different functions. They are mutually supporting, in spite of contradictions among some of them. Here are those functions:

F1) as a symbol and negative *totem operator* in the sense of Levi-Strauss (symbolic core for the tribe integration);

F2) as a transfer of evil's symbolics — for symbolization of evil is needed as a counterpart of the ideal of good;

F3) as an "empty space," or place-holder, of postmodern writing "in itself";

F4) as an intension, or object representation; and

F5) as an expression, or self-portrait of the discursive subject.

This means that the ordinary semiotic triad (syntax, semantics, pragmatics) is insufficient. Although some of these functions are mutually contradictory, together they make a functional whole.

(F1): "SERBS" AS A NEGATIVE TOTEM OPERATOR

In all-embracing discourse and its symbolic-integrative function, a totem always must be given that serves as a *topos* of self-identification and integration of the tribe in the face of Others. In that prospect, there is no demarcation between "primitive societies" and contemporary ones, for integration cannot be achieved without a suitable myth. Integration of community has myth and totem as its foundation.

On the one hand, the idea of a "new united Europe" (or of a New World Order) is a positive totem and *summum bonum*; the opposite symbol — "Serbs" — gets the role of the necessary counter-simulacrum that signifies and names *summum malum*. Both simulacra in totemic functional order[4] create a normative opposition: culture *versus* nature, civilization *versus* barbarianism. A totem operator serves to demarcate two tribes: first, the tribe of mondialism, or civilized people, who want the "world without frontiers" and who are calling for "the blood of the disobedient," and, secondly, the tribe of the "pre-moderns" and "primitives," who still believe in the anachronistic ideas of national sovereignty and who are "drinking the other's blood." "Modern and civilized" *versus* "pre-moderns" are delimited on their relation to the (geographical) frontiers.

We are talking here about mondial tribalism, with a sharp black-white division: *pro et contra*, on the principle of *exclusi tertii dive medii*. If you are not *for*, you must be *against*; that is to say, you are a victim of "national tribalism."[5] Stating that people who are in favor of world community "without frontiers and national states" are integrated in the "mondial tribalism" could sound strange, but it is a brute fact of our time.

Therefore, the intension of the term "Serbs" as a functional *simulacrum*,[6] is not only attached to the members of one nation, as a tribe of "pre-modern savages," but, at the same time, it represents an anti-norm or paradigm of the "kind of behavior one must not exhibit" if one has the wish to be part of the "international community." Integrative ties of civilization are made stronger under the treatment of the negative totem as a symbol of "dangerous nature."

(F2): THE SYMBOL "SERBS" WORKS AS AN ACTUAL *transfer of an invariant scheme of evil in the modus of the contingent picture*; JUST AFTER THIS TRANSFER THE SYMBOL IS FUNCTIONING AS A NAME FOR EVIL.

We have seen that the symbol "Serbs" is functioning as an antipode to the idea of the "new Europe" in its status of *summum bonum*. As an actual totem operator, "Serbs" provides a contingent empirical picture of an invariantly present transcendental scheme of evil.[7]

The "Modern and Civilized," integrated in a narcissistic collective consciousness, *versus* the Monster of "national tribalism" are ready to perform a group ritual of bloody sacrifice for the sake of mondial tribalism and the future "community of citizens of the world." The victim of the ritual must be a Monster. This Monster is necessary for Narcissus to enjoy his own perfection.

A mass of people covered with a negative totemic operator must be a "wild tribe," which is to be destroyed. This operation of "semantic killing" allows the real killing to be performed with free hands and even with applause. Given that the guarantees of humanistic hysteria are provided, the action of extermination would be a performance of good in itself, never mind the thousands or millions of people killed. After all, they are less than human.

(F3): THE SYMBOL "SERBS," AT THE SAME TIME, BEARS THE FUNCTION OF A *vacant place*, OR A PLACEHOLDER, WHICH IS AT THE DISPOSAL FOR A FREE-HAND INSCRIPTION OF A PICTURE OF PURE EVIL ITSELF.

In order to fulfill the function of a totem operator (F1), the "empty space" (*tabula rasa*) must be appropriately filled in. Its limits are contoured by the scheme of evil (F2), while the process of filling the provided empty space must result in its translation into a picture in the manner of *clara et distinctae*.

The symbol "Serbs" gets its function on the basis of this empty schema that is then "packed" by way of postmodern writing "in itself" (F2). This occurs quite spontaneously, in the cool logic of complete arbitrariness with which the humanist intellectuals devoid of knowledge and responsibility are armed. This filling-in of a blank page, this writing on an empty space, then generates the needed textual picture of the Monster *vis-à-vis* Narcissus. While the picture is new, the schema is very old, for it is invariantly present in modern culture and renews itself in every episode of the idea of a "New World Order." This is the same old schema of the twentieth century. Think of the picture the word "Bourgeoisie" created in Communist Russia in 1918, the picture the word "Jews" evoked in the Germany of 1933. Those are instances of the same schema of the Monster — the evil in itself — that must be eliminated.

This function reveals that anti-Serbian discourse is a discourse of suppressed and pathological desire operating by "projection" of the unconscious drive against the Other, which assigns to the Other the reality of this self-created picture of a Monster and deadly enemy. With this specific function, the symbol "Serbs" provided Western intellectuals with a way to vent their aggressiveness accumulated as a result of the oppression that "civilizational discontent" (in Freud's apt phrase) has placed upon them.

(F4): "SERBS" AS *intension* OR *institutional clue of all factual information* ABOUT SERBS IN THE STATUS OF EXTENSION.

Intension is the only proper semantic function of a sign. But, in the case of the symbol "Serbs," its range and scope of information has been limited in an *a priori* fashion by the three previously described functions.

The logic of semiological space dictates self-depicting in the range of how "you must be" in order to abide by simulacra given in the mixing of irresistible Western political power, rosy promises for naïve people, and the jangle of arms.

The simulacrum "Serbs" in the discursive universe of the Western media operates as the *intension* that embraces a plurality of members of a people.[8] In this function a symbol works as an *a priori* core for all possible empirical information about Serbs, whether on TV and radio daily news, papers, scientific and pseudo-scientific symposia, or essays.

That is to say, the word "Serbs" is an institutional fact[9] of the transatlantic Western community, a proto-fact that imposes choice and meaning for all given natural facts and their status of "news of the day." If information on the level of natural facts is disturbing for the sovereignty of the symbol, it must, in the ruling discursive regime, be devoid of its right in the *quid iuris* dimension.[10]

The media picture, reinforced by frequent repetition that those who are "against us" do not care to be in the club of democracy, is not a factual one. It is a picture offered by the symbol, and its intelligibility is transferred into the sphere of sensible experience or the empirical realm. But, if we are this picture's creators, it is our duty to advocate it as a picture of brute facts providing testimony about real Serbian brutalities and crimes. For this reason, scores of humanist intellectuals, together with politicians, have a militant, inimical attitude toward Serbs. That is how we can account for their demand, even back in 1992, that Serbia and Belgrade be bombed because they were a nest of Nazi criminals.

In this institutional frame just described, the postmodernist writing "in itself" [*an sich*] (F4) is performed as a writing on the Serbs [*auf Serben*], just as one would write on a blank piece of paper. (The procedure is not unlike tattooing.) This means that one must write *on them*, and must not write *about them*—if the aim is to gain the status of writing in the sense of information *about someone*.

(F5): AS A VARIABLE PICTURE WITHIN AN INVARIANT SCHEMA OF EVIL, AND ABOVE ALL, AS A "VACANT PLACE," THE WORD "SERBS" IS AN EXPRESSION *or a self-portrait of the contemporary or post-cold-war mind* IN ITS GENUINE TRUTHFULNESS.

This conclusion follows from the nature of language that reveals itself in every discourse: the discourse always mirrors the speaking subject who thus both expresses and reveals himself. (For this reason: "What it mirrors language cannot represent."[11] To "catch" what is mirrored, one must invent the second mirror, a meta-language.)[12]

While this symbol "Serbs" reigns, the living Serbs are thrown out of European space. The symbol itself, being a Western product *par excellence*, of course remains; it is a symptom that testifies to the transfer of the identity and character of the Western (and new European) mind to the Other. By this operation, a necessary alibi is provided for dealing with the Serbs in the specific way they are treated, for they, interpreted in the light of the evil symbol, are a danger for Europe and the West itself. The final dilemma vividly presents itself: this danger is either allowed expansion or the Serbs are to be destroyed.

A SUMMARY

To summarize the relation of "Serbs" as a symbol and Serbs as signified people, I will use a scheme I elucidated elsewhere:[13]

"Serbs"	=	Serbs
Oneness		Plenitude
Intension		Extension
Institutional	D	Natural fact
fact	I	(*brute fact*)
Culture	S	Nature
(*nomos*)	C	(*physis*)
Inside Europe	O	Outside Europe
Tyrant	U	Victim
(Hunter)	R	(Beast)
Nazi	S	Jew
Bolshevism	E	Bourgeois
International		National
Object of desire		Object of hatred
"Serbs"	≠	Serbs

This comparative table was constructed through a long content analysis of Western media (in France, Germany, England, and the US) in the period 1991 to 1996. The left side marks the propositive side of discourse; the right side its performative dimension. So, on the left side, the discourse describes the world, while the right side prescribes to the world and makes it quite contrary to the way it is represented. It describes Serbs as Nazis, but makes of them the new hunted Jews, prepared for exile or extermination; describes them as tyrants, but makes of them the victims of the technology of power. It portrays them as a threat to civilization, but places them under the threat of genocide, which was easily attempted in the spring of 1999 without fear of much protest.

Let us now consider the exact relations among entities in the equations at the top and bottom of the table. Namely, if according to the function of intension or information it holds:

"Serbs" = Serbs (F4)

But according to the contrary function of expression, it holds:

"Serbs" = West (F5)

Then it can not hold:

Serbs = West

Instead it amounts to:

West ≠ "West"

In other words, it follows that the West in its prosaic truth is something very different than its own picture of itself suggests — namely, it is something very different then the set of values it supposedly promotes (values so attractive to the rest of the World): freedom, democracy, human rights, the division of power, and the division of private and public, etc.

Therefore, due to the fusion of contradictory functions (F4 and F5) at the same time it must hold:

"Serbs" = Serbs (F4)

And

Serbs ≠ "Serbs" (F5)

It is worth considering two conclusions that follow.

This "impossible" (non)reversible equation — that connects both verticals in the given table — is a result of eliminating a primary semantic rule by a pragmatical principle (within the technology of power) and thus performs the "shift" of sign function from informative to disinformative. At the same time, this disinformative doublet (non-information) works and holds as true information — and precisely this makes the core of ideological and political simulation and manipulation. To explain this, two remarks are in order.

Functions of *information* (F4) and *expression* (F5) are, with the capacity of mutual substitution, conjoined in the "empty place" (F3). Informative function is fulfilled by the opposition made of the expression and self-portrait of the discursive subject, for this fusion works as uncontroversial information about Serbs themselves. Therefore, the function of dis-information is twofold:

1) on the one hand, we have disinformation about Serbs (F5) that has the validity of only truthful information;

2) on the other hand, inasmuch as it is a disinformation about Serbs, it is not devoid of informative value.

If we recall Russell's insight that a relation of meaning and denotation is not necessary in natural dimension,[14] the symbol "Serbs" as a core of information (F4) is in fact a floating relation of arbitrariness toward real Serbs. Contrary to this, the function of expression (F5) is anchored in the institutionally necessary relation between the symbol and the Western mind that bears it out and gets its institutional promotion through the regime of political discourse. In that prospect there is no freedom or arbitrariness.

As for the nature and effects of the doublet—informative/disinformative or expression/information—we could conclude that, while the symbol "Serbs" in its semantic function and capacity is disinformative as far as real Serbs are concerned, it is symptomatically informative as far as the West and its character, beyond its narcissistic picture of itself, is concerned. It is a necessary conclusion from the expressive function of the symbol (F5), and not from the function of any information clue, regarding extension (F4).

"Serbian crimes," therefore, are institutionalized facts and by the discursive hypnopedia are fixed as *brute facts*. In other words, "Serbs" first (in 1991) built a concentration camp in the medium of Western political discourse, and after that (1992-93) a "Serbian concentration camp" was not hard to find in some region of former Yugoslavia—because under pressure of the Western "anti-Serbian" institutional semiotics, it had to be there. What is in the sign and in the head must also be in reality. From the prospect programmed in this way, in the eyes of any European "monitor," even a Serbian refugee center must "in its very essence" be a concentration camp where Serbs torture other nations. Under the same conditions of validity, a camp that is not Serbian—i.e., a camp where Serbs are imprisoned and tortured—simply cannot and does not exist.[15]

As we can see, the symbol "Serbs," due to its functions in the technology of power, is too overloaded to accomplish successfully its semantic informative function. This sign was not invested with a function for knowledge, but of power promotion. For this reason, the above quoted "impossible" doublet does not obey logic, but dictates it.

"Nazification" as Morally Overloading

So far I have argued why the identification Serbs = Nazis cannot stand empirical ground. In short, the informative function of the term "Serbs" is, as it were, the Achilles' heel of the ruling discourse in the Western media universe. In the face of the reconstructed semiotic mechanism, it would be naïve to consider factual questions: who acted in what way, or how much crime took place? The war in former Yugoslavia was just as bloody as many other civil wars; combatants on all sides committed crimes. However, only the Serbs were and continue to be stigmatized as Nazis. This started from the very beginning in 1991. Our reconstruction shows how it worked.

If our reconstruction is correct, there is no reason to accept any information about Serbs, since it is mostly a false construction. Thus, as for contemporary Serbian "Nazism," the factual question (*quid facti*) will no longer occupy our attention. Instead, we will go further in the analysis on the level of *quid iuris*: of divided roles in the post-Cold-War war games for the sake of globalization on behalf of the remaining superpower (i.e., the US). In particular, we shall take a look at the functions the "Nazification of Serbs" performs within the technology of power. We are interested in both the rationale of its use and the moral position invested in the justification of military actions against the Serbs.

After all the norms of international law were neglected—from the Geneva Convention of 1947 and the UN Charter to the Statute of NATO itself, not to mention the total neglect of national parliaments of the countries involved in the action—justification, being still needed, could only turn to moral grounds. However, this kind of justification can be confronted with two potential objections: first, morality offers no firm ground for such justification. Second, the justification on moral grounds, if at all available, must be as strong as possible.

Generally, the prolonged Nazification can be seen as setting up a justification of a military action against Serbs as morally uncontroversial acts. The aim of the allegation is to achieve the belief that the victim has the non-controversial status of being a supreme murderer. If this is achieved, then any discussion becomes pointless, and we have a free hand to act. In further analysis, we will find various functions Nazification can fulfill and how this explains why so many have been involved voluntarily in creating an open "hunting season" on Serbs in the last eight years.

Among the functions of Nazification, we will mark out eight main and four collateral points.

1. "Nazification" is the most effective way of internationalizing internal quarrels in order for other states to intervene with the assurance that public opinion will approve.

"Hitler is among us! How can you stand still and be moral in your own eyes?" This is admittedly the most successful way of internationalizing the insurrection of Albanians in Yugoslavia. First, when such an internal conflict is (internationally) described using the Hitler metaphor, it ceases to be what it is in other states—a terrorist activity dealt with by police action. It becomes a pretext for a big power to intervene, followed by humanist and humanitarian excuses. State sovereignty must pay the price. Secondly, every person, being a human and moral being, is called on to become engaged by "contributing to solve the problem." That opens a flood of moralism, which is very useful for the political heavyweights to finish the job—a job, by the way, that has nothing in common with human rights, democracy, and emancipation of peoples but instead has to do with neocolonialism, subtle forms of slavery, and highly sophisticated totalitarianism (which will be glorified as "self-evident democracy" beyond any doubt).

2. "Nazification" as a theme primarily functions as a way of covering up the crimes committed against Serbs by presenting them as violators deserving of punishment. This should achieve two goals: a) to punish Serbs as the defeated side and b) to rehabilitate the real criminals. (This is especially true about NATO aggression.) Serbs really have committed two great crimes: first, for entering the combat and, second, for being defeated. Therefore, they must be punished for the defeat as a war crime[16] and for all that had to be done to them in the process.

3. Nazification provides moral justification for all the actions the US and NATO took. It had to be a moral justification in the strongest terms, in order to justify such obvious crimes as bombing hospitals, schools, TV stations, etc. This is achieved by using the word "Nazism," for nothing counts as a crime against a "Nazi." By contrast, tolerating the "Nazi" is a crime against the whole world.

4. Nazification allows the maximal widening of the fields of maneuver: *all means are permitted* if the end is elimination of (Serbian) "Nazism." Whatever is done, in the end the intervening state will enjoy the image of the Savior of mankind, an angel of mercy.

It is clear that such allegedly moral justification must provide compensation for charges about the illegitimacy of intervening actions. Reinforcing the moral dimension of the problem is the suggestion that the actor will act beyond all legal norms because his actions are morally justifiable. In other words, law will be suspended as superfluous or "inappropriate for the case."

5. The powerful West is provided an alibi to commit Nazi-type crimes *in stricto sensu*, while a wide array of humanists applauds thunderously. This was evident during the NATO aggression: some western intellectuals demanded the US State Department put an end to the whole matter by dropping a mid-size nuclear bomb on Serbia! And we must not kid ourselves—a possible use of a local-scope nuclear bomb was included in the plans of the US military. Hence, the sub-functions of the "Nazi" label were a) to provide camouflage to hide crimes committed against Serbs, since to kill a Nazi cannot be valuated as

a crime; and b) to immobilize living Serbs and make of them a herd of sheep prepared for slaughter.

6. The intervention in Yugoslavia was a stage rehearsal for all those who oppose those presenting "obstacles" to the globalization process. Look, here is what you are facing! You will be painted as genocidal monsters, in public and in all media; intellectuals will "discuss" your true identity and "demand action" against you. A huge power will unleash terror with free hands against you.

7. For humanist intellectuals (former admirers of internationalism, today of mondialism), engaged as collaborators in the lynch of Serbs as Nazis, the story serves as a comfortable way to ease their "conscience" and enables them to ask more and more. (Intellectuals in the West already in 1992 began to demand the bombing of Serbia.)

8. The story of the current need for deNazification of Serbs serves to mask a likely occupation of the country and its denationalization. This existing "Nazism" provides an alibi to devoid Serbs of national identity.

There are a few collateral functions too:

Collateral function 1: Nazification provides justification for colonial intervention (planned beforehand) and acquiescence to the plan by the Western public and especially by the humanist intellectuals in the country to be conquered.

Collateral function 2: In the country, insignificant and irresponsible political groups are repeating the story of Serbian Nazism: a) in order to provide western media attention for themselves; b) by aiding the humanist simulacrum to promote anti-Serbian nationalism—in Serbia; and c) to call for (more) foreign intervention, with a moral alibi, in order to overthrow the political regime at home, for these groups are too impotent to do this on their own through regular elections.

Collateral function 3: "Nazification of Serbs" brings a bonus in the form of deNazification of Germany, i.e., deNazification of the Nazis. Looking back, the German guilt or error during their genocidal exercise was that they did not act only against the Serbs (leaving all other groups alone). Furthermore, it amounts to a dangerous thesis that maximum evil cannot take place except in the "Nazi" form. The outcome is blindness regarding phenomena of real contemporary evils.

Collateral function 4: For Jewish intellectuals specially, the "deNazification" language game offered another opportunity to revisit the Holocaust. The price was twofold: a) a rebuff to the Serbs, the only people in Europe who during World War II protected Jews and gave them shelter; and b) a total devaluation of symbols such as "Nazi," "Auschwitz," "Genocide," etc; These symbols are becoming coins in a small trade, as Jewish intellectuals, whatever their true intentions, are engaged in accelerating a total oblivion of those crimes that "must not be forgotten."

Clearly, the Nazification thesis provides a strong, although not moral, justification for what passes as "human rights protection." In the rest of this chapter, I will focus attention on the main points 2 to 5 listed above.

A moral justification is often fabricated by mobilizing strong sentiments and sympathetic feeling for those who suffer. To be persuasive, in spite of breaking all legal norms, moral justification must be maximized. Further, justification of that sort, in its very logic, posits the absolute evil, so in the face of it is the phenomenon that all moral norms are neglected in the name of the supreme good. This maximizing is essential because moral justification must be absolute. As if it were a theater play with divided or imposed roles, the show must go on until the very end, for the sake of plausibility, even at the cost of the extermination of the "evil Serbs," if need be.

Let us consider the following situation: if we were facing absolute evil, would it be moral (and normal) not to act? If we are ready to act, are we not obliged to destroy the evil with all possible means at our disposal? Further: if we are engaged in this fashion, does the absolute evil not lead us, for the sake of morality, of course, to perform actions beyond the moral realm?

This is the logic seen in Western religious wars, in revolutions, and in the case of any fundamentalism.

This is why the game is so dangerous. The logic of maximizing (moral) justification includes a duty to exterminate the guilty ones, whether a few individuals or a large collective (collective punishment). This could be appreciated as an unintentional consequence of the game, but it does not change the reality of the outcome. These are some of the consequences of grasping so easily for the term "Nazi."

A Visit by the "Merciful Angel": A Justification

We had the vivid experience of the real face of humanitarian intervention in the form of night bombing, armed with a justification in terms of human rights. We are told that the whole action was named "Merciful Angel."

Is it moral to be moral in dealing with Hitler? Is a crime against a Nazi possible, at all? This question is a trap for moral judgment. Playing on sentiments, rather than appealing to reason, the question is seductive as, depending on the answer, it leads to two cardinal moral positions.

1. *The negative answer*: No, it is not allowed to be moral toward Hitler; therefore, all means are permissible to destroy him— *the end justifies the means.* This leads to permissivism and, further, to fundamentalism, manicheism, fanaticism, moral terrorism, and, in the last resort, totalitarianism. (Remember that totalitarianism goes along with moral justification, because it breaks all kind of norms.)

In this case a sort of heteronomy seems to dictate the right course of action, for morality depends on some outer force—the criminal nature of Hitler. But this is a mere illusion. This is neither heteronomy nor morality but, quite to the contrary, a case of deep arrogance—an immorality in its disregard for all others, disguised as a confession of love and care for "all the people in the world."

The negative answer thus leads to paternalism and to acting, though not behaving, as merciful.

2. *The positive answer*: Yes, it is moral to be moral in dealing with Hitler. Our morality depends not on the object but on our attitude toward ourselves, not only towards judged action. This is a case of moral autonomy, for our morality is not variable with respect to some outer instance, but depends on self-esteem and the esteem of others. For this position, any affirmation of love is superficial. Merciful action is allowed only for the sake of the disabled, who cannot take care of themselves.

Here is another point. Who is to say that we—being victims of the recent lecture in globalism and closed into a concentration camp by economic sanctions—are not disabled? We are disabled, because we are powerless and labeled as "Nazi." For those reasons we must take the intervention of the West as an act of mercy. We finally must understand that NATO aggression really was an act by the "Merciful Angel" above our heads.

The concept of mercy, contrary to forgiveness, stays in the relation to the Other, not in relation to the self.[17] For this reason, mercy could go hand-in-hand with punishment. If we are still apt to say that it is hard to understand bombs and missiles as a means of spreading mercy, we must remember that we are mortal beings and that the real end of God's plan must be secret to us.

Intervening action must be represented and justified as a merciful act, supported with humanism. In this procedure, especially, "humanrightsism" and labeling the victim as a "Nazi" are important in making the chief aims of the action as secret as possible for the common people at home and abroad. The open quest to reveal these ends and to yield justification for them are, no more and no less, acts of arrogance that must be punished, as our case demonstrated.

In the logic of the Merciful Angel some special distribution of rights and duties is included. For instance: you have no right to wage war—even if you are under assault. You have no right to have identity and a sense of pride—even if you are an old European nation—or to be autonomous in the judgment of your own future. You do not have the slightest right to be a victim—although you are victimized. You have only the right to surrender, to bow your heads, and to creep—above all, to make of yourself that that we are already making of you. Of course, you are allowed to protest against us—for not being more severe in our actions than we are.

In short, you have a right to prepare yourself for the gallows. If you do all to fulfill this demand, you can be liberated of that duty and receive entry into the company of civilized democratic countries. This would be mercy—because of the risk contained in the chance that the judge knocks out the bench below your feet, just after you put the rope around your neck. Risk is part of playing, for the game has to be played in a relation of mutual trust, as it is demanded.

What is this story about? In the Rambouillet ultimatum, we were given the rope and the call for mutual trust. Because we abandoned the relation of trust, we were visited by the "Merciful Angel" from the sky night by night, for 78 days, beyond the expectation of ourselves or of NATO leaders.

Intervention, therefore, could be seen in two ways: first, as a punishment, for we are so rotten that we are unworthy of mercy; we have not been able to stand the temptations of "fate" (i.e., the politics of the West toward us). Second, intervention could appear as a merciful act, regardless of the way it came about (whether it involved bombs and missiles or economic sanctions, or only diplomatic actions and political pressures). This has also two meanings: for Serbs as aggressors—the merciful act aims to change them, to eliminate their "Nazi character," and to civilize them. For the Serbs as victims—it aims to liberate them from inner aggressors and oppression and to civilize them too. Above all, the merciful act aims to join them in the brotherly love of a future global "international community."

Before bombing we were tacitly given the demand to cooperate, and this was presented as a merciful act. Bombing is our deserved punishment, with the educational function of showing us what mercy means in full.

That amounts to this conclusion: serious moral justification is not needed! Appearance is good enough. The morality of such humanitarian intervention is quite superficial and serves only to check the obedience and fidelity of the victim.

Justification as a rational form of argumentation cannot be performed without the Other, free in opinion, recognized in the right to oppose and to claim truth for statements.[18] In this case there is no such condition. Who, then, is asking for the moral justification of the humanitarian intervention in action? Only those who do not read out the rules of the game imposed by the global power, which acts beyond duty any time it cares to and can justify anything to anyone. (And philosophers, of course, who are not asked for anything, but have a professional need to ask themselves everything, in order to keep their language game in motion.)

This mockery of morality is the outcome of the above-mentioned "widening of the maneuvering field," which is revealed, for instance, in the doubtful status of the Hague Tribunal. We may agree that it is judicially problematic, but this changes nothing about the fact that this institution is counted on to legitimize the intervention in Yugoslavia. Its implicit message is that, although such a trial could not be used to solve internal disputes in Western countries, Serbs, as Nazis are outside any law, culture, morality, or custom. Why, then, should we have correct relationships with them, morally or legally? The point is not to judge them in fairness, but to subdue them once and for all.

Conclusion: Moral Image is All That is Needed

Regarding the usual story that "wealthy democracies have a duty to intervene," we should not be so naïve in believing that some of them, alone or in alliance, are ready to set in motion a huge military machinery and to spend billions of dollars solely because someone's human rights are jeopardized in some corner of the world. First, the cost of mobilization of the military could not be recovered by the mere fact that some human rights have been restored. Second, if justice is at stake, what about all the other oppressed ethnic groups on the globe? It seems that the Merciful Angel is not so merciful, after all.

Machiavelli first discovered that in politics one does not need to be moral in one's actions, but one does have to provide a moral image, or a moral justification; in other words, one must present a moral appearance in public, something like a moral veil that manages to make invisible actions of a real political nature that could not be approved by citizens. This is the scope or function of morality in politics: politics must be in pursuit of moral justification in appearance, but not of morality in a substantial sense.

In the theater of the NATO intervention and its justification, we have, in fact, seen an ordinary case of political manipulation with a moral veil. It is exceptional only because it has happened in our time and to us in Serbia. Something else is strange, however. How could so many philosophers ponder the problem of moral justification of military interventions and not recognize the thin connection between politics and morality or that all the reasons in favor of intervention must always be manipulated by politics?

The problem is not to find a set of necessary and sufficient conditions that can justify military intervention, but to find a case where all of that would not end in even better manipulation. In other words, we could ask the question: is it possible (and how) to avoid just those interventions which are apparently morally uncontroversial, but which, in fact, are deeply problematic morally? Today we intervene, say, because media reports that someone "over there" is eating children, and, of course, we want to stop the practice. *Ex post facto*, truth reveals itself that the story was a media fake.

If political power is interested in morality only to the extent that it offers a public veil, while at the same time philosophers trouble themselves to find moral justification for military intervention, the latter cannot avoid the following unpleasant consequences: 1) philosophers serve as window dressers for politicians, providing content for the moral veil politicians need; and 2) in our concrete case (due to dualism) they have created the ideology of "Humanrightsism," as on the surface a brand new American export product, tasteful for many East European intellectuals, while in reality it serves the purpose of neo-colonialism, an "old wine in a new bottle."

Notes

1. Jurgen Habermas, "Humanizam i bestijalnost" (*Die Zeit* 18, 1999*)*, *Nova srpska politicka misao*, Posebno izdanje 2 (1999) 64–71; Andre Glucksmann, "Evropa u prvoj godini novog milenijuma," *Nova srpska politièka misao*, Posebno izdanje 2 (1999) 81–82; Susan Sontag, "Zasto smo na Kosovu," *Nova srpska politicka misao*, Posebno izdanje 2 (1999) 25–29.

2. Cf. Pierre Bourdieu, "The Economics of Linguistic Exchanges," *Social Science Information* 16 (1977): 645-68; Pierre Bourdieu, "Symbolic Power," *Identity and Structure: Issues in the Sociology of Education*, ed. Denis Gleeson (Nafferton, UK: Nafferton Books, 1977) 112-19; John B. Thompson, "Symbolic Violence," *Studies in Ideology* (London: Polity Press, 1984) 42-72.

3. Notice that throughout the article the relation of the sign "Serbs" (in quotation marks) and the signified people — the Serbs — are related identically as meaning, always given in quotation marks, and denoted object, or denotation, in the sense of Russell. See Bertrand Russell, "On Denoting," *Meaning and Knowledge: Systematic Readings in Epistemology*, ed. E. Nagel and Richard B. Brandt (1905; New York: Harcourt Brace, 1965) 81–83, *et passim*.

4. Claude Levi-Strauss, *Divlja misao* (Belgrade: Nolit, 1978) 223. Also: "Kind of things that serve to collective signification of clan is called its totem. Totem of the clan is totem of every one of its members.... Usually, totem is not individual, but species or subspecies.... Totem is collective significant ... and in relation to it things are classified on the sacred and profane"; Emile Durkheim, *Elementarne forme religijskog života* (Beograd: Prosveta, 1982) 94, 96, 110.

5. Karl-Raimund Popper, *Open Society and its Enemies* (Princeton, NJ: Princeton University Press, 1971) 316, 318.

6. "Simulation starts ... from a sign as a reversion and killing of any reference whatsoever." A decisive turn is made with passing from signs that are hiding something to the signs

that are hiding that there is not anything— that could be hidden." Sharl Bodriard, *Simulacije i simulakrumi* (Novi Sad: Bratstvo-jedinstvo, 1991) 9-10.

7. There is invested a Kantian sense and connection of scheme and picture, as given in his Transcendental Analytics of *KrV.*

8. "The intension is what is actually conveyed by the designator from the speaker to the listener; it is what the listener understands. The reference to the extension, on the other hand, is secondary; the extension concerns the location of application of the designator, so that, in general, it cannot be determined by the listener merely on the basis of his understanding of the designator, but only with the help of factual knowledge." Rudolph Carnap, *Meaning and Necessity. A Study in Semantics and Modal Logic* (Chicago, IL: Phoenix Books, The University of Chicago Press, 1956) 157; "... *semantical rule for a sign has to state primarily its intension; the expression is secondary*, in the sense that it can be found *if the intension and the relevant facts are given.* On the other hand, if merely the extension were given, together with all relevant facts, the intension would not be uniquely determined." (Carnap, *Meaning and Necessity* 112); also, Rudolph Carnap, *The Logical Structure of the World* (London: R. and K. Paul, 1967) 74-75. Carnap's demarcation of intension and extension of statement is equivalent to Frege's difference of sense— *Sinn and referent: Bedeutung* (Frege, 1892), or to Russell's difference of meaning and denotation. *Cf.* Frege (1892), "Sinn und Bedeutung," in Gottlob Frege, *Funktion, Begriff, Bedeutung. Fünf logische Studien*, ed. G. Patzig (Göttingen: Vandenhoek und Ruprecht, 1962) S. 38-63; also, Russell (1905), "On Denotating," *Meaning and Knowledge. Systematic Readings in Epistemology*, ed. E. Nagel and Richard B. Brandt (New York: Harcourt Brace, 1965) 109; Carnap, *Meaning and Necessity* 125, 236.

9. Institutional facts: institutions of relations of intersubjectivity, of mutual rights and duties. *Cf.* Babic (1976); Renate Bartsch, "Die Rolle von pragmatischen Korrektheitbedingungen bei der Inter-pretation von Außerungen," *Sprechakttheorie und Semantik*, ed. Günther Grewendorf (Frankfurt am Mein: Suhrkamp, 1979) 218-19; J.R. Cameron, "Sentence-Meaning and Speech Acts," *The Philosophical Quarterly* 20 (1970): 103.

10. Regime of discourse— Michel Foucault, "Truth and Power," *The Foucault Reader*, ed. Paul Rabinow (Harmondsworth: Penguin, 1986) 112, 133— holds the "field of discursive events"— Michel Foucault, *Archäeologie des Wissens* (Frankfurt am Mein: Suhrkamp, 1973) 42— or sustains "the power which constitute domain of objects in relation to which truthful and false statement could be affirmed"; Michel Foucault, "Discourse on Language," *Archaeology of Knowledge* (New York: Harper Colophon, 1972) 234. "Regime also holds discursive formation that defines objects, types of utterances, correlations, and flow of statements under the rules of formatting (*Formationsregeln*) which are not relating to the language but to discourse as a practice" (Foucault, *Archäeologie des Wissens* 58, 70). Therefore: "Disciplines are constituting a control system in discourse production ... wherefrom it follows: "it is possible to be right only if rules are obeyed of given discursive 'police' that are reactivated in every event when someone is speaking" (Foucault, "Discourse on Language" 224).

11. Ludwig Wittgenstein, *Tractatus*, 4.121; also: "No statement could say anything on itself " (3.332); "Statement can not maintain on itself that is truthful" (4.4442). Ludwig Wittgenstein, *Tractatus Logico-philosophicus* (Sarajevo, 1989).

12. "We must always distinguish clearly between the language about which we speak and the language in which we speak (...) The names of the expressions of the first language, and of the relations between them, belong to the second language, called the *metalanguage.*" *Cf.* Alfred Tarski, "The Concept of Truth in Formalised Languages," *Logic, Semantics, Mathematics: Papers from 1923 to 1938* (Oxford: Clarendon Press, 1956) 167, 210-211; also, Tarski (1936) 353; Carnap, *Meaning and Necessity* 242; Carnap, *The Logical Structure of the World* 74-75, 293.

13. *Cf.* Brdar, "Srbi i/ili Evropa: preispitivanje odnosa," *Srpska politicka misao* 2.2-3 (1995): 47, *et passim*.

14. Russell 83.

15. The whole operation was the "masterpiece" of the agency Ruder & Finn Global Public Affairs. What was at stake was discovered by its director Mr. James Harff in a revealing interview given to Mr. Jacques Merlino in Paris in October 1993. Ruder & Finn are a public relations company, currently registered as foreign agents. Here are Harff's statements, slightly abridged. [End of quote from the periodical and beginning of the quote from the book:]

> Harrf: For 18 months, we have been working for the Republics of Croatia and Bosnia-Herzegovina, as well as for the opposition in Kosovo.
>
> Question: What achievement were you most proud of?
>
> Harff: To have managed to put Jewish opinion on our side. This was a sensitive matter, as the dossier was dangerous looked at from this angle. The Croatian and Bosnian past was marked by a real and cruel anti-semitism. Tens of thousands of Jews perished in Croatian camps. So there was every reason for intellectuals and Jewish organizations to be hostile towards the Croats and Bosnians. Our challenge was to reverse this attitude. And we succeeded masterfully.
>
> At the beginning of August 1992, the *New York Newsday* came out with the affair of (Serb) concentration camps. We jumped at the opportunity immediately. We suggested to them [Jewish organizations] to publish an advertisement in the *New York Times* and to organize demonstrations outside the UN.
>
> This was a tremendous coup. When the Jewish organizations entered the game on the side of the (Muslim) Bosnians, we could promptly equate the Serbs with the Nazis in the public mind. Nobody understood what was happening in Yugoslavia... But, by a single move, we were able to present a simple story of good guys and bad guys, which would hereafter play itself.
>
> We won by targeting the Jewish audience. Almost immediately there was a clear change of language in the press, with the use of words with high emotional content, such as "ethnic cleansing," "concentration camps," etc. which evoked images of Nazi Germany and the gas chambers of Auschwitz. The emotional charge was so powerful that nobody could go against it.
>
> Question: But when you did all of this, you had no proof that what you said was true. You only had the article in *Newsday*!
>
> Harff: Our work is not to verify information. We are not equipped for that. Our work is to accelerate the circulation of information favorable to us, to aim at judiciously chosen targets. We did not confirm the existence of death camps in Bosnia, we just made it known that *Newsday* affirmed it.
>
> Question: Are you aware that you took on a grave responsibility?
>
> Harff: We are professionals. We had a job to do and we did it. *We are not paid to be moral.*

Interview was tape recorded when it was transmitted on French TV2, Paris, October 1993. It was published in Jaqcues Merlino, *Les Verites Ne Sont Pas Toutes Bonnes A Dire* (*The Truth from Yugoslavia is not being Reported Honestly*), published by Albin Michel, Paris, 1993.

16. Jovan Babic, *Moral i nase vreme* (Beograd: Prosveta, 1998) 171–72, *et passim*.

17. Cf. Jovan Babic, "Justifying Forgiveness," *Peace Review* 12.1(2000): 92-93.

18. *Cf.* Johnson, 1964: 1.

8

The Aftermath of the Kosovo Intervention: A Proposed Solution

Aleksandar Jokic

Introduction

In this last chapter of our book devoted to the issues raised by the notion of "humanitarian intervention," I shall take a brief look at the aftermath of the Kosovo intervention. Specifically, I focus on the events that have unfolded since the signing of the Kumanovo peace agreement when NATO troops rolled into the Serbian province of Kosovo and Metohija. The items to be analyzed and subjected to philosophical scrutiny all have to do with the language used to describe events, appropriate policies, and recommendations for change in the region. As this language is in many ways distorting the reality both on the ground and globally, the goal of obtaining clarity should facilitate efforts to formulate a meaningful solution for long-term stability and peace in the region. Somewhat unrealistically, for the sake of analysis, I will assume that peace is the ultimate goal of all the players involved. Hence, I begin by describing the need for developing an ethics of international activism, followed by an examination of "word games" that may obscure the goals of peace; in the final section of the chapter I propose a solution that involves more than just Kosovo and Metohija.

The Ethics of Peace Activism

Elsewhere I have argued that there are important similarities between (international) activism, ideology, and the declarative meaning of the key phrases deployed as part of the discourse about Balkan conflicts.[1] Here, therefore, I shall only briefly sketch out these points of similarity in order to set up the context for discussion in the coming sections of the chapter.

In describing activists, what readily comes to mind are phrases like "well-meaning," "ready to sacrifice," or "peace-loving." This means that their motivation is not only good in the ordinary sense that the activity in question is in itself good, or taken to be good, but it is good because the objectives guiding the action—e.g., peace, de-nuclearization or human rights—are themselves *conceived* as unquestionably good. This motivation stems from the activists' increased sensitivity to evil that exists in the world. Without that sensitivity there would be no engagement in the first place. Their motives, therefore, are not only good when their actions are assessed in retrospect, but the motivation is good in the deeper sense that its very source is the good itself (or opposition to and distaste for evil as such). Their motivation is not contingently good, but it is necessarily so, for it is aimed at and focused toward the good. Evil is not only something merely negative, but for these sensitive souls it is something unbearable. They are, therefore, unable to just contemplate, attempt to understand, or simply perceive evil, they must actively engage in eradicating it.

This (tacitly assumed) account of motivation is at the bottom of activists' preoccupation with matters that strictly speaking are of no direct concern to them. The activist is not fighting to gain something for herself; she is engaged because she cannot stand evil suffered by others (call this, foreign or external evil). The *per assumption* absence of the activist's direct interest in the matters of her *engagement* shows that this peculiar impetus that gets her going must be purely moral in nature. This is exactly what defines the (international) activist's position.

A picture emerges according to which, for the activist, given the axiological nature of the cause she is fighting for, all that is required to set her on the right path is that she be sincere and firm in her decision. Are there no obstacles to getting the purpose right, to honing in on what is unquestionably the right goal for which to make personal sacrifices? What could be the source of such infallible knowledge? These are appropriate questions! The activist possesses not only a firm conviction that the cause is right, but also a persuasion that no consideration could possibly put it in question. The position is tantamount to a person who has all the answers in advance, with no need to engage in the search for evidence. It is a position that readily presents answers, while the procedure that supplied them remains forever hidden, unexplored, and insignificant. Does this, therefore, mean that it is not, strictly speaking, important *what will really be achieved* (as in the saying "Don't look a gift horse in the mouth"), but that whatever is accomplished is good enough—in the sense of being sufficient? Put differently, since the activist's motivation procures the act's rightness and its goodness, does this mean that *there is no possible question to be raised here*? Or, that no argumentation of any kind is required or possible in this case? The last remark indicates an *ideological* character of the situation—we are trading in a context wherein *reasons* do not function in their customary fashion, or not at all.

Ideologies function precisely in this way: no reasons are presented, and to any argumentation offered, everything is *already* settled (prior to any questioning). What is more, attempting to ascertain the real nature of anything—when this is done from an independent point of view, i.e., from the perspective that fails to *pre*determine it with respect to the basic (ideological) tenet as concordant or perhaps not—is viewed as a way of *putting in question* what is *already clear* (and *accepted*)! Ideologies, as is well known, incorporate no debate, no argumentation, and no uncertainty. What we do find is that all reasons have already been "distributed": some are favorable (and hence they are the "right" ones) while others are not (in which case they are either "wrong" or, worse, a dangerous attempt at deception).

This mechanism, common to activism and ideology, is also, however, quite prevalent with many words and phrases in the current discourse about the decade-long Balkan crises. Language functions in similar fashion whenever the meaning remains on the *declarative* level, i.e., when the speaker's intention is not to take on an obligation in any (strong) sense that would permit scrutiny, but only to express agreement with some assessment that is already (contextually) current. No discussion, no deliberation, no *pro et contra* argumentation is even hinted at, there is no compromise either, nor any withdrawal (except total treason); there is only "battling" for the right cause, as soldiers in a just war only can.

This is the basis for many of the word games that can easily sway even the best and the brightest in the direction of causing harm rather than good. Examples of two such phrases are examined in detail in the next two sections. Let us here examine, very briefly, another one in order to point more precisely to what the game consists of and what one, particularly peace activists, should be on guard for. Consider the phrase "democratic revolution" widely used to describe the events of October 5, 2000, in Yugoslavia that saw the transition of power from Milosevic rule of more than a decade to a new government. What does "democratic revolution" really mean, and what does it describe? The phrase, in fact, describes nothing; it simply expresses approval through the positive meaning inertia contained in the word "democratic." One element, therefore, of this phenomenon is the *non-descriptive* meaning of the key phrases, though they are in fact authoritatively presented precisely as if their main role was objectively descriptive, providing the true nature of things thus referred to. The other is what I call the *attitudinal* (Stevenson calls it "propagandistic")[2] character of the chosen language, and it is precisely these two elements taken together that make the word game in question possible. What this does in real life, however, is to move us away from correctly understanding what really happened, in particular, such improprieties as foreign governments meddling with another country's elections by "illegally" funding a side in the electoral process (i.e., it is illegal in their countries, e.g., in the US, to receive such funds). To the extent that it moves us away from the real questions, this particular language game also represents a contribution to the lexicon of denial.[3]

Serbian Nationalism

Let us first consider the phrase "Serbian Nationalism." Recalling the period immediately preceding elections in Yugoslavia, on September 24, 2000, a careful observer could have noticed an interesting dynamic with the use of the phrase "Serbian nationalist." It occurred in the media daily, alternatively prefixed either by the words "moderate" or "hard-line" when *intending* to describe the opposition candidate Dr. Vojislav Kostunica. This dynamic deserves closer scrutiny.

Let us start by asking the following question. What is wrong with Serbian nationalism? No one will tell you exactly, but that there is something seriously wrong is taken for granted. It is such an affront to human decency that just mentioning it suffices to justify the most savage bombing since Dresden, or almost a decade of severe economic sanctions by the "international community." Yugoslav President Milosevic, we were repeatedly told, must not be allowed to play yet again the card of "Serbian nationalist sentiments."

All the way up to the day after the elections, Vojislav Kostunica, the opposition presidential candidate, had consistently been labeled in the Western media as "a moderate Serbian nationalist." What is a moderate Serbian nationalist? At best all this phrase could mean is that the man is not as bad as Milosevic, the hard-line Serbian nationalist.

Things only got worse, and very quickly, just one day after Kostunica's impressive show in the first round of presidential elections. (He indeed might have scored an outright victory over Milosevic.) Just one day after the elections, Kostunica had been up-graded to "another hard-line Serbian nationalist" by the influential, supposedly independent, intelligence outlet Stratfor (Strategic Forecasting, LLC) in their weekly analysis entitled "Checkmate in Yugoslavia?"[4] What is more, in this very short piece, Kostunica was called a Serbian hard-line nationalist no less than three times. Others quickly followed this practice. So, how does one go from moderate to hard-line Serbian nationalist so quickly? The transformation, a cynic might say, occurs as one gets closer to power in Yugoslavia. By definition, therefore, a bad guy must always be in power in Yugoslavia. It is that easy. All one has to do is evoke the evil of "nationalism," and that is enough to absolve the US of its once and future crimes against the people of Yugoslavia.

But, let us return to that awesome phrase "Serbian nationalist sentiments." One has to be extra careful here, for its meaning, as the phrase was used throughout the 1990s in the context of the Yugoslav tragedy, implies a kind of collective guilt on the part of Serbian people. It appears that any other nation in the world is allowed to have "nationalist sentiments" except them. The term was interchangeable with "greater Serbia" ideas (or ideology attributed to all Serbs) which included the (alleged) practice of removing all non-Serbs from an area.

I define "nationalist sentiments" as signifying concern for the well-being of one's own group in a way that gives preference to the well-being of the members of that group rather than another. In the case of people in Yugoslavia in the period before Kostunica's victory, these sentiments had to be directed against two sources of evil: the regime then in place and the international community (primarily the US that took the most active role in NATO bombing of the country). In fact, the "nationalist sentiments" were not at the time acting in support of any political party, but rather against these two sources of evil. That is, there was no such thing as nationalist sentiment in favor of the government in Yugoslavia. Rather, it was an anti-attitude, since the misfortune and misery of people in Yugoslavia consisted precisely in the fact that they had to choose between two evils, one having to be judged as a lesser evil.

Nationalist sentiments in Serbia dictated, in real life, an anti-regime and an anti-international community attitude. People knew that these were their two oppressors. However, when considering which is the greater source of misery, those who drop bombs (all the while threatening to do it again) and keep austere economic sanctions endlessly in place (by far a bigger killer over the longer run than cruise missiles) are clear winners. By choosing them as a greater source of evil, an illusion of support for the regime was created, when in fact it was essentially a negative attitude. This is then played out in the mainstream media as "nationalist sentiments" that can justify whatever punishment the international community cares to mete out to Serbs, and the other 26 nationalities living in Yugoslavia.

Finally, we could ask why would Kostunica be branded a nationalist, in the negative sense of the word? Two reasons were often cited. First, Kostunica condemned the 1999 war and labeled NATO's prosecution of the air campaign as a series of "criminal acts." And second, he does not recognize the legitimacy of the ad hoc criminal tribunal in The Hague. But the opinions that NATO committed war crimes and that the Hague tribunal is a political ploy serving the very same purpose as sanctions and bombing campaigns are universally held in Serbia and well beyond its borders. Would this make all those who think so, whether they are in India, Russia, China, or the anti-war activists from the US and elsewhere, the hard-line nationalists? Of course not!

Again we see at play here what I have called the non-descriptive attitudinal character of language. The difference this time is that rather than turning on the positive meaning inertia of the word "democratic," the game unfolds on the basis of the negative meaning inertia of the phrase "Serbian nationalism" carefully crafted through the years of satanization of Serbs in the Western media.[5] And again, the phrase serves the purpose of covering up the activities of the "international community" that should really be at issue, and of preventing real questions from being raised. The lexicon of denial expands.

"Reverse Ethnic Cleansing" and "Revenge Killing"

Going further back to the time soon after the NATO bombing of Yugoslavia, to the second half of 1999, after NATO troops moved to Kosovo, we encounter two most curious phrases ubiquitously employed by journalists, political analysts ,and even academics: "reverse ethnic cleansing" and "revenge killing." These innocent sounding phrases harbor a dangerous attitude of complacency toward true massacres of countless civilians.

In sharp contrast to the spring of 1999 when citizens of the Western nations were being literally barraged with anecdotal accounts of alleged atrocities in Kosovo, supposedly committed by Serbian troops against ethnic Albanians, the media were largely silent during the summer of 1999.

The media chose, for the most part, not to report on the most recent wave of Kosovo Liberation Army (KLA) atrocities against the non-Albanian (and even non-Muslim Albanian) population in Kosovo. Nor have they reported about the mass destruction of Serbian houses, farms, and Orthodox churches.[6]

This muted response is curious for two reasons. First, we ought to remember that the avalanche of stories in spring 1999 came despite the fact that all international observers were evacuated from Kosovo in the wake of NATO bombings. By contrast, there is a deafening silence during the summer and fall of 1999 (and to this date) despite the overwhelming international presence: massacres of Serbs, Gypsies, and others by KLA-Albanians are happening in front of about 50,000 NATO-dominated "peacekeepers."

The second curiosity has to do with the language found in the few reports on the current situation. In particular, as noted, two newly concocted phrases abound: "revenge killings" and "reverse ethnic cleansing." Look at the built-in bias of these phrases of choice. These words not only seem to justify military intervention based on initial violence, they also appear to justify the choice to do nothing but sit and watch the latest massacres. Because they are "revenge" and "reverse," these killings and the ethnic cleansing bear the marks of approval. As long as politicians and journalists continue to play these word games, their words will encourage massacres.

For those who might think that these words were well-chosen, consider this: the distinction between "ethnic cleansing" and "reversed ethnic cleansing" does not help describe any particular situation. The use of these phrases is simply an indication of the precise point in time those who use them first got really interested in the ongoing events. Had they chosen to start paying attention at some earlier point, say in relation to what Kosovo Albanians did to the Serbs in the 1970s and 1980s, the order of these phrases would have been different.[7] We would have had "ethnic cleansing" of Serbs from Kosovo in the 1980s, then "reverse ethnic cleansing" of Albanians at the end of the 1990s, and finally "reversed reverse cleansing" of Serbs now. Maybe the story would be even more complicated than this.

The same applies to the phrases "killings" and "revenge killings." By adding words "reverse" and "revenge," an impression of justification for those acts is created which leads to general inaction in trying to prevent the latest round of violence. This word game is particularly dangerous as it fosters mass murder, violence, and homicide while hiding inactivity. The lexicon of denial grows even further.

The Solution[8]

Is there a long-term solution to violence in the Balkans? Will peace and stability ever come to this troubled region? I believe there is a chance, and here is the solution peace activists ought to support.

Democratic Serbia provides an opportunity for thousands of American troops stationed in the Balkans to return home, and return soon. A comprehensive resolution of *all* issues generated by the dissolution of former Yugoslavia is now easily achievable with all but minimal US military presence (a small number will have to remain in Macedonia).

Many think that Kosovo remains an intractable problem, even after a "democratic revolution" in Belgrade. It is not! The obvious and inexpensive solution is to partition Kosovo between Serbs and Albanians. The Serbian part of Kosovo would then become a part of Serbia proper, while the Albanian part would become independent. Albanians have made it abundantly clear that they want nothing short of full independence. If possible, this genuine desire ought to be satisfied. Some give-and-take would be necessary, however, but partition is the only natural way to go. What would it take to accomplish this?

First, the myth that Serbs would not find this option palatable must be rejected. In fact many Serbs, including members of the Serbian Academy of Sciences and Arts (SANU), and in particular the former president of Yugoslavia, the novelist Dobrica Cosic, have long advocated this sort of solution. Back in 1992 Cosic recommended partition (and even membership in NATO — which Washington rejected after he made an official overture).[9] During 1996 and earlier D. Despic, then SANU president, ran a series of newspaper interviews advocating the same idea. This appears to have also been the position favored by the Serbian Orthodox Church. Where exactly the lines of partition should be drawn is another matter, but it is a feasible step for both Serbs and Albanians.

In fact, convincing Serbs that a specific partition is good will seem less of a problem than divorcing the Kosovo issue from the Republika Srpska issue. And this is where the key policy move by the US administration could lead to a happy return of American servicemen and women from both Kosovo and Bosnia. A carefully crafted package of financial incentives (such as, for example, forgiving Yugoslavia's $14 billion foreign debt) and a policy of compensating the Serbs' loss of territory in Kosovo by empowering Republika Srpska to join Yugoslavia would provide a long-term security and stability solution for the Balkan puzzle. This proposal would have to be further fine-tuned, such as offering a provision that the UN would guarantee that the Holy Orthodox sites that remain in Albanian-dominated Kosovo would enjoy protection from destruction and that access is secured to all Serbian pilgrims, etc.

The policy of partitioning Kosovo together with the unification of Republika Srpska with Yugoslavia (which would perhaps acquire a new name: Serbia and Montenegro) offers long-term security and stability for the region. Also, it is no less a natural outcome than was the unification of Germany, for example. Once NATO troops pull out of Bosnia, Serbs in Republika Srpska will be safe from possible attack coming from the Muslim and Croatian Federation as the strength of VJ (Yugoslav Army) will function as a decisive deterrent. On the other hand the Muslim and Croatian side would have nothing to fear from a democratic government in Belgrade. Similarly, after partition of Kosovo, KFOR can pull out without worry of a renewed full-scale war between Serbs and Albanians there. A small contingent of NATO troops (preferably Americans, because of their credibility) would have to maintain a long-term presence in Macedonia to prevent a conflict erupting in the western part of the country where Albanians have a majority similar to the Kosovo situation. Albanians there might be tempted to repeat a Kosovo-style uprising. American troops in Macedonia would guard against this, further contributing to the long-term security of the Balkans. The cost would, however, be an insignificant fraction of the current expenses of maintaining both the Bosnia and Kosovo missions (currently surpassing $3.5 billion annually).

This entire enterprise is likely to provoke fierce resistance only from one side: the ethnic Muslims in Bosnia. However, American diplomats should have no serious problem convincing them to go along, as Muslims have enjoyed American protection and favors from the beginning of the Yugoslav crisis.

Notes

1. Cf. Aleksandar Jokic, "Activism, Language and International Law," *International Journal for the Semiotics of Law* 15.1 (2002); pp. 107-20. The middle sections of this chapter are based on the material from this article, reproduced here with permission.

2. *Cf.* Charles L. Stevenson, *Ethics and Language* (London: Oxford University Press, 1944), particularly chapter XI "Moralists and Propagandists."

3. Just days before the elections in Yugoslavia, the *Washington Post* indicated that the National Endowment for Democracy has concluded that they have been too open about the fact that they pay the "democratic" opposition. The article is entitled: "$77 Million Helps Foes of Milosevic." It is written by John Lancaster and appeared on Tuesday, 19 September 2000.

4. Analyses by Stratfor are available on their web site, <http://www.stratfor.com/>.

5. A veteran foreign correspondent, Russell F. Anderson, who covered events starting from the Spanish Civil War, reveals in a letter to the Editor of the *New York Times* (30 October 1994) that he was troubled with the new practice of reporters voicing their own opinions about events. The reporter he had in mind particularly was CNN's Christiane Amanpour. He writes, "during my time as a journalist, the watchword was to beware of half-truths because you may have got hold of the wrong half." When it comes to reports dealing with Serbia during the 1990s many "wrong halves" have been hastily reported, apparently on purpose. This attitude, approaching genocidal journalism, is perhaps best crystallized in the shocking words of Thomas L. Friedman, who exclaimed during NATO bombing: "Like it or not, we are at war with the Serbian nation and the stakes have to be very clear: ... every week we will set your country back by pulverizing you. You want 1950? We can do 1950. You want 1389? We can do 1389 too." *New York Times* (23 April 1999): A25.

6. On its web site (<http://www.decani.yunet.com/home2.html>) the Serbian Orthodox Church offers a detailed report of suffering titled "Golgotha of Kosovo Serbs and Minority Groups in Post-war Kosovo."

7. In this respect early reports by David Binder of the *New York Times* are a must read. In his column "In Yugoslavia, Rising Ethnic Strife Brings Fears of Worse Civil Conflict" (1 November 1987), he writes: "Slavic Orthodox churches have been attacked, and flags have been torn down. Wells have been poisoned and crops burned. Slavic boys have been knifed, and some young ethnic Albanians have been told by their elders to rape Serbian girls." And earlier, on 12 July 1982 also in the *New York Times* in a piece entitled "Exodus of Serbians Stirs Province in Yugoslavia," Binder reports that already 57,000 Serbs were forced to leave Kosovo, and the idea of an "ethnically clean Kosovo" appears perhaps for the first time in the press.

8. This section is reproduced with permission and slight changes from my "What Should American Peace Activists Know About the Balkans," *Peace and Change* (Blackwell Publishers, 2002).

9. Cf. Svetozar Stojanovic, *Serbia: The Democratic Revolution* (forthcoming).

Contributors

MILAN BRDAR is Professor of Social Science and Philosophy at Novi Sad University, Yugoslavia. He was President of the Serbian Philosophical Society in 1997-2000. He is the author of *Critique of Philosophy of Science and Methodology of Karl Raimund Popper* (1981); *Praxis Odyssey: A Study in Genesis of Bolshevik Totalitarianism 1917-1929*, in two volumes (2000-2001); and *Philosophy in the Pissoir* (2002). He is editor of *Philosophy, Language, Community* (1999). His most recent published papers deal with issues in political science and geopolitics, as well as in philosophical methodology.

MARJORIE COHN is Associate Professor at Thomas Jefferson School of Law in San Diego, California. She teaches international human rights law. Co-author of *Cameras in the Courtroom: Television and the Pursuit of Justice*, she has published numerous articles and does media commentary about criminal justice, human rights, and US foreign policy. In addition to her monthly columns in the *Los Angeles Daily Journal*, the *San Francisco Daily Journal*, and *Jurist: The Legal Education Network*, she publishes regularly in major newspapers. She sits on the National Executive Committee of the National Lawyers Guild; is editor of the *Guild Practitioner*; co-chairs the Guild, Äôs international committee; and is on the Roster of Experts at the Institute for Public Accuracy. Professor Cohn has served on international delegations in Iran, China, and Cuba, as well as Yugoslavia.

ERNST-OTTO CZEMPIEL is Professor of International Relations at the University of Frankfurt. He co-founded the Peace Research Institute Frankfurt (PRIF) in 1970 and was its co-director from 1970 to1996. He is Chairman of the Kuratorium Peace Prize of Hesse, 1994-2002. He has authored numerous books and journal articles.

RICHARD FALK is the Albert G. Milbank Professor of International Law and Practice at the Woodrow Wilson School, Princeton, NJ. He has authored more than a dozen books including *Law, Morality, and War in the Contemporary World* (1984) and *Legal Order in a Violent World* (1968). He was counsel to the International Court of Justice, research director of the Coming Global Civilization project, and honorary vice-president of the American Society of International Law.

ROBERT M. HAYDEN is Professor of Anthropology, Law, and Public and International Affairs and Director of the Center for Russian & East European Studies at the University of Pittsburgh, Pennsylvania.

ALEKSANDAR JOKIC is Professor of Philosophy at Portland State University, Director of the Center for Philosophical Education at Santa Barbara City College, and co-founder with Jovan Babic of the International Law and Ethics Conference Series (ILECS). He is the author of *Aspects of Scientific Discovery* (1996), editor of *War Crimes and Collective Wrongdoing* (2001) and *From History to Justice* (2001), and co-editor with Quentin Smith of *Time, Tense, and Reference* (2003) and *Consciousness: New Philosophical Perspectives* (2002). His most recent published papers deal with issues in Kantian ethics, the morality of economic sanctions, fetal rights, and ethics of international activism.

GEORG MEGGLE is Professor of Philosophical Foundations of Anthropology and Cognitive Sciences at the University of Leipzig. He is the founder and first president of the Society for Analytical Philosophy (GAP-*Gesellschaft für Analytische Philosophie*). His research is mainly on topics of action, communication, language (*Grundbegriffe der Kommunikation*, 1997), interpersonal relations, meaning of life (*Sinn des Lebens*, dtv, 2002), and ethics of war.

ALEKSANDAR PAVKOVIC is Associate Professor in Politics and Head of the Department of Politics at Macquarie University, Sydney, Australia. He is the author of *The Fragmentation of Yugoslavia: Nationalism and War in the Balkans* (2000). His recent work focuses on theories of secession, liberation ideologies, and nationalism.

BURLEIGH WILKINS is a Professor of Philosophy at the University of California in Santa Barbara. He has made a substantial contribution to the analytic philosophy of history and the study of Burke's political philosophy. He is the author of *Terrorism And Collective Responsibility* (1992), *Hegel's Philosophy Of History* (1974), and numerous journal articles including "A Third Principle Of Justice," *Journal of Ethics* (1997).